SOCIAL THEORY

A Guide to Central Thinkers

edited by Peter Beilharz

ALLEN & UNWIN

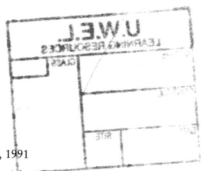

First published in 1992
Allen & Unwin Pty Ltd
8 Napier Street, North Sydney, NSW 2059 Australia

National Library of Australia
Cataloguing-in-Publication entry:

Beilharz, Peter.
  Social theory: a guide to central thinkers.

  Bibliography.
  ISBN 1 86373 163 6.

  1. Social Sciences — Philosophy. 2. Philosophers. I. Title.
300.1

Set in 10/11pt Sabon by Adtype Graphics, North Sydney
Printed by Chong Moh Offset Printing Pte Ltd, Singapore

Contents

Preface

This book grows out of an event, and out of a culture. The event—the 1989 Annual Conference of the Australian Sociological Association; the culture—that diverse but keen and passionate bunch of people concerned with social theory in Australia, some of whom attended the Conference, some of whom appear in this volume as contributors. For the 1989 TASA theory stream, I had decided to prevail upon contributors to give short, pithy presentations on their (usually) favourite theorists—to make their enthusiasms intelligible to outsiders, to undo a little of that professional idiocy which all specialists suffer, to produce cameos for those better versed, in order to draw out the vitality of the different theories. That idea then produced another—a book, including some of the classics as well as the moderns, hoping again to introduce social theories to newcomers and outsiders but also to canvass some substantive issues in social theory. The result, this book, can hopefully be read as a book, too, and not just used as a 'tool', because for all the difference in approach and emphasis, there are some shared concerns here.

Many people contributed to this process, not least of all the participants at the conference. Katy Richmond, the key organiser of TASA 89, actively supported the idea from the beginning. Evan Willis mooted the idea of a book. Patrick Gallagher liked the idea, and was patient of the more than usually complicated process of its creation, as was Elizabeth Weiss. Karen Ward was a terrific desk-editor, and Jo Jarrah a lynx-eyed copy editor. Elizabeth Grosz and Vicky Kirby, Johann Arnason and Michael Taveira helped with connections. Paul Harrison acted as reader and adviser on the contributions as they came in. Dor, Nik and Rhea were supportive of what could have been just another Harold Hare idea. My greatest debt is to the contributors themselves. They are indeed creating a theoretical culture, endeavouring to keep us all thinking in an epoch where critique is often either marginalised or else posturing and precious. Their efforts help us to see, at the end of the day, that social theory is also a practical interest.

Peter Beilharz
February 1991

INTRODUCTION

Peter Beilharz

Why do social theory? Ours is an instrumental culture, presided over by a utilitarian regime which looks favourably upon quick results. No time to think. Even those of us who are students or teachers find that we are compelled to do social theory furtively, selectively, between all the other demands of everyday life. Why bother? A moment's reflection tells us that there are different ways of knowing. Commonsense privileges experience; philosophy tells us that there are other, 'theoretical' ways of knowing. This is not a new predicament. Classical philosophy distinguishes between *theoria*, pure contemplation, *praxis*, or transformative activity, and *techné*, or technical knowledge. The sense that there are different ways of knowing is not brought about by 'postmodernity', nor by the proliferation of knowledges sometimes referred to as the 'information explosion'. Almost two centuries ago de Tocqueville advised that no single person could know what they might hope to, and Goethe used one of his characters in *Elective Affinities* to lament the growing list of things one really must read. Thus we turn to 'authority', and to theory. If we need, in sociology, to know about capitalism we turn to Marx, or in politics, to know about legitimation, we turn to Weber, or about gender, to feminist theory.

Theory is useful; it enables, it helps us better to understand what we already knew, intuitively, in the first place. But theory is always plural, *theories*, and multicentred. This makes theory in general difficult, so we turn to theorists in particular—for communication, we see Habermas, for social movements, Touraine, modernity, Heller, and so on. This remains difficult, for each theorist has a different story to tell, and there are different interpretations of each theorist. But this is the way social theory works. It depends on enthusiasm, passion, suspicion, scepticism, tolerance, patience and judgement. The theoretical attitude is open-ended, for theory is culture and not an instrument. The theoretical attitude does not rest well with the cult attitude of individual thinkers as

SOCIAL THEORY

heroes (and yet this is one of the most common dispositions in social theory, as though theories were mere totems, like football teams, sports stars or guitar players).

This book is a guide to some central social theories. It is a guide, neither a tool nor a dictionary, neither a form guide nor a Top Forty. It is aimed at students, undergraduates and others, explicitly as an introduction, an invitation to the culture of social theory, one possible beginning and not a conclusion. It rests on the premise that social theories work something like maps—they are metaphors for society, for regions, for the world system, but no substitute for the complete journey in pursuit of understanding, and never one-to-one in their attempts at representation or interpretation. This book is not by any means comprehensive. It sets out to cover the work of some central theorists, presupposing that there is always a multiplicity of centres. The view from Melbourne or Sydney, Bundoora or North Ryde is both central and peripheral, as, in a different sense, is the view from London or Boston.

Knowledge is perspectival, so these entries on theories reflect the biographies and locations of their authors, as the principles of selection reflect the path of the editor. There will, of course, need to be more books, more essays, more introductions—feminist introductions, postmodern 'introductions' or departures, readers, essays and so on (see variously Shanley and Pateman 1990; Lovell 1990; Tong 1989; Benjamin 1989; Foss and Pefanis 1990). There *are* more theories than there used to be, and there is increased disputation around what constitutes significant theory. Partly these issues are perspectival. Those who view themselves as outsiders, nomads or rebels will be attracted to postmodernism, as their forebears were to existentialism earlier in the twentieth century and to romanticism since the eighteenth. Foucault will be more attractive to those working on the failures of the legal system, Habermas to those concerned to argue against the excessive juridicalisation of everyday life. More, there is an undeniable element of disposition in the choice of theories. As the romantic socialist William Morris pointed out in criticism of Edward Bellamy's mechanical socialist utopia *Looking Backward*, personalities orient theories. Agnes Heller's is an undeniably optimistic if sober theory—it attracts people of similar orientation. Theorists such as Marcuse in the 1960s were immediately attractive to libertarians who also had some need to claim the unchangeability of the world. Althusser was powerfully influential upon those in the 1970s for whom science was a high priority. People involved in social movements are likely to be attracted to action theory in the manner of Touraine.

Are all theories then equal, and merely a matter of taste? This view is increasingly popular, part and parcel of the relativism which is such a striking sign of the malaise and fear of judgement characteristic of our times. There are, arguably, some theories which are more important than others, and there is no necessary relationship between the popularity of a theory and its fruitfulness. Some leading theorists are still marginal. Castoriadis, for example, has never received the bouquets of some other theorists, and still works against the current. Others who are less marginal—Derrida, for example—still take on the stand of marginality. Others included here will raise the odd eyebrow. Dumont fails to register as a social theorist in part because of the dubious hegemony of disciplinary thinking: he is an Indianist, not a theorist. Seabrook would similarly elude the net, most often, because he is a journalist (shame!), the result being that too many view his work as something less than what it is, an attempt to expand the English ethical socialism of Ruskin, Morris and Tawney by stretching it over the frame of the world system. Thus Wallerstein would typically be seen as a central social theorist, but not Seabrook. Here, both are included, as is Gramsci, who some would see as a political theorist but not a social theorist.

As well as the inclusions, there are of course also exclusions. Some of the classics are included, some not. Marx, Weber, Durkheim and Freud appear because they are classics in the strong sense. They offer vocabularies which provide a frame of reference which allows us to shorthand, to condense, to simplify the complex and thus actually to speak with each other (Alexander 1987). 'Capitalism', in this sense, conjures up 'Marx' for us, so that when I make a particular claim about capitalist civilisation, I invite you to respond with 'You mean in the Marxian sense?': without sacrificing our differences, we make a point of contact. This is what Foucault refers to when he comments that the great theories become dissolved into our own attempts to explain (Foucault 1980: 52).

The bias of this collection is toward the classical and the modern. Postmodernism has received more press that any other recent phenomenon since the Sex Pistols; whether this will last is the question. The critical observation frequently made of postmodernism is that it only puts anew questions about reason and imagination, thinking and the senses, prose and poetry that were earlier put by modernists around the turn of the century. When a significant writer such as Richard Rorty defends himself as a postmodern bourgeois liberal, it is difficult to avoid the sense that each term becomes more weighty, respectively, from left to right (Rorty 1982: 206–7). Stephen Toulmin suggests a similar temperament when he indicates that we need to go 'back to postmodernity', his own favoured thinkers being moderns like Wittgenstein and Dewey, and Renaissance humanists such as Montaigne (Toulmin 1990; Beilharz 1991).

Rorty has no entry in this book, partly because his own work is both available and accessible; the modesty of its claims make its intelligibility straightforward. While people will still be talking about Rorty in ten years, it is difficult to know whether they will still be speaking of Lyotard; but again, those who are curious can simply turn to the admirably lucid Postscript to the *The Postmodern Condition* (Lyotard 1984). Probably neither Parsons nor Althusser would be included in such a book published ten years hence. As for Baudrillard, my suspicion is that readers will take his own advice, and forget the cool memories (Baudrillard 1987).

The central fact of recent social theory, which is evident in some postmodern theory but strongest in theories such as Weber's and Heller's, is the turn away from grand theory to the celebration of contingency (Rorty 1989; Heller 1991). Grand theory is out, contrary to Quentin Skinner's innuendo in *The Return of Grand Theory in the Human Sciences* (Skinner 1985). The idea of highly systematic and synthetic theory is increasingly discredited, in my view, rightly so. Reflect back upon some theoretical attempts which took place in sociology in the 1970s and the 1980s, to develop comprehensive theories of exploitation and domination: Marxism, feminism, racism, ageism, etc. Partly because of the excessively ideological environment of this period, there seemed to be some sense that a theory which did not address everything did not address anything. This tyrannical attitude is now far less frequently encountered, as the plurality of domination and of perspectives upon these forms of domination is recognised. This is not so much a matter of the end of grand narratives—as various critics have pointed out, postmodernism, too, is a grand narrative. It is rather the end of what now look like unconvincing and immodest attempts to get the intellectual head around the social world.

The issue at risk here, more often the subject of heated than enlightening argument, is the question of how social theory is created at all. In the classical conception *theoria* is produced *ex nihilo* in the empirical or experiential sense: it offers primary understanding, or foundational knowledge. The classical Greek cosmos looked down upon *techné*, and in many ways rightly so; when we look now at the civilisation we have produced, we can only wonder at how rampant and pervasive technical thinking has become. Weber and the Frankfurt School declaimed the predominance of technical rationality, as did Habermas after them, but to no apparent avail. Yet our intellectual culture also, at the same time, privileges theory over other practices. There is a hierarchy to be observed, with theory superior, at the acme: philosophy on the top floor, statistics in the basement.

Ought we to trust our capacity to think, or our capacity to experience? Conspicuously, we do both, but the divide occurs when we argue about how to create social knowledge. Each position knows all too well the faults of the other. Those who incline to the general warn us not to universalise the particular, while those who favour contingency begin to twitch when others think from the general to the particular. According to arguments such as Dewey's, which will doubtless become more influential into the nineties, knowledge is more adequate (not more certain) when it also refers to making/doing. Knowing/making/doing—not Theory in one corner and Practice in the other room—is the pragmatist approach to the creation of knowledge (Dewey 1929). Grand theory is thus on the decline. Grand theoretical claims are increasingly likely to attract sceptical, if not cynical responses from the denizens of modernity/postmodernity.

How did all this come about? To cut a long story short, the real culprits are arguably less those who conducted the dialectic in distant Athens than the positivists: sociologists such as Comte, for whom a series of law-like propositions about society could basically sum it all up. In one sense it is indeed sociology, and not philosophy, which is responsible for the trouble, for it is sociology that, to use Windleband's distinction, took up its claim to legitimacy in terms of arguments concerning the *nomethetic*, or law-like, leaving historians to pursue the *ideographic*, or empirical dimensions of the social world. Viewed from the perspective of the struggle between historians and sociologists, the decline of grand theory must be seen in some quarters as a decisive victory for the theory and practice of history, just as Edward Thompson's *The Poverty of Theory* was widely—and quite mistakenly—viewed as the last historical word against the excessively theoretical bent of French structural Marxism or its local echoes.

The attack upon general theory as excessively general, or 'theoreticist' has taken on other forms as well. Grand Theory was most famously attacked by sociology's maverick, C. Wright Mills, in *The Sociological Imagination*—not, this time, a defence of the ideographic against the nomethetical, so much as a pox on the houses of both 'Grand Theorists' and 'Abstracted Empiricists' (Mills 1959). Skinner's claim is that the 1970s, however, were a period of grand theoretical reprise, probably with Habermas as the most eminent representative of the trend. Yet while some central theorists, such as Habermas, have certainly become more systematically ambitious, shifting in this case from Marx to Weber to Parsons and systems theory, others, like Foucault, continued to produce case studies, monographs illustrative of a larger, though often implicit general theory of power.

At the same time, as Skinner rightly indicated, there has been a strengthened resistance to the model of natural science in the human sciences, which echoes back to Windelband and especially to Dilthey, and follows through the legacy of hermeneutics. Hermeneutics, the theory of interpretation which emerges from biblical analysis via Scheiermacher and finds its most substantial recent representatives in Gadamer and Ricoeur, in some respects avoids the dualisms characteristic of disputes between empiricists and theorists. This is because it takes texts and traditions or classics seriously, but it also acknowledges the reader, proposing a possible fusion of horizons between the worlds of the text and the interpreting subject. The theorist ceases to be a hero or iconoclast and becomes a partner in conversation (Gadamer 1975; Ricoeur 1978; and generally see Mueller-Vollmer 1986).

This kind of approach to knowledge resonates throughout the German tradition and surfaces also, in variations, as deconstruction. Certainly it summons up the spirit of Max Weber, the idea of understanding in sociology, and the preference, often, for the essay form. The trend in social theory today is apparently toward the partial, the fragmented, against general theories such as, say, Habermas' *Legitimation Crisis*. It is apparently, and hopefully, a trend toward taking the classics seriously as sources of insight, thinkers of fields, forgers of metaphors, and partners in dialogue, but away from the project which would see the classics as able to generate all insight out of themselves (Alexander 1987). But if there is a shift away from 'high theory' or philosophy in the Aristotelian sense, what then happens to the activity of theorising itself? One earlier solution offered by Robert Merton and still exhumed periodically when in doubt is the idea of 'middle-range theory' (Merton 1957). By middle-range theory Merton meant to provide a solution to the problem of theory, but all he succeeded in doing was naming it.

Some historians conventionally speak of a 'toing and froing' or dialectic between 'facts' and 'theory', and though the vocabulary is clumsy, the point is clear enough: 'facts' and 'theories' are mutually related and effective upon one another (see, for example, Carr 1961). In sociology we find a related claim for something called 'grounded theory' as a possible way out of a labyrinth (Glaser and Strauss 1968). Again, this response names the problem rather than solving it, by indicating that theory needs to be grounded. But all theory, after all, is grounded: Marx's and Weber's in the textile mills of the early industrial revolution, and in their political commitments; Habermas' in the biographical problem of how to explain and avoid Nazism; Castoriadis' in Athens and in the politics of *Socialisme ou Barbarie*; the Frankfurt School in its social research program and in the Holocaust; Touraine's in the sociological intervention; Heller's in the politics of reform communism in Hungary and radical republicanism in the United States. The implication of 'grounded theory' advocates, that some theories (their own) are 'grounded' and others not, merely turns professional necessity into virtue. More fundamentally, the question also arises whether empirical social research can itself generate adequate theoretical understanding.

Certainly some social theories are more empirical than others. Against the theories of, say, Wallerstein or Elias, which lie within the realms of historical sociology, the arguments of Habermas or, even more, Alexander, are more 'purely' theoretical. But there is, at the same time, no reason to presume that a philosophical argument concerning history or experience is inadmissable; there is a historical argument about history, and there is also philosophy or theory of history; there is the chronicling of experience, and the attempt to explain experience in a theory of everyday life. Thus it may be worth pausing for a moment here to wonder whether the alleged stand-off between empiricists and theorists is authentic, for empiricists of course also use theory but do not privilege it, while theorists more or less consistently orient themselves to practical concerns but refuse 'empiricism'.

Consider a case of the interpretation of 'theory' and 'practice' in, say, Castoriadis' analysis of the future of the Soviet Union. Predating the fall of the Berlin Wall, Castoriadis proposes that there are three possible outcomes of the Gorbachev phenomenon (Castoriadis 1988). In the first scenario, Gorbachev pushes, the apparatus reacts and deposes him. In the second, he waters down his reforms and 'succeeds'. In the third scenario, there is social rupture, or popular revolution, and subsequent military intervention. When Castoriadis published these views, in the early, cosy optimism of the Gorbachev phenomenon, some radicals scoffed at the second and third possibilities. The third, or course, has since become even more ominous.

The point in the present context, however, is that the whole exercise is deeply theoretical, drawing on a long project of the analysis of Soviet-type societies as representing certain configurations of power, legitimacy, and ideology or imaginary signification, involving particular ways of thinking and doing that refer back to the Russian Revolution, the weight of history, and to Marxism. The particular is there, but so is the general, the interest in trend or pattern, the willingness to speculate. It is difficult to imagine what, by comparison, an 'empirical' analysis of Gorbachev would look like. In 1988, it probably would have been 'all well, moving too fast'; by 1992 it might be guns or butter. Empiricism here borders on impressionism, compounded by our increasing reliance on the spectacles presented to us by television 'news'.

Social theory matters because it addresses social problems, questions of the human condition in modernity. Theory is generalising, but this does not mean that it needs to be systematising or totalising. This is the logic of the pragmatic turn in social theory. Like the linguistic turn before it, it places emphasis upon the moment of construction and on the contingency of meaning. It speaks against certainty and finality. And it directs our attention to the possibility that perhaps we have simply demanded too much of social theory, reading it as though it were the last word and the end of the story when it was rather offering us the invitation to puzzle through the mess with which modernity confronts us.

Perhaps part of the problem has been that our reluctance to ponder sufficiently has led toward too easy an acceptance of theoretical maxims we would not otherwise entertain. The idea, for example, that capitalism is a smart economic machine which is only ever capable of maximising profits is not only empirically untrue, but also theoretically unconvincing, for capitalism is also about the politics of power, which sometimes can be traded off against profitability (Kalecki 1943). The proposition that the state is an actor, similarly, rests on a unifying and homogenising logic which represses the fact that states are complex, riddled by internal differences and jealousies, and are staffed by human beings (Beilharz, Considine and Watts 1991; Allen 1990). If the world is the mess that it is, then theorists need to recognise this, and so do the users of theory. The logic of the pragmatic turn in social theory is a turn to partial rather than synthetic theories. This is entirely consistent with the project of social theory, for it enables it more closely to aspire to the prospect of an open culture.

If the status of postmodernism is difficult to establish, so too is the place and impact of feminist social theory. Postmodernism and feminism are often now hyphenated, as previously were socialism and feminism, or yet earlier liberalism and feminism. The difference is that whereas both liberalism and socialism correspond to a feminism which chooses to draw upon the legacy of the Enlightenment, postmodernism typically turns its back on all this, or at least as much as it can. The postmodern rejection of Enlightenment rests upon an act of homogenisation of difference which has to be experienced to be believed, for the Enlightenment also had its attraction to empiricism and scepticism, all here obliterated. For its part, feminism still has, among others, the choice to operate within the hitherto existing sphere of social theory, or else to construct its own, and in very rough terms this is one difference between the strategy of Anglo-American and French feminisms. This returns us again to questions about how social knowledge is created. Some feminisms find sympathy in romanticism, postmodernism and in history because all, alike, are drawn to the category of experience. Romanticism, postmodernism and the practice of history are all originally 'masculine' endeavours. What this would seem to suggest is that sources of inspiration in theory are not exclusively gendered.

To pick up two cases diametrically opposed in 'theory', yet aligned in 'gender', consider again the case of Thompson and Althusser. The dispute between Thompson and Althusser was one of the most vicious in recent memory, at least as far as Thompson's invective was concerned. The core of the dispute was fairly simple: Althusser argued somewhat literally that philosophy was the best way to know, Thompson responded pompously that History was the Queen of the Sciences. While the sparks were flying, feminist historians and philosophers were doing their work. Some, like Catherine Hall, acknowledge the impact for them of Thompson's emphasis on experience and the view from below in his *Making of the English Working Class*, while others, such as Elizabeth Grosz and Michèle Barrett, were to explain that even though Althusser was no feminist, their own projects nevertheless drew upon his inspiration (Hall 1990; Grosz 1989; Barrett 1980). Or think of the influence Foucault has had on feminism, even though, again, his politics were those of male homosexuality rather than those of feminism.

None of this is new. If Nietzsche, the misogynist, stands behind Foucault, then we would expect Nietzsche, too, to be a source for feminist social theory. But here there is a longer story, as well. Nietzsche's public opposition to feminism and to socialism did not prevent his own influence overwhelming just those movements. His influence was evident not just in the fringes of the German radical movements, but also in the arguments of moderates such as Lily Braun (Braun 1987; Hinton-Thomas 1983). Socialists and feminists took the inspiration they needed from Nietzsche and ignored the rest. Probably what they did was typical, for ideas influence and fuse in all kinds of apparently random ways, ways which are neither obviously rational nor irrational. This is a highly significant theme, for it serves to illustrate something about the contingency of everyday life in the practice of social theory.

If we return to the eternal question of how social knowledge is created, what social theory is for, one answer is that we do not 'know'. We are not able easily to explain how social insight happens; as Weber says, it can sometimes come of hard labour, sometimes arrive out of the blue. Social theory is mediated into our lives by all sorts of contingent circumstances—who teaches us, how and where, what we read, when and with what resonances in our memories, senses of experience and identity. This is not to say that theory cannot be constructed 'anew', but it is to wonder what the basis of creation might be, for postmodernism and for feminism alike. If theories are likely to be more regional and partial, then there are clearly all kinds of possibility for specific feminist theories of reproduction or 'labour', sexuality or family. Whether there need be a specific and independent feminist aesthetic, or science, is partly a matter of position (Felski 1989). To some degree the question of position returns to the theme of insiders and outsiders, and this also raises the related issue of whether feminism is seen primarily as critique or as substantive alternative theory (Soper 1986). Probably feminism needs to be both liberal and postmodern (Yeatman 1990), but this is obviously a dispute between feminists. Given the tendency to fragmentation and to partial, pragmatic theories, there seems to be little reason to expect a new synthesis, here or elsewhere.

Such a healthy scepticism, however, need not lead to nihilism. Ever since the belated realisation, after Foucault, that knowledge had something to do with power, there has been a tendency for intellectuals to be afraid of knowledge claims which may possibly and maliciously become claims to power. In their silliest forms, these fears generated hypotheses regarding intellectuals as the new ruling class, as though technocrats were intellectuals in any substantive sense at all. As Bauman expressed it, nevertheless, the worry was that intellectuals had become legislators; they needed, once again, to return to the safer pastures of interpretation (Bauman 1987). There is no doubt that intellectuals or theorists can become dangerous when they become technocrats or legislators, or even when they believe they have some special eligibility for these roles. But if intellectuals flee from legislation, they, too, leave it to others who cannot easily be trusted.

The internal politics of social theory may not always be good politics, but this is no reason for intellectuals to turn their backs on politics as such. This remains, indeed, one area of concern, for political theorists and political actors draw upon social theories in their practices. An encyclopedia of social theorists which omitted the name of Keynes would be remiss, as scholars now recognise (O'Donnell 1990), not simply because Keynes was a philosopher *manqué* but also because of the social theoretical implications of his own *General Theory* and *Essays in Persuasion*. Social theory turns up in some funny places. Social policy, in particular, depends and calls on social theory (Williams 1989; Beilharz 1987). Social theory need not be utilitarian, but it should be worldly. Social theory is interested, never disinterested.

The world of the 1990s and after 2000 will be a different world to that into which we were born. The end of communism and the realignment of world forces will not, however, reinstate capitalist civilisation as anything other than an incremental success story. Into the 1990s modesty will be one motif of social theory, but this modesty and circumspection will need constantly to be balanced against regional concerns and global sensibilities. This is no time to return to the medievalism implicit in some claims for 'local knowledge' (cf Geertz 1983), for while we are locally placed we have never before been so simultaneously cosmopolitan. The proposition that social theory is dead or in crisis thus has its sting, but only and especially when it is aimed at the verbose and bloated claims of some of the grander theories. We need social theory now, perhaps more than ever before, for it demands of us also that we clarify our norms and values, our politics and our ethics. It is a way of operating in the world, a way of respecting its complexity and that of theory. These are some of the reasons why we do social theory.

BIBLIOGRAPHY

Alexander, J. (1987) 'The centrality of the classics', in A. Giddens and J. Turner (1987) eds *Social Theory Today* Cambridge, Polity
Allen, J. (1990) 'Does feminism need a theory of the state?', in S. Watson (1990) ed. *Playing the State* Sydney, Allen & Unwin
Barrett, M. (1980) *Women's Oppression Today* London, Verso

Baudrillard, J. (1987) *Forget Foucault—Forget Baudrillard* New York, Semiotex(e)

Bauman, Z. (1987) *Legislators and Interpreters* Cambridge, Polity

Beilharz, P. (1987) 'Reading politics: social theory and social policy' *Australian and New Zealand Journal of Sociology* 23(3)

——(1991) 'Back to Post Modernity' *Thesis Eleven* 29

——Considine, M. and Watts, R. (1991) *Arguing About the Welfare State* Sydney, Allen & Unwin

Benjamin, A. (1989) *Lyotard Reader* Oxford Blackwell

Braun, L. (1987) *Selected Writings on Feminism and Socialism* Bloomington, Indiana University Press

Carr, E.H. (1961) *What is History?* London, Macmillan

Castoriadis, C. (1988) 'The Gorbachev interlude' *Thesis Eleven* 20

Dewey, J. (1929) *The Quest for Certainty* London, Allen & Unwin

Felski, R. (1989) *Beyond Feminist Aesthetics* London, Hutchinson

Foss, P. and Pefanis J. (eds) (1990) *Jean Baudrillard. Revenge of the Crystal* Sydney, Pluto

Foucault, M. (1980) *Power/Knowledge* Brighton, Harvester

Gadamer, H. G. (1975) *Truth and Method* New York, Seabury

Geertz, C. (1983) *Local Knowledge* New York, Basic Books

Glaser, B. and Strauss, A. (1968) *The Discovery of Grounded Theory* London, Weidenfeld and Nicholson

Grosz, E. (1989) *Sexual Subversions* Sydney, Allen & Unwin

Hall, C. (1990) 'The tale of Samuel and Jemima', in H. Kaye and K. McClelland (eds) *E.P. Thompson. Critical Perspectives* Cambridge, Polity

Heller, A. (1991) 'Contingency, irony, solidarity' *Thesis Eleven* 29

Hinton-Thomas, N. (1983) *Nietzsche in German Politics and Society, 1890–1918* Manchester, Manchester University Press

Kalecki, M. (1943) 'Political aspects of full employment' *Political Quarterly* 14(4)

Lovell, T. (1990) *British Feminist Thought. A Reader* Oxford, Blackwell

Lyotard, J. F. (1984) *The Postmodern Condition* Manchester, Manchester University Press

Merton, R. (1957) *Social Theory and Social Structure* New York, Free Press

Mills, C.W. (1959) *The Sociological Imagination* New York, Oxford

Mueller-Vollmar, K. (1986) *The Hermeneutics Reader* Oxford, Blackwell

O'Donnell, R. (1990) *Keynes: Philosophy, Economics and Politics* London, Macmillan

Ricoeur, P. (1978) *The Philosophy of Paul Ricoeur* Boston, Beacon

Rorty, R. (1982) *Consequences of Pragmatism* Brighton, Harvester

——(1989) *Contingency, Irony, Solidarity* Cambridge, Cambridge University Press

Shanley, M.C. and Pateman, C. (1990) *Feminist Interpretations and Political Theory* Cambridge, Polity

Skinner, Q. (1985) (ed.) *The Return of Grand Theory in the Human Sciences* Cambridge, Cambridge University Press

Soper, K. (1986) 'Qualities of Simone de Beauvoir' *New Left Review* 156

Tong, R. (1989) *Feminist Thought. A Comprehensive Introduction* London, Unwin Hyman

Toulmin, S. (1990) *Cosmopolis. The Hidden Agenda of Modernity* New York, Free Press

Williams, F. (1989) *Social Policy* Cambridge, Polity

Yeatman, A. (1990) *Bureaucrats, Technocrats, Femocrats* Sydney, Allen & Unwin

PETER BEILHARZ

1

Louis Althusser

Louis Althusser was born in 1918 in Algeria and died in Paris in 1990. He was, as one obituary put it, the last Marxist philosopher (*Le Monde* 31 October 1990). His work was extraordinarily influential in France, England and Australia throughout the 1970s and 1980s. Yet those who come to Althusser afresh, into the 1990s, would be justified in wondering what all the fuss was about. Titles like *For Marx* and *Reading Capital* are hardly likely to be as alluring to postmodern eyes as good narratives like Foucault's *Discipline and Punish* or his *History of Sexuality*. Yet Althusser and Foucault were very much part of the same milieu. Althusser, for his part, brought together two of the dominant streams in postwar social theory—Marxism and structuralism. More than Sartre, he was a Marxist, a lifelong member of the French Communist Party, the leading defender of the work of the 'mature' Marx, *Capital*.

Althusser was the leading theoretical antihumanist in Marxism, playing an equivalent role, in effect, to Lévi-Strauss, but explicitly within Marxism and as a philosopher. His interest was in structure, not in action or praxis, and yet he remained committed to the possibility of socialism. Like the later Marx, and like Durkheim, however, he was also concerned to explain the problem of order: how capitalist societies could reproduce themselves even against (or with) the will of those who sought to transform them. This concern took Althusser, finally, into the realms of social theory charted by Gramsci: ideology and consciousness.

Althusser was thus a vital transitional figure in postwar social theory. His contribution was to raise some good questions (less uniformly often did he provide good answers, but such is the task of social thinking). His work made it possible for him, and for others after him, to ask further questions about, among other things, economy and society, ideology, philosophy of science, and interpretation.

ECONOMY AND SOCIETY

Marx identified his own central contribution to social theory as the recognition that economy was the most influential or determinant instance of society. Ideology, belief, culture, law, language and religion each made sense only with reference to economy (1859 *Preface*). Subsequent Marxists were given to puzzle over the exact relation between economy and society. Could cultural forms be deduced from or read off the economy? Was economy the basis of society and all else mere superstructure? If so, then how could the residual existence of traditional elements in modernity (such as the church) be explained?

Althusser made two advances here. First, he insisted that all societies or social formations combined different modes of production. Capitalist societies such as France always contained residual elements of feudalism; France could simultaneously be a highly technocratic and thoroughly traditional society, combining nuclear physicists on the one hand and peasants on the other. Russia could simultaneously carry elements of bourgeois and socialist revolution (see Althusser 1969: 94–116). The observation itself was not new—Gramsci had made it in *The Southern Question*, Trotsky in *1905*. There was no such thing as a pure capitalist society; rather, all existing societies were characterised by uneven development. Althusser's insistence was that this be registered theoretically, something which Marx had failed to do in the general theory of capitalist production which he offered in *Capital*.

Second, this meant that while economy was determinant, it would not always be dominant: residual or 'secondary' elements could in fact dominate societies. Economy, politics and ideology were thus necessarily related to each other, but sometimes in such a way that the dominant economic class (the bourgeoisie) would not be the leading political class (as, for example, the petite-bourgeoisie might be, under fascism). While Althusser was not a world system theorist, this ideal of mixed modes of production and implicitly interrelated social formations reintroduced into theory the problem of imperialism or the structures of global capitalism. For while, say, Russia at the turn of the century did not have its own entrepreneurial bourgeoisie, it did have a small but strong capitalist sector in which the proletarians were local, and the bourgeoisie French, English or American in origin.

These elements of Althusser's work were influential both upon anthropology (see, for example, Godelier 1972; Terray 1972; Seddon 1978) and on political economy (see Taylor 1979; and see generally *Journal of Australian Political Economy*). What Althusser avoided here was the question of how the transition from capitalism to socialism might occur. His interest in the systemic or synchronic dimension sometimes resulted in the charge that his theory simply bolted Marxism onto structural functionalism in order to explain how the world could *not* be changed at all (see, for example, Clarke 1980).

IDEOLOGY

Althusser's proposal that economy was ultimately, but not practically, determinant of social life opened the theoretical possibility that societies were held together not by economy but by ideology or consent—the insight most usually attributed to Gramsci. Althusser's work, even though itself distant from Gramsci's, actually helped to produce the Gramsci boom of the 1970s. Moreover, while Althusser gave all the external appearances of being a good and reliable communist, he also helped to legitimate the importance of Freud and Lacan for social theory. Both psychoanalysts were structuralists, in the sense that they viewed surface signs as symptoms of other, deeper orders or disorders. This approach resembled Marx's distinction in *Capital* between appearance and essence as levels of reality.

The crucial concept here is that of overdetermination, that something incidental or contingent can actually cause or at least represent something apparently more fundamental; the Freudian slip is not a slip but represents something meaningful (Freud 1939; Althusser 1969: 101–16; Laplanche and Pontalis 1973: 292f). Overdetermination thus introduces into Marxism the possibility of a far more nuanced conception of causality than the orthodox would allow. The truth of a society will no longer be where Marxists claim to find it—in economy—but can be displaced elsewhere, and needs therefore to be read symptomatically. This was to open the possibility of a radical escape hatch from Althusserianism, for if ideology was the overdetermining factor, then the determinant nature of the economy was a kind of bluff, a slumbering last instance never to be called on. Althusser's attempt to modify the base–superstructure theorem, to moderate the economism within Marxism, led to the explosion of orthodoxy in other hands, and to the transformation of communism into the reconstruction of the project of radical democracy (Laclau and Mouffe 1985).

Althusser's interest in social reproduction thus became focused on the institutions which seek to naturalise the status quo: the school, the political party, the trade union, media, the church. His was not a stress on what Marx had called the dull compulsions of everyday life—get up, work, eat, sex, sleep—but on the ideologies and belief systems of capitalism and their agencies. Althusser addressed these concerns in the influential essay 'Ideology and Ideological State Apparatuses' (Althusser 1971) which again betrays the influence of the Gramsci whom Althusser textually marginalised. Althusser's approach confuses the issue by arguing as though society is the state; this is one other point of contact with Foucault's temptation to argue that capitalist democracies are in fact totalitarian. The Gramscian component was developed by Poulantzas—especially in his last work, *State, Power, Socialism* (Poulantzas 1978)—by Laclau and Mouffe, and by Stuart Hall and others within cultural studies. Similarly, Althusser's enthusiasm for Lacan played a part in the opening of Marxism to psychoanalysis, sexuality and feminism. Like Foucault, Althusser was no feminist, but this has not prevented his work from serving as a path in the development of French–English–Australian feminism in the 1970s and 1980s (Barrett 1980; Grosz 1989).

PHILOSOPHY OF SCIENCE

In a less significant register, arguably, than in economy or ideology, Althusser also enabled further questioning about the philosophy of science, or the conditions of the creation of knowledge. His defence of the work of the later Marx was posited on the premise that Marx initiated, around 1845, an epistemological break, or scientific rupture. Marx was not always a Marxist: he came to produce Marxism as a new science only later in his life, as he created a new vocabulary and theory (Althusser and Balibar 1970). In some places, for example in the General Philosophy Department at the University of Sydney, Althusser's affinities with Kuhn were recognised, for Kuhn's idea of a process of scientific revolution or paradigm shift in knowledge was in some respects analogous to Althusser's epistemological break or theoretical–scientific rupture (see Althusser 1969: 31–9; Lecourt 1975; Kuhn 1962). This particular dimension of Althusser's work—his relation to Bachelard, Canguilhelm and others—was relatively underdiscussed, with the exception of Sydney journals like *Working Papers in Sex, Science and Culture*.

While the idea of rupture seems now, in retrospect, significantly to overstate the possibility of breaking with traditional languages and ways of knowing and the novelty of Marxist concepts, Althusser did here usefully raise the question of shifts in the creation of knowledges. Notable examples are the discussion of Engels' use of Lavoisier's 'discovery' of phlogiston and of Montesquieu's discovery of the continent of history (Althusser and Balibar 1970: 150–8; see also 1972). What these signify, perhaps more than Althusser ever understood, is the theme of Marx's *Eighteenth Brumaire* or the message of Freud, that we always confound our pursuit of the new by constructing it in terms already known to us, re-enacting the past while we fancy ourselves trailblazing into the future.

INTERPRETATION

Perhaps Althusser's greatest, if unwitting, contribution was his partial and halting exposure of the necessity of interpretation. In the politically overcharged atmosphere of the 1960s—after the death of Stalin,

Khruschev's secret confession of Stalin's crimes, the invasion of Hungary and the Sino–Soviet split, as well as the discovery of the young Marx—Althusser declared that the question was clear: the challenge was how to read or construct Marx. His own version was single-minded—the question for Althusser was how to read *Capital*, and how to read it in a certain authorised manner, repressing or ignoring its Hegelian dimension (in chapter 1, volume 1). Althusser did not exhort his readers to read the *Grundrisse, The German Ideology* or the *Paris Manuscripts,* but the logic of his argument was to shift interpretation away from the text and toward the reader. His demand that we 'return to Marx' was unintentionally hermeneutic, for if we read symptomatically, then the question of interpretation is thrown open: there are logically as many possible readings of Marx as there are readers of Marx, as many Marxes as there are interpretations of Marx.

In Althusser's own terminology, overdetermination warranted overinterpretation: the notion of the talking cure introduced the theme of knowledge as conversation or dialogue between reader and author (and potentially between readers). Althusser was thus unwittingly subversive of Marxism, for he invited readers to open the Pandora's box of interpretation. He thus helped to set the scene for the more favourable reception of both hermeneutics and deconstruction. And even if in dogmatic inflexion, he did require of us that we *read Marx*—and his students began to read not only *Capital* but the young Marx, and Hegel, Hyppolite and Kojève, Gramsci, Weber and Nietzsche ... to *read,* to think theoretically, to seek out the problematic or constellation of concepts within theories and how they worked.

There is, of course, a great deal more than this to Althusser, and to the retrospectively bizarre yet ultimately fruitful phenomenon of the Althusserian moment. Althusserianism was a cult and is, in this sense, reminiscent of the 1960s as such. Here I have emphasised the positive dimensions. The negative are equally striking: we need think only of Althusser's peculiar demand that we treat Lenin as a philosopher, his posturing Maoism, the internality of his logic or the pompous jargon of his lexicon, the extraordinarily hermetic conception of theory outside of history, and the resultant intellectual gangsterism practised by his English and Australian enthusiasts.

The extremity of his theory invited the intellectual execution of Althusser by Edward Thompson in the work of his own excess, *The Poverty of Theory;* more balanced assessment was offered by Richard Johnson (1982: ch. 5) and by Perry Anderson (1980). Althusser had already pre-empted much of this response in his own *Essays in Self-Criticism* and had come closer again to Gramsci in his last writings (see, for example, 1978). The story ended in sadness. The manic depressive finally strangled his wife, and disappeared into an institution. Poulantzas, his most brilliant follower, committed suicide in 1979. Althusserianism disappeared as a formal force, like a message in a bottle into the depths of the channel. It would be hard to imagine Althusser's theory as a central influence into the twenty-first century, but equally difficult to deny its centrality to our own time.

BIBLIOGRAPHY

Primary sources

Althusser, L. (1969) *For Marx* Harmondsworth, Penguin
——(1971) *Lenin and Philosophy and Other Essays* New York, Monthly Review
——(1972) *Politics and History* London, New Left Books
——(1976) *Essays in Self-Criticism* London, New Left Books
——(1978) *Le marxisme aujourd'hui,* unpublished
——and Balibar, E. (1970) *Reading Capital* London, New Left Books

Secondary sources

Anderson, P. (1980) *Arguments Within English Marxism* London, Verso
Barrett, M. (1980) *Women's Oppression Today* London, Verso
Benton, T. (1984) *The Rise and Fall of Structural Marxism* London, Macmillan
Callinicos, A. (1976) *Althusser's Marxism* London, Pluto
Clarke, S. (1980) *One Dimensional Marxism* London, Allison and Busby
de George, R. and F. (1972) *The Structuralists From Marx to Lévi-Strauss* New York, Anchor
Descombes, V. (1980) *Modern French Philosophy* Cambridge, Cambridge University Press
Elliott, G. (1987) *Althusser—The Detour of Theory* London, Verso
Freud, S. (1939) *Psychopathology of Everday Life* Harmondsworth, Penguin
Godelier, M. (1972) *Rationality and Irrationality in Economics* New York, Monthly Review
Grosz, E. (1989) *Sexual Subversions* Sydney, Allen & Unwin
Hindess, B. and Hirst P. (1975) *Precapitalist Modes of Production* London, Routledge
Johnson, R. (1982) 'Reading for the best Marx', in R. Johnson et al. eds *Making Histories* London, Hutchinson
Kuhn, T. (1962) *The Structure of Scientific Revolutions* Chicago, Chicago University Press
Kurzweil, E. (1980) *The Age of Structuralism* Princeton, Columbia University Press
Laclau, E. and Mouffe, C. (1985) *Hegemony and Socialist Strategy* London, Verso
Laplanche, J. and Pontalis, J.B. (1973) *The Language of Psychoanalysis* London, Hogarth
Lecourt, D. (1975) *Marxism and Epistemology* London, New Left Books
Poulantzas, N. (1978) *State, Power, Socialism* London, New Left Books
Seddon, D. (1978) *Relations of Production, Marxist Approaches to Economic Anthropology* London, Frank Cass
Soper, K. (1986) *Humanism and Antihumanism* London, Hutchinson

Taylor, J. (1979) *From Modernization to Modes of Production* London, Macmillan
Terray, E. (1972) *Marxism and 'Primitive' Societies* New York, Monthly Review
Thompson, E.P. (1978) *The Poverty of Theory* London, Merlin
Vincent, J.M. (1974) *Contre Althusser* Paris, 10/18

2

American and British Feminisms

The term 'Anglo-American feminism' is often used to describe the body of thought which has emerged from the second-wave women's movement in England and the United States since the late 1960s. In spite of a similar heritage of ideological assumptions and intellectual traditions, significant differences exist in the development of feminism in these two countries, most notably the greater influence of Marxism upon English feminism as compared to closer links to both liberalism and anti-racism campaigns in the USA. The use of the term 'second-wave' points to a significant prior history of feminist activism, which resulted in women gaining the vote in England and the US in the 1920s (Banks 1981).

The re-emergence of feminism in the late 1960s has been attributed to a number of factors, including expanding female entry into higher education and the paid workforce, which led to a widening gap between women's own expectations and dominant representations of their role as that of full-time wife and mother (Friedan 1965). Furthermore, women's politicisation in New Left and civil rights struggles, where their own political concerns were largely ignored or ridiculed, in turn inspired them to form an autonomous liberation movement (Mitchell 1971). Thus, feminist thought does not exist in isolation but forms part of a social movement opposing women's oppression and this in turn accounts for its breadth and diversity.

Of course, schools of thought cannot be rigidly circumscribed within national boundaries, particularly in the case of feminism, which has drawn on the ideas of women from many different cultures. The following survey therefore includes references to women who were either born or now live in Australia and whose work has significantly contributed to the development of Anglo-American feminist thought.

HISTORICAL DEVELOPMENT

In one of the most influential texts of early second-wave feminism, *Sexual Politics* (1971), Kate Millett developed a groundbreaking analysis and critique of the various ideological processes through which patriarchy reproduced itself, demonstrating how sex roles—the notion of 'natural' and opposed male and female characteristics—served to reinforce and legitimise male power over women. Millett's account challenged prevailing conceptions of politics, arguing that the intimate sphere of romantic and sexual love, traditionally defined by men as a 'private' refuge from the demands of the public world, was permeated by relations of domination and subordination.

In another important early feminist text, *The Dialectic of Sex* (1970), Shulamith Firestone argued for a feminist materialist theory of history grounded in biological reproduction as the basis of women's oppression. Women's child-bearing capacity combined with the long period of dependency of the human infant were the primary causes of a gender division of labour which resulted in public power and authority residing in the hands of men. A necessary condition of feminist revolution was thus the abolition of motherhood and the family; here Firestone placed her hope in the liberating potential of new reproductive technologies as a means of overcoming the tyranny of biology, an optimism which some later feminists have found misplaced (Corea 1985).

These and similar works argued that women's differences from men constituted the basis of their oppression, frequently appealing to an ideal of androgyny which would free both women and men from the constraints of sex roles. As the 1970s progressed, however, some feminists became critical of what they saw as an attempt to gain equality with men by becoming like men and hence devaluing female difference. For example, Adrienne Rich (1976) developed a distinction between motherhood as an institution which served to oppress women, and as a potentially empowering experience rooted in women's distinctive psychological and biological characteristics.

The celebration of women's culture and the 'women-identified woman' was an important theme of 1970s feminism, often defined in opposition to a male affinity with abstract rationality, destruction and violence (Griffin 1978). This kind of dualistic framework shaped Mary Daly's (1978) indictment of patriarchal myths and institutions, which included a global survey of such ritualised forms of violence against women as Indian suttee, Chinese footbinding, African clitoridectomy, European witchburning and American gynaecology. Reappropriating mysogynistic terms (hag, crone, spinster) for feminist ends, Daly's creative and witty word play shaped her vision of woman-centred forms of knowledge uncontaminated by patriarchal thought.

More recently, this woman-centred perspective has in turn been

SOCIAL THEORY

called into question for a tendency towards essentialism and universal-
ism, i.e. defining aspects of women's experience as innate or making false
generalisations about the lives of all women. Socialist feminists have been
critical of what they regard as a shift toward a quietistic celebration of a
separate women's sphere grounded in female psychology or biology and
a consequent abandonment of issues of economics, class and history
(Eisenstein 1984; Segal 1987). In the US, women of colour have demonstrated the racist assumptions of a primarily white, middle-class
women's movement which has generalised unthinkingly from its own
relatively privileged position and glossed over conflicts between women
in the name of a spurious ideal of sisterhood (Hooks 1984; Moraga and
Anzaldua 1981).

The premises of Anglo-American feminism have also been challenged
by feminists influenced by poststructuralist thought and French feminism, who have been critical of appeals to female experience, subjectivity
and truth which pay insufficient attention to the linguistic mediation of
reality (Alcoff 1988). Contemporary Anglo-American feminist thought
has sought to respond to these criticisms by defending and refining its
arguments and currently embraces a range of views regarding the possibility and difficulty of theorising woman as an autonomous category
(Harding 1986).

ANALYTICAL OVERVIEW

One of the traditional ways of classifying Anglo-American feminist
thought is by making a distinction between *liberal feminism,* which
seeks equality for women through reforms to existing institutional structures, *socialist feminism,* which believes that gender cannot be understood in isolation from class and the structures of inequality operative in
capitalist society, and *radical feminism,* which identifies the domination
of men over women as the most fundamental and deeply rooted form of
oppression (Jaggar 1984). Such taxonomies are helpful in highlighting
significant differences between feminists as to the nature and causes of
women's oppression and the specific intellectual traditions on which
these positions draw (Donovan 1985).

However, they also obscure the distinctive features of feminist
thought which cannot be neatly assimilated into traditional political
categories on the left/right spectrum. These are best encapsulated in
terms of the early feminist slogan, 'the personal is political'. Feminism's
most significant contribution to social and political thought lies in its
far-reaching challenge to the private/public distinction embedded in
Western thought. On the one hand, it has politicised the so-called private realm by rendering visible gender hierarchies which structure all
aspects of everyday life; on the other, it has demonstrated that an
ostensibly 'rational' realm of work and politics is itself shaped by deep-
rooted emotional and psychic investments in gender identity. The

22

feminist critique has radical implications for understanding the entire spectrum of social relations.

PATRIARCHY

Patriarchy is the term used to describe a social system in which men as a group wield power over women. Engels (1972) argued that the origins of patriarchy were linked to the advent of private property and inheritance, which led to the regulation of female sexuality within a monogamous family unit. However, his account has been criticised for its reduction of women's subordination to economic factors and an inability to account for gender inequality in pre- and post-capitalist societies.

Feminist debates have centred around the possibility of developing a general theory of patriarchy. According to anthropologist Michele Rosaldo (1974), sexual asymmetry is a universal fact of all human cultures arising from male monopoly of public life and women's containment within the domestic sphere. Similarly, Sherry Ortner (1974) suggested that the devaluation of women is a result of the invariable association of feminity with nature rather than culture in all societies. Other feminists have been more sceptical regarding the possibility of making such cross-cultural comparisons and have questioned the value of unicausal explanations of women's subordination, which may take significantly different forms in different cultures (Brown 1981).

Marxist and socialist feminists have addressed the task of accounting for both the autonomy and the interrelatedness of capitalism and patriarchy. In a systematic coverage of the issues, Barrett (1980) indicated the weakness of functionalist arguments which assumed that patriarchy was necessary to the reproduction of capitalism, as well as some of the difficulties arising from the deployment of patriarchy as a trans-historical category. Feminists have expressed different views on the value of trying to reconcile Marxism and feminism into a single, 'dual-systems' theory, given the gender blindness of Marxist theory and the need to account for other forms of oppression such as that based on race (Sargent 1981; Kuhn and Wolpe 1978).

It seems important to recognise both the ubiquitous nature of patriarchy and its historically changing and culturally diverse forms. Sylvia Walby (1989) has argued that contemporary Western societies are undergoing a gradual shift from private patriarchy, where individual men benefit from women's subordination within the household, to public patriarchy, where women gain access to, but remain subordinate within, the arena of paid work, state and cultural institutions.

REPRODUCTION

A distinction is often made between the spheres of production and reproduction, with the latter designating the various processes through which life is reproduced and maintained, such as the bearing and rearing of children. Many feminists have identified the sphere of reproduction as a crucial determinant of gender inequality, agreeing with Engels that 'the modern individual family is founded on the open or concealed domestic slavery of the wife' (1972: 137).

Women's work in the home, because it is unpaid, has frequently not been acknowledged as work, a blindness reflected within sociological theory until Ann Oakley's (1974) groundbreaking investigations into the sociology of housework. The domestic labour debate in Marxist feminism centred around the economic significance of housework in the functioning of capitalism and the question of whether it could be understood in terms of the Marxist category of surplus value. Later discussions gave greater emphasis to the sphere of ideology, suggesting that dominant representations of the nuclear family as a privatised realm of intimacy and community played a crucial role in reinforcing a 'natural' association of women with house-keeping and child-care (Barrett and McIntosh 1982).

Radical feminist analyses have placed greater stress on the biological aspects of reproduction. Mary O'Brien (1981), affirming the importance of motherhood as a female experience which must remain central to feminist philosophy, argued that male alienation from the cycle of biological reproduction was a central factor in understanding the existence of patriarchy. The development of new reproductive technologies is often seen in this light as an example of increasing control over women's procreative power by a male-dominated medical profession (Corea 1985).

GENDER IN THE WORKPLACE

Feminist analyses of paid employment have focused on several issues: why women do less paid work than men, why they earn less money and why they do different jobs (Walby 1989: 25). Women's association with the reproductive sphere interacts with their subordinate position in the paid workforce (Hartmann 1981). Thus gender segregation in employment echoes that in the home, with women often working in jobs which require them to cook, clean, look after the children, provide emotional support, etc. In turn, the low pay and status allotted to women's work, which is typically defined as 'unskilled', renders them economically dependent upon a male wage-earner, ensuring their continuing responsibility for housework and child-care. Hartmann suggests that the concept of a 'family wage' as the legitimation for male access to better paid jobs embodies a set of interrelations between patriarchy and capitalism which is crucial to understanding the oppression of women.

While the notion of what constitutes 'women's work' changes significantly over time, it is always redefined in such a way as to remain separate from 'men's work'. Australian feminists Game and Pringle (1983) argue that the persistence of gender segregation in the workplace must be understood as a symbolic as well as economic phenomenon, i.e., in terms of the various social meanings with which gender identity is invested. More recently, Pringle (1988) has criticised Weberian theories which equate modern bureaucratic organisations with a public world of impersonality and instrumental rationality, showing that gender and sexuality saturate the workplace and remain central to its functioning.

SEXUALITY AND DOMINATION

The relationship between sexuality and power has been a key theme of second-wave feminism, with radical feminists focusing on the sexual objectification of women as the primary mechanism of patriarchal oppression: 'Sexuality is to feminism what work is to Marxism: that which is most one's own, yet most taken away' (MacKinnon 1981: 515). Whereas male sexuality is expressed in terms of the conquest and control of women, femininity is culturally defined in terms of the arousal of and submission to male desire.

A major aspect of feminist theory and politics has been the validation of lesbianism as a sexual preference and the critique of 'compulsory' heterosexuality. Adrienne Rich (1980) developed the notion of a 'lesbian continuum' which could encompass the diversity of friendships between women as well as the sexual relationships of self-identified lesbians. Asserting a primary intimacy between women stemming from the early mother–daughter bond, Rich argues that heterosexuality, rather than being a 'natural' desire, was an oppressive social institution which isolated women from each other by rendering them dependent upon individual men.

Feminism had brought to light widespread forms of sexual abuse or violence against women which have traditionally been ignored or trivialised: rape, domestic violence, incest, sexual harassment. Brownmiller's *Against Our Will* (1975) was an influential early radical feminist text which argued that rape functioned as a major form of social control over women. Other feminist writers offered passionate indictments of the ubiquity of pornographic images in Western culture as embodiments of a sadistic masculine desire to objectify and control women's bodies (Dworkin 1981).

Sexuality has been one of the most contested areas of debate within feminism, with some feminist theorists being critical of what they perceive as the moralism implicit in the radical feminist condemnation of pornography and its denial of female sexual desire and agency (Snitow et al. 1984).

SEX-GENDER DISTINCTION

A primary concern of feminist theory has been the question of *how* individuals acquire an identity as male or female. Here the distinction between *sex* and *gender* was of crucial significance; while sex described biological differences, gender designated the culturally imparted attributes of masculinity and femininity, which, most feminists believed, were historically variable and open to change. Theorists addressed the socialisation processes through which gender identity was inculcated and maintained, investigating gender hierarchies in such domains as language, education, religion, the mass media, etc. (Greer 1970; Spender 1980; Oakley 1981).

However, some feminists felt that socialisation theory did not provide an adequate explanation for the tenacity of gender differences, which seemed deeply embedded in the psychic structure of the individual and often resistant to change. As a result, they turned towards psychoanalysis as a means of accounting for such resistance. Gayle Rubin's model of the 'sex–gender' system combined Lévi-Strauss' work on the exchange of women within kinship systems with a selective appropriation of Freud, while Juliet Mitchell (1975) also argued for the value of Freudian theory in understanding the mechanisms of patriarchal oppression.

More recently, feminists have sought to develop specifically woman-centred forms of psychoanalysis. Because it is invariably women who mother, according to Chodorow (1978), girls acquire a sense of female self by identifying with a primary caretaker of the same gender, while the acquisition of male identity requires boys to separate themselves from and to reject the mother. Girls thus develop a greater sense of relationship and connectedness to others, which in turn encourages them to become mothers themselves, whereas male identity is characterised by an emphasis on separation, autonomy and clearly defined ego boundaries. In a related account, Dorothy Dinnerstein (1976) also resorted to the fact of universal mothering to explain deep-rooted cultural hostility towards the feminine, suggesting that men seek to overcome their infantile experience of helpless dependency on an all-powerful mother by exercising control over women in adult life.

Finally, it should be noted that the sex/gender distinction has been increasingly subject to criticism for adhering to, rather than questioning, a dualistic opposition between nature and culture, the biological and the social (*Australian Feminist Studies* 1989).

GENDER AND THOUGHT

Feminism has gone beyond the critical analysis of social institutions to reveal the gender asymmetry underpinning the conceptual frameworks and categories of Western thought. An examination of the history of

Western philosophy reveals a systematic equation of human rationality with masculinity, defined through the exclusion of a femininity equated with nature and the irrational (Lloyd 1984). Feminist philosophers of science have criticised the subject/object dichotomy enshrined in the scientific world view; the development of scientific thought has been permeated by metaphors of male domination over a nature codified as feminine (Keller 1985). Such interrogations of claims to objectivity and impartiality have in turn inspired reflections on the status of feminist arguments. Can women's experiences provide a grounding for feminist thought or does feminism rather problematise the status of that experience by exposing its socially constructed nature?

Sandra Harding (1986) provides a helpful distinction between several different feminist theories of knowledge or epistemologies. *Feminist empiricism* aims to identify and eliminate systematic biases against women in existing bodies of knowledge as a means of achieving a more accurate and objective understanding of reality. *Feminist standpoint* theories question this goal of objective, value-free knowledge, arguing that women's distinctive psychological and social experiences provide the potential basis for a superior understanding of the nature of social relations. *Feminist postmodernists* by contrast are sceptical of any such claims to truth and of attempts to attribute a privileged status to women's experiences.

Similar debates have occured in the sphere of ethics. Gilligan (1982) exposed the male bias of prevailing psychological models of moral development, showing that women opted for an approach to moral problems which emphasised responsibilities to others rather than abstract rights. Sara Ruddick's (1989) notion of maternal thinking also exemplifies an attempt to ground an ethical theory in the caretaking relationships commonly experienced by, though not unique to, women.

CONCLUSION

The last twenty years have seen a remarkable expansion of feminist scholarship. This work has demonstrated that taking woman rather than man as the reference point of academic inquiry requires a shift in perspective which has the effect of relativising and destabilising existing intellectual paradigms. Feminist theory thus has implications not just for the study of women but for the entire domain of social theory, because it suggests that existing theoretical frameworks which claim general validity have in fact relied tacitly or explicitly on a masculine norm.

BIBLIOGRAPHY

Alcoff, L. (1988) 'Cultural feminism versus poststructuralism: the identity crisis in feminist theory' *Signs* 13 (3): 405–36.
Australian Feminist Studies (1989) 10, Sex/Gender Issue
Banks, O. (1981) *Faces of Feminism: A Study of Feminism as a Social Movement* Oxford, Martin Robertson

Barrett, M. (1980) *Women's Oppression Today: Problems in Marxist Feminist Analysis* London, Verso

——and McIntosh, M. (1982) *The Anti-Social Family* London, Verso

Brown, P (1981) 'Universals and particulars in the position of women', in Cambridge Women's Studies Group *Women in Society: Inter-disciplinary Essays* London, Virago

Brownmiller, S. (1975) *Against Our Will: Men, Women and Rape* New York, Simon and Schuster

Chodorow, N. (1978) *The Reproduction of Mothering: Psychoanalysis and the Sociology of Gender* Berkeley, University of California Press

Corea, G. (1985) *The Mother Machine: Reproductive Technologies from Artificial Insemination to Artificial Wombs* New York, Harper and Row

Daly, M. (1978) *Gyn/Ecology: The Meta-Ethics of Radical Feminism* Boston, Beacon Press

Dinnerstein, D. (1976) *The Mermaid and the Minotaur: Sexual Arrangements and Human Malaise* New York, Harper and Row

Donovan, J. (1985) *Feminist Theory: The Intellectual Traditions of American Feminism* New York, Continuum

Dworkin, A. (1981) *Pornography: Men Possessing Women* London, Women's Press

Eistenstein, H. (1984) *Contemporary Feminist Thought* London, Allen & Unwin

Engels, F. (1972) *The Origins of the Family, Private Property and the State* New York, International Publishers

Firestone, S. (1970) *The Dialectic of Sex: The Case for Feminist Revolution* New York, Bantam

Friedan, B. (1965) *The Feminine Mystique* Harmondsworth, Penguin

Game, A. and Pringle, R. (1983) *Gender at Work* Sydney, Allen & Unwin

Gilligan, C. (1982) *In a Different Voice* Cambridge, Harvard University Press

Greer, G. (1970) *The Female Eunuch* New York, McGraw-Hill

Griffin, S. (1978) *Woman and Nature: The Roaring Inside Her* New York, Harper and Row

Harding, S. (1986) 'The instability of the analytical categories of feminist theory' *Signs* 11 (4): 645

Hartmann, H. (1981) 'The unhappy marriage of Marxism and feminism: towards a more progressive union', in L. Sargent (ed.) *Women and Revolution* Boston, Southend Press

Hooks, B. (1984) *Feminist Theory: from Margin to Center* London, Southend Press

Jaggar, A. (1984) *Feminist Politics and Human Nature* Brighton, Harvester

Keller, E. (1985) *Reflections on Gender and Science* New Haven, Yale University Press

Kuhn, A. and Wolpe, A. (1978) (eds) *Feminism and Materialism: Women and Modes of Production* London, Routledge & Kegan Paul

Lloyd, G. (1984) *The Man of Reason: 'Male' and 'Female' in Western Philosophy* London, Methuen

MacKinnon, C. (1981) 'Feminism, Marxism, method and the state: an agenda for theory' *Signs* 7 (3): 515–44

Millett, K. (1971) *Sexual Politics* London, Rupert Hart-Davis

Mitchell, J. (1971) *Women's Estate* Harmondsworth, Penguin

——(1975) *Psychoanalysis and Feminism* Harmondsworth, Penguin

Moraga, C. and Anzaldua, G. (1981) (eds) *This Bridge Called My Back: Writings by Radical Women of Color* Watertown, Mass., Persephone Press

Oakley, A. (1974) *The Sociology of Housework* Oxford, Martin Robertson

——(1981) *Subject Woman* Oxford, Martin Robertson

O'Brien, M. (1981) *The Politics of Reproduction* London, Routledge & Kegan Paul

Ortner, S. B. (1974) 'Is female to male as nature is to culture?', in M. Z. Rosaldo and L. Lamphere (eds) *Women Culture and Society* Stanford, Stanford University Press

Pringle, R. (1988) *Secretaries Talk: Sexuality, Power and Work* Sydney, Allen & Unwin

Rich, A. (1976) *Of Woman Born: Motherhood as Experience and Institution* New York, W. W. Norton

——(1980) 'Compulsory heterosexuality and lesbian existence' *Signs* 5 (4): 631–60

Rosaldo, M. Z. (1974) 'Women, culture and society: a theoretical overview', in M. Z. Rosaldo and L. Lamphere (eds) *Women, Culture and Society* Stanford, Stanford University Press

Rubin, G. (1975) 'The traffic in women: notes on the "political economy" of sex', in R. R. Reiter (ed.) *Towards and Anthropology of Women* New York, Monthly Review Press

Ruddick, S. (1989) *Maternal Thinking: Towards a Politics of Peace* Boston, Beacon Press

Sargent, L. (ed.) (1981) *Women and Revolution* Boston, Southend Press

Segal, L. (1987) *Is the Future Female? Troubled Thoughts on Contemporary Feminism* London, Virago

Snitow, A. Stansell, C. and Thompson, S. (1984) *Desire: The Politics of Sexuality* London, Virago

Spender, D. (1980) *Man-Made Language* London, Routledge & Kegan Paul

Walby, S. (1989) *Theorizing Patriachy* Oxford, Basil Blackwell

3

Hannah Arendt

Hannah Arendt (1906–1975) was born and raised in Königsberg, a provincial German town in East Prussia which had become well-known through two of its most famous citizens, the German philosopher Immanuel Kant and the pioneer of western Jewish Enlightenment Moses Mendelssohn. She grew up in a well-established bourgeois German–Jewish family, a fact that gave her both a secure childhood and set the scene for her life history and intellectual development.

Her life can be divided into three major phases. The first (1906–1933) encompasses the years of her childhood, her student years in Germany, and her first political work against the rise of Nazism. Arendt studied philosophy under leading philosophers of her time. With two of them, Martin Heidegger and Karl Jaspers, close relationships persisted well into the post World War II years, albeit for very different reasons. Heidegger became a Nazi and was promoted in academia, but for a brief period he had been her lover. Karl Jaspers, on the other hand, lost all of his academic privileges and positions because he steadfastly refused to submit to the Nazis. He became Hannah Arendt's friend for life, and, when Jaspers was awarded the German Peace Prize in 1958, it was she who gave the address in his honour. As an adolescent Arendt showed little interest in politics and Judaism but the rising power of the Nazis persuaded her to regard her own position with growing political astuteness.

The second phase of her life (1933–1951), beginning with her forced departure from Germany after Hitler's rise to power, were years of persecution and intense struggle for survival, first physically in France and later financially in New York. In this period she devoted most of her energies to the Jewish cause: the survival of Jews and the retrieval of Jewish culture after the war. From this time stems the writing that Feldman edited later into the volume *The Jew as Pariah* (1978). In some of these papers and a series of lectures, she prepared the ground for her book entitled *The Origins of Totalitarianism* which was first published in 1951 and made her famous overnight. A year later, she was finally granted American citizenship.

In the third phase of her life, from 1951 to her sudden death in 1975, Arendt rose to the stature of a major twentieth-century thinker, whose honesty in the concern for the nature and causes of twentieth-century crises gained her both fame and fierce disapproval. Indeed, she was considered an enfant terrible of intellectual life, not only in New York but in the entire Western world. She came into the crossfire of criticism on countless occasions, most severely after the publication of her book *Eichmann in Jerusalem*. Her quality as a thinker was never in doubt and much of her reputation rested on a *succès d'estime*, even though few liked her criticisms and even fewer her conclusions (Hill 1979: x). She continued to be a prolific writer until her death. It is also important to note that she lived what she preached. Hannah Arendt, who raised the concept of the pariah to new importance and made it central to her thinking, also lived her life as a pariah.

Every account of Hannah Arendt's works begins almost peremptorily with the statement that Arendt was an original thinker. Indeed, Arendt's political ideas are striking and controversial, and she is not easily fitted into any 'school' of thought. At times she attacked the disciplines of history, sociology and politics, on many occasions argued against Marx, and dreamt about the ideal polis, which often had a conservative tinge. At the same time she was a radical thinker. She was an explicit critic of the cult of growth and the distortion of freedom under a system that called itself a free market and subsumed all other activity, chiefly the political sphere, under its dictates (Feher in Kaplan, 1989). But she also criticised the French Revolution for its fateful error of mixing a concern for social issues with that of political freedom. Finally, she attacked democracy itself as too inadequate a system to result in political freedom. Democracies were ultimately very deficient systems that functioned by suppressing dissent and oppressing minorities. In her view, only a republic provided the political space for political action and allowed for free expression of irreducibly pluralistic views.

She does not give answers on how to solve our modern ills but was content to debunk and build paradigms of thought. At least she has not fallen into a trap of her own making here for she claimed that, since Plato, and later also under Christianity, the Western tradition of political thought had been a philosopher's tradition, and thus, in a sense, it was apolitical. The very people, she argued, who engaged in political thought were men of contemplation rather than of political action and thus diametrically opposed to those who practised politics in everyday life (Canovan 1974: 11). She thought that theorists had no business telling practitioners how to think. The political *actors* themselves had to learn to think and to decide. Furthermore, her concern about the atrophy of the public sphere in modern times led her to urge that the capacity for action be reclaimed (Hill 1979: xii).

In her first major work, *The Origins of Totalitarianism,* Arendt argues that totalitarianism is essentially different from all other forms of political oppression (despotism, tyranny, dictatorship) and this difference finds its clearest expression in the ideology and terror that systematically destroyed Jews in Hitler's Germany and kulaks in Stalin's Russia. Totalitarianism, as a crisis of the twentieth century, is seen here as a phenomenon applicable to both Russia and Germany. However, much of her book deals with Nazism, and it is in this context that her explanations are most convincing. She is interested in understanding why the existence of the Nazis and the mass extermination of Jews were possible and why anti-Semitism formed such an essential part of Nazi totalitarian rule. To answer these questions she mustered the entire history of the *Abendland* or occident, or, rather, strands and elements of it which might explain the sudden collapse of morality in twentieth century Europe and the fall into publicly approved barbarism.

One of her chief contentions is that three main changes in nineteenth–century Europe undermined and eventually dismantled the structure and self-understanding of nation states. These were racism, imperialism and, as an obverse side to imperialism, movements such as Pan-Slavism and Pan-Germanism, which provided the raw material for totalitarianism in the twentieth century. Imperialism, most pronounced in Britain, combined several forces destructive of the political sphere: expansion for its own sake, which was itself built on racism and the development of bureaucracies to service overseas possessions. In contrast to Weber, Hannah Arendt perceived these administrative bodies as distinctly destructive and negative. The issue in the colonies was not to establish responsible governments but to 'administer' possessions gained by immoral means. Colonial governments were therefore ruling by decrees, by secret decisions, and by arbitrariness devoid of any sense of personal responsibility, and at the same time creating an atmosphere in which racial domination became historically justifiable destiny. Colonialism taught that violence alone can establish racial supremacy. Its tenets became inflammatory when, within Europe, these ideas merged into and partly fuelled an inverted imperialism at home, especially in Russia and in Germany. These movements were based on race and expansionary claims vindicated not by institutions and political structures but solely by the claim of the group as being superior to others. They arose, she argues, in the absence of a fully developed nation state and were in themselves inimical to it (cf Canovan 1974: ch2).

Essential here is the concept of the pariah. Feher suggests (1989: 18–21) that one of the most interesting aspects of her explanations of totalitarianism is the truly astonishing structure of Arendt's book. More than the first quarter of the book is devoted to a very detailed account of Jewish emancipation and the rise of political anti-Semitism. Here an attempt is made to explain the rest of society by understanding the exception. It is here that the historical role of the Jew as pariah finds new application, an idea she had already fully developed in her first major work *Rahel Varnhagen* (1974). The pariahs of European society, paradigmatically the Jews, were definable by their lack of belonging to a political community. Unlike her predecessors, however, Arendt's analysis endows the position of pariah with the new qualities and potentialities of a rebel who can turn resentment into political action. Jewish emancipation, as it evolved in nineteenth-century Europe, however, was merely a social emancipation which gave rise to the social climber, who won for himself a better life, but not political freedom.

The idea of the pariah was indeed also a personal position at which Arendt had arrived in response to the persecution of Jews in Europe. This position, which she termed 'conscious pariah', was closely tied to her concept of natality. By natality she refers to the unalterable and contingent qualities of the circumstances (personal, historical, ethnic) of one's birth that circumscribe 'what' one is. Having been born a pariah, a Jew for example, one should acknowledge that one is a Jew because only by being true to oneself can one have the integrity to act from a position of strength. Attempts at assimilation, as she had already observed in *Rahel Varnhagen,* would and could only lead to the assimilation of new prejudices and to self-denial.

Another set of concepts was crystallised in *The Human Condition* (1958). In this book Arendt casts three categories for human activity: labour, work and action. Labour referred exclusively to those activities which were essential for survival. Work, on the other hand, concerned human productivity, while action belonged to neither group. It is this latter category which deserves most attention for in it she spells out the problematic distinction between 'social' and 'political'. Indeed, she draws a sharp line between the two. By 'social' she refers to any human activity and any issue and concern that is grounded in the social and economic world. Issues such as poverty, housing, social equality, women's movements etc. are 'social' questions and, in Arendt's schemata, do not belong in the realm of the 'political'. Action in turn is only possible in the political realm.

This separation has troubled many political theorists, for it seemed to have extremely reactionary implications. Would she want to see the big social questions of the nineteenth and twentieth centuries—such as class disadvantage, minority status and specific issues such as housing and the management of poverty—struck again from the political agenda? In a sense, she would, as far as her specific idea of the 'political' realm is concerned. However, it is clear from other contexts that she also vehemently argued that poverty was entirely unacceptable because all it did was to create mobs and elites, and neither group was capable of disinterested political action. For the same reason, i.e. because of the political destructiveness of structured inequalities, she despised the philosophy of growth of capitalist free markets.

Her ideal of a republic, as distinct from a democracy, emphasises the idea of political freedom based on human rights. Those human rights in a fully-fledged republic should express the irreducibly pluralistic nature of the political community and would potentially give everyone the right to fully participate. Democracies, by contrast, falsely assume a rule by consensus when indeed they represent only the interests of a powerful mainstream lobby that could degenerate into oligarchy or even tyranny. Moreover, democratic practice had shown a steady atrophy of the political sphere. In her view, politics is neither a superstructure imposed on conflicts and social interests nor is it or should it be a guardian of private interests. The origin of politics lies in the Greek polis, which distinguished between the private household and the public space of the polis. The former lies in the realm of necessity; the latter describes the realm of freedom. The important point here is that in her view of the Greek understanding, the private existed for the public and not vice versa, as is assumed today. The obfuscation of political action lies in the confusion of work and action. Much of what politicians and democratic governments do today is 'making' things, such as programs, building houses, devising policies, and they are, in her sense, therefore not engaged in political action. In each case, consensus has to be reached and decisions have to be made. It is achieved at the expense of plurality. Thus, in Arendt's unusual treatment of sovereignty, the concept becomes the very opposite of freedom, but, as she explained more fully in *On Revolution* (1963), power and freedom are not compatible.

But who are its actors? The keyword here is the citizen, in sharp contrast to the bourgeois. She put her hopes for the future into citizenship, agreeing with Marx that the bourgeois victory in nineteenth-century Europe was the single most catastrophic event for political man and woman. She argues that human speech and action are in fact basic needs and the loss of a public realm is the loss of freedom, or vice versa, and only through the creation and maintenance of a public sphere can citizens be free. She thus invests human beings as citizens with the capacity for action through which they will not just fulfil their own potential but through which the republic will be sustained. Her view of unpredictable, spontaneous political action ran very much counter to predominant sociological theories of role assignment and role-play, categories which she regarded as deterministic and passive. Against political theories based on descriptions of institutions, systems and roles, she defends the individual, the original action and the capacity to achieve such originality via a process of thinking, as shown especially in her collection *Between Past and Future* (1961). Her emphasis on diversity and the right of individual action clearly has very radical and positive implications for minority groups.

There is no doubt that her vision of 'true politics', of the ideal form of citizenship in a republic, and of strong individual actors, has more than a tinge of the romantic about it. But one needs to recall here that these views were nurtured by one of the greatest catastrophes of human history: a world war larger and more devastating than any previous war, followed by a cold war, and a holocaust which horrified not just because it was barbaric but because it was so carefully planned, administered and executed on the very principles of the modern world. The 'banality of evil', an expression she used in describing Eichmann at the trial in Jerusalem, showed to her how extremely average people could become instruments and executioners of monstrous designs. Eichmann had no opinions. Yet opinions are essential for the public political sphere. Freedom lies in the diversity of opinions, in the right to express them without any coercion. Her rallying against ideologies, her mistrust of endeavours in political thought for finding out generalities and 'truths' is after all firmly rooted in the experience of the crises of the twentieth century.

BIBLIOGRAPHY

Primary Sources

Arendt, H. (1951) *The Origins of Totalitarianism* New York, Harcourt Brace (also called *The Burden of Our Time* London, Secker and Warburg)
——(1958) *The Human Condition* Chicago and London, Chicago University Press
——(1958) *Rahel Varnhagen: The Life of a Jewish Woman* London, East and West Library
——(1961) *Between Past and Future* New York, Viking; London, Faber and Faber
——(1963) *Eichmann in Jerusalem: A Report on the Banality of Evil* New York, Viking; London, Faber and Faber
——(1963) *On Revolution* New York, Viking Press; London, Faber and Faber
——(1968) *Men in Dark Times* New York, Harcourt Brace
——(1970) *On Violence* New York, Harcourt Brace; London, Allen Lane
——(1972) *Crises of the Republic* New York, Harcourt Brace Jovanovich
——(1978) *The Jew As Pariah: Jewish Identity and Politics in the Modern Age* A collection of essays and letters written from 1942–66, edited and with an introduction by R. H. Feldman, New York, Grove Press Inc.
——(1978) *The Life of the Mind* New York, Harcourt Brace Jovanovich; London, Secker and Warburg
——(1982) *Lectures on Kant's Political Philosophy* London, Harvester Press

Secondary Sources

Bernstein, R. J. (1977) 'Hannah Arendt: the ambiguities of theory and practice', in T. Ball (ed.) *Political Theory and Praxis: New Perspectives* Minneapolis, University of Minnesota Press

Canovan, M. (1974) *The Political Thought of Hannah Arendt* London, J. M. Dent

Cooper, L. A. (1976) 'Hannah Arendt's political philosophy: an interpretation' *Review of Politics* April, 38:145–76

Coser, L. A. (1984) 'Hannah Arendt (1906–1975) : self-proclaimed pariah', in L. A. Coser *Refugee Scholars in America. Their Impact and Their Experience* New Haven and London, Yale University Press

Heather, G. P. and Stolz, M. (1979) 'Hannah Arendt and the problem of critical theory' *The Journal of Politics* February 41: 2–22

Hill, M. A. 1979 (ed.) *Hannah Arendt: The Recovery of the Public World* New York, St Martin's Press

Mack, A. (1977) (ed.) *Social Research* 44 (Spring). Special New School issue on Hannah Arendt, with contributions by J. Habermas, H. Jonas, G. Gray, R. Nisbet, J. N. Shklar, S. Wolin, B. Crick, H. Morgenthau, D. Sternberger, E. Heller, E. Vollrath, and E. Young-Bruehl

Kaplan, G. and Kessler, C. (1989) (eds) *Hannah Arendt. Thinking, Judging, Freedom* Sydney, Allen & Unwin

Kateb, G. (1984) *Hannah Arendt. Politics, Conscience, Evil* Totowa, N.J., Rowman & Allanheld

May, D. (1986) *Hannah Arendt* Harmondsworth, Penguin

Nelson, J. S. (1978) 'Politics and truth: Arendt's problematic' *American Journal of Political Science* 22: 270–301

Parekh, B. (1981) *Hannah Arendt and the Search for a New Political Philosophy* Atlantic Highlands, Humanities Press

Quinton, A. (1983) 'Hannah Arendt', in A. Bullock and R.B. Woodings (eds) *20th Century Culture: A Biographical Companion* New York, Harper and Row

Whitfield, S.J. (1980) *Into the Dark. Hannah Arendt and Totalitarianism* Philadelphia, Temple University Press

Young-Bruehl, E. (1982) *Hannah Arendt. For Love of the World* New Haven and London, Yale University Press

4

Pierre Bourdieu

This analysis of the academic world is the end product of the critical reflection on scientific practice which I have never ceased to conduct as part of the very process of my research, since the time when, as a young ethnologist, I took my own native region as the object of my ethnological investigation (Bourdieu 1962).

Thus, my sociological analysis of academic world aims to trap *Homo Academicus,* supreme classifier among classifiers, in the net of his own classifications. It is a comic scenario, that Don Juan deceived or The Miser robbed ...

The sociologist, who chooses to study his own world in its nearest and most familiar aspects should not, as the ethnologist would, domesticate the exotic, but, if I may venture the expression, exoticise the domestic, through a break with his initial relation of intimacy with modes of life and thought which remain opaque to him because they are too familiar.
... (Bourdieu 1988:xi)

This passage from one of Bourdieu's latest '*objectifications*'—the making public or conscious and problematic of that which is unconscious, taken-for-granted (*doxic*) and unproblematic—reveals the heart of Bourdieu's academic practice. The perspective he brings to bear on his own society, that of the marginalised, estranged observer for whom all is exotic and strange, springs from his anthropological/ethnographic experience studying another, non-Western society, and from the experience of a class-based cultural marginality within the Parisian academic scene resulting from his provincial and lower middle-class origins. Despite his unquestioned status as one of the current *patrons* of French sociology (along with Crozier, Touraine, Boudon ...) and as the reigning star at Editions de Minuit (they have published 14 of his books over the past 26 years and 9 since 1977), Bourdieu constantly cultivates this sociocultural marginality as an essential ingredient in the maintenance of his particular sociological perspective and of his position within the intellectual *field* (*champ*—a field of battle; a space of action), free of academic factions, fads and fashions, uncategorised and uncategorisable —as a Durkheimian, a Weberian, a Marxist, phenomenologist, structuralist ... He seeks constantly to subvert the hegemonic domination of our consciousness and action by ideological principles which are taken for granted as 'commonsense', revealing how banal are so many of the things we treasure as rare, how widespread are qualities and behaviours we assume to be unique, how public and shared are the things we assume to be private and personal (see Bourdieu 1980: 40–1). His sociology is overtly political as he aims at the transformation of culture and society through subversive revelation, through exposure.

Pierre Bourdieu, Professor of Sociology at the College de France, was born in 1930 in the province of Bearn in the south of France, the son of a civil servant. He was educated with the elite, though in a way not one of them, at the Ecole Normale Superieure. Honneth, Kocyba and Schwibs (1986) conducted a revealing interview with Bourdieu about the various academic influences of his intellectual development, revealing a clear statement of his claim to sociocultural and intellectual marginality. He carried out ethnographic research in war-torn Algeria from 1958 to 1961, in particular among the acephalous Kabyle, the site for the development of many of the concepts central to his theory of practice as he struggled to understand the reproduction of sociocultural cohesion and of law and order in the face of an absence of overt rules and authority. He returned to France to research the processes by which structured cultural differences were reproduced within French society, seeking the clues to the reproduction of structured social inequalities. Convinced of the need to locate theorising in the context of ongoing empirical research, Bourdieu looked for the clues to the processes of cultural differentiation in the French education system, secondary and tertiary, and in the formation and transformation of artistic taste. In the process he has also explored the complexities of language use and the logics they employ.

Bourdieu rose to prominence on the French intellectual scene in the late 1960s when the book *Les Heretiers,* coauthored with his colleague Claude Passeron (Bourdieu 1979b), became a source book for the student revolt of 1968, evidence of poor education and economic prospects and, most importantly, of the complicity of the French educational establishment in the promotion of a class-ridden society. However, awareness of his work in the Anglo-American scene lagged behind. His early work, *Sociologie de L'Algerie* (1958), had been translated and published as *The Algerians* in 1962 (1962b) but it received little attention. Since then a spate of books has been translated.

Bourdieu's work combines a theoretical rigour compatible with Anthony Giddens, with whose work there is much in common, particularly with regard to the concern with reintroducing time and space into theories of social action and social structure (the process of 'structuration' in Giddens), with constant and widespread empirical research. Like Durkheim and Mauss, and more recently Louis Dumont and Maurice Godelier among others, he sees the ethnological experience, or at least a firm grounding in the ethnography of non-Western societies, as vital for the effective study of one's own social milieu. While refusing the labels that encompass others, his work is constantly a dialogue with varieties of Marxism, structuralism, phenomenology and poststructuralism (Derrida was a fellow student at the Ecole Normale and a political compatriot: see Honneth et al. 1986).

Contemptuous of academic gamesmanship, of the academic dilettantes who maintain 'a coquettish relationship with selected works' (Bourdieu 1967:182), Bourdieu has nonetheless been so dealt with in the Anglo-American scene, characterised/caricatured as a 'reproduction theorist', by those who would dismiss his work on the basis of a misreading of bits of his work, usually to construct a foil to their own assumed brilliance. As we indicate below, when Bourdieu seeks to discover the sociocultural processes which lie behind the reproduction of structured inequalities, he refers not to a process by which static structures are reproduced in an identical way over and over again—that would be classically structural functionalist and completely antithetical to Bourdieu—but rather to the processes by which the ongoing structuring of social relationships are formed and transformed (reproduced). His theory of practice is the linchpin of all his work; his *Outline of a Theory of Practice* (1977a) is the work that must be read if the studies of education, art, language and the state are to be placed in perspective.

While Bourdieu's sociology constantly clarifies the relationship between the individual and society, he is careful not to succumb to the temptation to use an intensely ideological category such as 'the individual' as a unit of analysis. When operating *as a social scientist* he is concerned with our socialness, with our behaviour as *agents* of and creative elements in the social process. So he consciously transcends both the ideology of individualism and subjectivism. Individuals are the clue, as objects of empirical/ethnological study, to an understanding which lies beyond any particular individual: 'The substantialist mode of thought which stops short at directly accessible elements, that is to say individuals, claims a certain fidelity to reality by disregarding the structure of relations whence these elements derive all their sociologically relevant determinations . . .' (Bourdieu 1977c: 487).

It is our agency, not 'us', that dominates his theorising.

For Bourdieu the *agents* of social interaction are *strategists* and time and space are integral to their strategies. Their strategic practice is structured by their sociocultural environment, by what Bourdieu has called their *habitus,* involving structured *dispositions* which in turn are the basis for ongoing structuring (structuration) (1977a: 71). So the strategic agents are disposed via their habitus to compete for honour, for *symbolic capital,* on the myriad but related *fields* of thought and action. The culturally competent strategists, agents embodying the habitus, are neither mechanistic puppets nor calculating game players. Their behaviour does not involve obedience to rules, it does not 'presuppose a conscious aiming at ends or an express mastery of the operations necessary to attain them and [yet is] . . . collectively orchestrated without being the product of the orchestrating action of the conductor' (p. 72).

Once we grasp such a view of strategic agents operating through and transforming culture, we are on the road to a transcendence of the simplistic schemes that have dominated anthropological and sociological writing. Ideologies are no longer either sets of rules and regulations oriented towards order or reflections of the material conditions of existence; kinship is no longer a clear unambiguous field of rules and terminologies understood through arbitrarily devised concepts; and culture is anything but a field of symbols with clear unambiguous referents. Knowledge is fluid, shifting, manipulable. As people orient their action they do so not in terms of rules but in terms of shifting possibilities. There is no claim to voluntarism, no reversion of Schutzian phenomenology or Geertzian 'theatre'. For to reject rules is not to reject structure or hegemonic domination. But first, what does Bourdieu mean when he calls for the substitution of 'strategy for the rule', when he concentrates on dispositions and rejects obedience to rules?

Bourdieu explores the structures beyond individual consciousness by stressing that the agent must thus be understood as 'a producer and reproducer of objective meaning' (p. 79) whose 'actions and works are the product of a modus operandi of which he or she is not the producer and has no conscious mastery'. 'It is because subjects do not, strictly speaking, know what they are doing that what they do has more meaning than they know.' Moving from a demonstration of the way the Kabyle of Algeria operate not through 'rules' of honour but a 'sense' of honour, Bourdieu turns to the analysis of Western capitalist society to show that we, too, despite (or because of) our codified rules and laws, are agents engaged in constant strategic practice; with 'the practical mastery of the symbolism of social interaction—tact, dexterity, or savoir-faire . . . accompanied by the application of a spontaneous semiology, i.e. mass of precepts, formulae, and codified cues' (p. 10). We are doubly blind to the informal aspects *because* of the existence of rules.

To transcend this blindness we must engage in a *methodological objectivism:* 'Only by constructing the objective structures (price curves, chances of access to higher education, laws of the matrimonial market, etc.) is one able to pose the question of the mechanisms through which the relationship is established between the structures and the practices or the representations which accompany them' (p. 21). But the resultant model of reality is only the start. Bourdieu warns of the tendency 'to slip from the model of reality to the reality of the model' (p. 29): 'Methodological objectivism, a necessary moment in all research, by the break with primary experience and the construction of objective relations which it accomplishes, demands its own supersession' (p. 72). We must, says Bourdieu, escape 'the realism of the structure' by passing 'from the *opus operatum* to the *modus operandi,* from statistical regularity or algebraic structure to the principle of the production of this observed order'. The consequent construction of a theory of practice 'or, more precisely the theory of the mode of generation of practices' is 'the precondition for establishing an experimental science of the *dialectic of the internationalization of externality and the externalization of internality,* or, more simply, of incorporation and objectification'.

The 'symbolism of social interaction' and our 'spontaneous semiology' are, as mentioned above, coordinated through the *habitus,* 'the strategy-generating principle enabling agents to cope with unforeseen and ever-changing situations' (p 72), the dynamic element of culture, the basis upon which we are disposed to order the symbolism available to us, through which the colours, shapes, sounds, words etc. *become* symbolic: '. . . systems of durable, transposable *dispositions,* structured structures predisposed to act as structuring structures, that is, as principles of the generation and structuring of practices and representations'. The practices and representations generated by the habitus can therefore '. . . be objectively "regulated" and "regular" without in any way being the product of obedience to rules, objectively adapted to their goals without presupposing a conscious aiming at ends or an express mastery of the operations necessary to attain them and, being all this, collectively orchestrated without being the product of the orchestrating action of a conductor'.

So the people we study regain their individuality, their creativity and we the sociologists, via a *methodological objectivism,* expose the meaning that they do not know but which they unknowingly create. Thus Bourdieu, through his studies of education, the arts and the state exposes the unconscious complicity of the upper- and middle-class in the reproduction of the structured inequality basic to capitalist relations of production. The contours of social inequality are structured through patterns of unequal access to *symbolic capital,* through unequal cultural competence as defined, accorded honour/acceptance by those in economic, political and cultural control. The dominant classes engage not only in political and economic domination but exercise this domination via *symbolic violence,* via *judgements of taste,* often via the violence of silence, as those denied access not only to the means of production but to cultural competence, *cultural capital,* consistently fail. Bourdieu provides a devastating summary of the vital role that the formal education system plays in the reproduction of classes:

Indeed, among all the solutions put forward throughout history to the problem of the transmission of power and privileges, there surely does not exist one that is better concealed, and therefore better adapted to societies which tend to refuse the most patent forms of the transmission of power and privileges, than that solution which the educational system provides by contributing to the reproduction of the structure of class relations and by concealing, by an apparently neutral attitude, the fact that it fills this function (1977c: 488).

By doing away with giving explicitly to everyone what it implicitly demands of everyone, the education system demands of everyone alike that they have what it does not give. This consists mainly of linguistic and cultural competence and that relationship of familiarity with culture which can only be produced by family upbringing when it transmits the dominant culture (p. 494).

Bourdieu not only reveals the nature of the cultural capital that must be accumulated to succeed but explores the linguistic codes via which this cultural capital is transmitted, revealing the way in which ambiguity is manipulated by and to the advantage of the dominant classes. He is at pains to stress that the logic of everyday life is not the logic of science, that people tolerate a wide range of ambivalence and ambiguity, of contradiction, basic to strategy. *Practical logic* 'functions practically only by taking all sorts of liberties with the most elementary principles of logic' (1977a: 141–2).

Through the study of education (1971a and b; 1977b, c and f; 1979b; 1988), through the study of language (1977e; 1980; 1982; 1989b), through the study of taste (1965b; 1966; 1968a; 1984) and through the study of the relationship between the state and education (1989), Bourdieu consistently demonstrates that class structures are not imposed from above or created by the ethnographer but are subtly reproduced through the containment of cultural dispositions within class groups. Class power is the exclusive control of cultural capital, the subtle retention of cultural privilege to restrict access to economic and political privilege. The working classes are trapped in their habitus through cultural impoverishment and cultural difference.

Bourdieu is of course not without his critics, but there is one critique which deserves particular attention, namely that by Noel Bisseret (1979). Bisseret claims that for all its critical intent, Bourdieu's (and Passeron's) sociology of French education fails to transcend 'essentialist' ideology, remaining in the dominant ideological mode and thus unwittingly supporting it. Their discourse is subverted by their recourse to ideologically laden terminologies, by logocentric taxonomies and their dependence on a *unitary subject* (see p. 138–9). Bisseret's critique is cogent and telling, particularly in light of the fact that Bourdieu has on the whole failed to apply his theory of practice to gender-based inequalities, despite its immediate relevance to the understanding of gender as a culturally constructed and culturally reproduced phenomenon, and the need, as so much feminist analysis makes clear, to take fundamental epistemological factors into account (see Branson & Miller 1979 and Miller and Branson 1989). His dismissal of Derrida's deconstruction theory in the final pages of *Distinction* (1984) fails entirely to understand the fundamental and intensely subversive nature of the political praxis that deconstruction can entail (see Spivak 1987), which provides further evidence of his failure to transcend Western logocentric epistemologies. Despite these problems, Bourdieu leads us further toward an adequate theory of sociocultural practice than any other social theorist. The criticisms mentioned by no means negate his theories, rather they are the basis for constructive development.

BIBLIOGRAPHY

Primary sources

Bourdieu, P. (1962) *The Algerians* Boston, Beacon Press
——(1963) 'The attitude of the Algerian peasant toward time', in J. Pitt-Rivers (ed.) *Mediterranean Countrymen: Essays in the Social Anthropology of the Mediterranean* Paris, Mouton & Col
——(1965a) 'The sentiment of honour in Kabyle society', in J. Peristiany (ed.) *Honour and Shame* London, Weidenfeld & Nicholson
——(1965b) (with L. Boltanski, R. Castel, and J.C. Chamboredon) *Un Art Moyen, Essai sur less Usages Sociaux de la Photographie,* Paris, Les Editions de Minuit
——(1966) (with A. Darbel and D. Schapper) *L'Amour de l'Art, Les Musees d'Art Europeens et leur Public* Paris, Les Editions de Minuit
——(1967) (with J.C. Passeron), 'Sociology and philosophy in France since 1945: death and resurrection of a philosophy without a subject' *Social Research* 34 (1)
——(1968a) 'Outline of a theory of art perception' *International Social Science Journal* 20 (4)
——(1968b) 'Structuralism and theory of sociological knowledge' *Social Research* 34 (4)
——(1971a) 'Intellectual field and creative project', in M. Young (ed.) *Knowledge and Control* London, Collier Macmillan
——(1971b) 'Systems of education and systems of thought', in M. Young (ed.) *Knowledge and Control* London, Collier Macmillan
——(1976a) 'The specificity of the scientific field' *Social Science Information* 14(6) (also in Lemert 1981)
——(1976b) 'Marriage strategies as strategies of social reproduction', in R. Forster and P. Ranum (eds) *Family and Society: Selection from the Annales* Baltimore, John Hopkins University Press
——(1977a) *Outline of a Theory of Practice* London, Cambridge University Press
——(1977b) (with J.C. Passeron) *Reproduction in Education, Society and Culture* London, Sage
——(1977c) 'Cultural reproduction and social reproduction' in J. Karabel and

A.H. Halsey (eds) *Power and Ideology in Education* New York, Oxford University Press

——(1977d) 'Symbolic power' in D. Gleeson (ed.) *Identity and Structure: Issues in the Sociology of Education* Nafferton, Nafferton Books

——(1977e) 'The economics of linguistic exchanges' *Social Science Information* 16 (6)

——(1977f) (with L. Boltanski) 'Formal qualifications and occupational hierarchies: the relationship between the production system and the reproduction system' in E.J. King (ed.) *Reorganizing Education: Management and Participation for Change* London, Sage (also in Lemert 1981)

——(1979a) *Algeria 1960* New York, Cambridge University Press

——(1979b) (with J.C. Passeron) *The Inheritors: French Students and Their Relation to Culture* Chicago, University of Chicago Press

——(1980) *Le Sens Pratique* Paris, Les Editions de Minuit

——(1982) *Ce que parler veut dire* Paris, Fayard

——(1984) *Distinction: A Social Critique of the Judgement of Taste* London, Routledge & Kegan Paul

——(1988) *Homo Academicus* Cambridge, Polity Press

——(1989a) *The Logic of Practice* Cambridge, Polity Press

——(1989b) *La Noblesse d'Etat: Grandes Ecoles et Esprit de Corps*, Paris, Les Editions de Minuit

——(1990) *In Other Worlds: Essays Toward a Reflective Sociology* Cambridge, Polity Press

Secondary sources

Bisseret, N. (1979) *Education, Class Language and Ideology* London, Routledge & Kegan Paul

Bowles, S. and Gintis, H. (1976) *Schooling in Capitalist America: Educational Reform and the Contradictions of Economic Life* London, Routledge & Kegan Paul

Branson, J.E. (1980) 'Sociology and the sociology of education in Australia' *The Australian and New Zealand Journal of Sociology* 16 (2)

——and Miller, D.B. (1979) *Class, Sex and Education in Capitalist Society: Culture, Ideology and the Reproduction of Inequality in Australia* Melbourne, Longman-Sorrett

Featherstone, M. (1986) 'French social theory: an introduction' *Theory, Culture and Society* 3 (3)

Garnham N. and Williams, R. (1980) 'Pierre Bourdieu and the sociology of culture: an introduction' *Media, Culture and Society* 2 (3)

Giddens, A. (1979) *Central Problems in Socal Theory: Action, Structure and Contradiction in Social Analysis* London, Macmillan

Honneth, A. (1986) 'The fragmented world of symbolic forms: reflections on Pierre Bourdieu's sociology of culture' *Theory, Culture and Society* 3 (3)

——Kocyba, H. and Schwibs, B. (1986) 'The struggle over the symbolic order: an inteview with Pierre Bourdieu' *Theory, Culture and Society* 3 (3)

Lemert, C. (1981) (ed.) *French Sociology* Columbia, Columbia University Press

Media Culture and Society (1980) 2(3): Special issue on the work of Bourdieu

Miller, D.B. and Branson, J.E. (1987) 'Pierre Bourdieu: culture and praxis', in

D.J. Austin-Broos (ed.) *Creating Culture* Sydney, Allen & Unwin

——(1989) 'Pollution in paradise: Hinduism and the subordination of women in Bali', in P. Alexander (ed.) *Creating Indonesian Cultures* Sydney, Oceania Monographs

Nice, R. (1978) 'Bourdieu: a "vulgar materialist" in the sociology of culture' *Screen Education* 28

Spivak, G.C. (1987) *In Other Worlds* London, Methuen

Theory, Culture and Society (1986) 3 (3): Special issue on French social theory

5

DAVID AMES CURTIS

Cornelius Castoriadis

Cornelius Castoriadis was born in Constantinople in 1922. He studied economics, politics and law at the University of Athens. As an underground Greek Communist Youth anti-fascist activist, he was placed under threat of death from Stalinists and fascists for joining the Trotskyists in 1942. He arrived in France in 1945 and founded *Socialisme ou Barbarie* (1949–1965) which became a key source for the non-communist New Left, influencing the May 1968 student-worker rebellion. He was an economist at the OECD from 1946–1970, and is now a practising psychoanalyst and director of studies at the Ecole des Hautes Etudes, Paris.

For the student of social theory, the social thought of Castoriadis presents a challenge because, in as much as society exists through its institutionalisation and as there can be no theory of its institution because of our instituted situatedness (1985), Castoriadis is a critic of social theory and the claims of social science. He also presents a challenge because no doctrinal exposition of his sociological methods and practices exists apart from his political and philosophic aims; reconstructing these views, one risks distorting or eliminating essential elements. Yet this also provides an opportunity, for Castoriadis' study of the *imaginary institution of society* is of such richness that it invites a creative continuation.

Castoriadis' social thought is inseparable from the 'socialism or barbarism' theme found in Marx, Engels, Luxemburg and Trotsky, but he was the first to express it as a present contending alternative. Castoriadis fleshed out this alternative in relation to the fate of the Russian Revolution and the prospects for socialism, challenging the 'inevitability of socialism' as he explored the implications of Trotsky's prediction that if war did not end in socialism, the Soviet Union and Nazi Germany would have to be examined as forerunners of a new form of barbarism. *Socialisme ou Barbarie's* inaugural editorial and 'The relations of production in Russia' (1949a) offered a Marxist analysis of the contemporary world at a stage of capital concentration theoretically foreseen, but not actually seen, by Marx: control of the means of production by 'one or a few capitalists', now on an international scale. Historical changes wrought by this concentration via war had consequences for the system thus engendered: a world divided into an American bloc still allowing monopoly competition but increasingly directed by managers as capital became more concentrated and production more technically complicated, and a Russian bloc whose means of production were administered collectively by a new class: the bureaucracy, given political expression through, but not synonymous with, the Party. Castoriadis' thesis of *bureaucratic capitalism* differed from others in its premises—based upon production relations expressing the bureaucracy–proletariat class division between 'directors' and 'executants', not simply upon forms of ownership—in the conclusion it drew—workers' management as the proletariat's response to Stalinism (confirmed by the 1956 Hungarian Revolution)—and in its worldwide scope.

Not content with this critical and unorthodox, yet faithful, Marxist analysis, Castoriadis began a four-decade critique of Marxism itself, focusing upon bureaucratisation and people's struggles against it. It led to his rejection of materialism as he articulated a new form of revolutionary social thought based upon the imaginary dimension of social institutionalisation and the possibility of an autonomous society.

The critique starts with economics. Contrary to Marxism's idea that capitalism inevitably will collapse due to a falling rate of profit, pauperisation, etc., Castoriadis showed (1953–54) that the two central variables—class struggle and the rhythm and nature of technical change—were not determinable but determining, thus throwing the entire system into a state of *indetermination*. People's class actions and technical innovations have actual effects upon capitalism; no theory of capitalism could predict its course—its downfall or its stability.

Castoriadis maintained his unorthodox Marxist view of the director–executant division as the key to *all* class societies when he expanded his anthropological conception from one focused narrowly on economics to one which also took in 'cultural' and 'sexual functions' (1955). After the Hungarian Revolution and as he fleshed out the content of socialism as an autonomous society of workers' councils establishing wage equality, elected and immediately revocable delegates at all decision-making levels, and a simplified circulation of information through elimination from the workplace and society of a separate ruling bureaucracy (1957), Castoriadis revised his class analysis to comprehend capitalism's specificity. The uniqueness of capitalism, 'whether private or bureaucratic', is that it is 'the ultimate negation of this autonomy . . . its crisis stems from the fact that the system necessarily creates this drive toward autonomy while simultaneously being compelled to suppress it'. His unique conclusion was that 'the proletariat enables the system to continue by acting *against* the system', for capitalism, with its technical complexity (compared to slave-based or feudal societies) and its stratum of managers separated from the work process they plan, 'can function only insofar as those whom it exploits actively oppose everything the system seeks to impose on them'. Workers must resist the capitalist plan of organisation with half of each of their gestures—(filling in gaps, opposing excesses), and this 'half' is what keeps the system running—while also expressing the autonomous tendency toward socialism the system must combat.

Castoriadis once said he merely pulled a loose string in Marxism—bureaucracy—until its whole system unravelled. While revealing his playful, critical side, cited alone it hides the subversive *and* positive features of his social analysis. Castoriadis asks (1958) not in what a day's work consists (Marx's question during the ten-hour-day struggle) but in what an *hour of work* consists. Using his new conception of the unique capitalist division between order-givers and order-takers and stressing the workers' actual critique of Taylorism and of the industrial relations sociology (Mayo) which replaced it, he analyses the permanent struggle over output and pay. He thus explodes the supposedly neutral 'rationality' of capitalist production as he reveals an informal counter-organisation among workers. Capitalism is not simply despotism in the workplace and anarchy in the marketplace (Marx) or a disenchanting but rigorous application of rationality (Weber) but despotism *and* anarchy *both* in the workplace and in the marketplace (or in 'the Plan') and characterised by a permanently contested irrational rationality of separate control.

Breaking even further with Marxism as he described the changes class struggle has wrought upon capitalism, Castoriadis focused his analysis on this form of irrational rationalisation that is the *modern bureaucratic-capitalist project* (1960–61). After a century of combating workers' struggles for higher wages (which Marxism said it could not grant), capitalism has learned that such wage increases and (relatively) full employment have become conditions for its continued existence and expansion. Along with this 'success', however, has come a waning of working-class resistance (except at the point of production) and the bureaucratisation of its organisations (presented not as a Michelsian 'iron law' but as a historical process). 'Consumption for the sake of consumption in private life and organisation for the sake of organisation in public life' have become the goals of a bureaucratised society which encourages (and results from) privatisation at all levels and mass irresponsibility as it destroys meaning in work. The basic contradiction of capitalism, a system which must both solicit and discourage participation, remains, but has expanded to all fields (not only production and the economy but politics, culture, sports). Yet the tendency toward autonomy also remains and expands as traditional relations and practices are destroyed. In as prescient an analysis as one could ask for, Castoriadis stated in 1960 that women and youth would soon create new sites of revolutionary struggle.

The final issues of *Socialisme ou Barbarie* mark Castoriadis' definitive break with Marxism (1964–65). Examining the 'two Marxes'—the one whose intuition was that people make their history and must conquer their freedom, and the one who buried this intuition under a system sharing basic assumptions with his capitalist environs (productivism, economic expansionism and rationalisation, neutrality of technique)—he said the choice had become one of remaining Marxist or remaining revolutionary; he opted for the latter. The tenet Marx shared with Hegel and all 'inherited philosophy' was *determinism,* the conviction that the world is made of real and/or rational elements whose existence is definable in its manipulable determinateness. This view occults the work of *creation/destruction* and *the imaginary* in history as the positing of new images, figures, forms of the social, irreducible to closed real–rational systems because creative and determinative of them. With his rejection of historical–materialist functionalism came a critique of structuralism when today's 'poststructuralists' were still drawing kinship grids. And as he criticised the idea of an exhaustive social theory, Castoriadis advanced a new conception of *praxis as autonomous activity* aimed at the development of the autonomy of the other and socially incarnated in pedagogy, psychoanalysis, and political activity.

Here Castoriadis' social thought comes into its own. As individuals, we have not created the meaning of autonomy; and the *project of autonomy* is directed not simply at other individuals but at an indefinite number of them in an indeterminate future. Praxis, and more generally conscious making and doing (*le faire*), are not, *pace* Habermas, merely 'intersubjective' activities but expressions of *'the social–historical',* or the 'collective anonymous'. This sphere consists of 'given structures ... institutions and works ... and ... *that which* structures, institutes, materialises ... [I]t is the union *and* the tension of instituting society and of the instituted society, of history made and history in the making'.

Castoriadis' elucidation of the social–historical, a realm he was the first to describe, is a principal task of his magnum opus (1975a). What is this form of being which exists as socially instituted only to the extent that it is always already historical and which can 'have' a history only to the extent that it has always been socially instituted? Why does it realise itself in a plurality of societies and a plurality of histories (something for which no system of real–rational elements could account)? An unprecedented relation which may be described as 'objectively reflexive' or 'mutually inherent' and as creatively determinative without being fixed in its elements or in their succession, it challenges all received notions of society, history and even ontology.

The true opposition is not between the social—erected into a 'collective (un)conscious' or reduced to 'intersubjectivity'—and the individual. Individuals are always already social, are socially fabricated, and fabricated each time in a unique way (or in a uniquely complementary set of ways) by the society which fabricates them—by means of individuals, among others of its creations. The true opposition to society is the psyche, which Castoriadis describes in an original Freudian conception as a *psychical monad,* closed upon itself, characterised by its *radical imagination* (the capacity to posit images, while 'leaning on' its bodily constitution and its environment, without being fully determined by the real–rational), and opened to a society's *social imaginary significations* only via the *violence of socialisation,* a process the psyche is incapable of performing on its own. Yet without the psyche's radical imagination there would be no *social imaginary,* and thus no society—nor vice versa (the psyche cannot survive unsocialised and its continued resistance to socialisation is conditioned by the society in which it is socialised: another unique relation of mutual inherence, unique to each society).

This relation exists even in the most instrumental activities. Technique—e.g. in tool-making and tool-using activities—presupposes the society in which such instrumental activities are reproduced and proceeds according to the choice of techniques, or *technology,* of that society. Yet a society exists only as it instruments itself through the fabrication/use of *its* tools. And to make/use such tools, which help make this society, its individual representatives must themselves be 'instrumented' as maker/users of these tools; to be a society, the society must institute an instrumental or *'ensemblist-identitary'* ('ensidic') aspect in its members. Castoriadis identifies two such dimensions: that of 'assembling, adjusting, fabricating, construction', or *teukein,* and that of 'distinguishing, choosing, positing, counting, saying', or *legein.* There is no articulate *legein* without a constructive *teukein* of that *legein* (itself internally articulated so as to presuppose itself), just as there is no socially constructed *teukein* without its articulation as a *legein.* And neither one exists without a cultural dimension that gives a specific social character to its instrumental or ensidic activities—which activities are the means by which the cultural dimension of making/doing and saying/representing is instrumentally instituted in that particular society.

The purpose of elucidating the mutual inherence of instituting and instituted society is not an exhaustive social theory but a contribution to the collective and individual project of autonomy: positing one's own laws, knowing that one is doing so. Society is capable of making this project its imaginary goal, as it has also been capable of *heteronomy*— the representation of society as the work of *extrasocial* social imaginary significations (God, Nature, Reason, the Laws of History). Technique, to use the example above, consists of techniques but is not in itself a technique nor an end in itself, though it may be made into one (at which

CASTORIADIS

point one loses control). Instrumental activity, itself a historical creation, is each time immersed in a *magma* of social imaginary significations through which it instruments itself and these significations, including, in our society, that of technique as end in itself. Autonomy too is a social creation, not to be confused with the mere self-institution of society. This project can be rendered explicit with the aid of deliberation and reflection upon society—first instituted in ancient Greece with the advent of philosophy, democratic politics and the study of history (1983b).

Castoriadis has elucidated the magmas of significations of various societies, especially the two core imaginary significations of modern society: the (capitalist) goal of unlimited expansion of (pseudo)rational (pseudo) mastery, with its momentous ecological consequences, and the project of autonomy, today on the wane in a society which produces only 'the greedy, the frustrated and the conformist'. Appropriately, no systematic enumeration of social imaginary forms has been attempted. Castoriadis has instead concentrated on philosophical and methodological issues. In his critique of Weber (1988b), for example, he argues that what the latter calls 'ideal types' are social imaginary significations irreducible to 'individual behaviour' or 'meaning' for an individual and not the construction of the social theorist but existent first as the forms of a given society instituted in relations of *coherence* and *complementarity* and through the social dimensions of *the intentional, the representational and the affective,* the last being the most difficult to elucidate (1991). Yet, few have made specific applications of his work or undertaken studies of particular problems, let alone developed his ideas. Whether this unique and rich form of social thought will remain singular and without sequel remains to be seen.

BIBLIOGRAPHY

Primary sources

Castoriadis, C. (1949a) 'The relations of production in Russia', reprinted in *Political and Social Writings* (1988) Vol 1
——(1949b) 'Socialism or barbarism', reprinted in *Political and Social Writings* (1988) Vol 1
——(1953) 'Sur le dynamique du capitalisme' *Socialisme ou Barbarie* 12
——(1954) 'Sur le dynamique du capitalisme' *Socialisme ou Barbarie* 13
——(1955) 'On the content on socialism I', reprinted in *Political and Social Writings* (1988) Vol 1
——(1957) 'On the content of socialism II', reprinted in *Political and Social Writings* (1988) Vol 2
——(1958) 'On the content of socialism III', reprinted in *Political and Social Writings* (1988) Vol 2

——(1960–61) 'Modern capitalism and revolution', reprinted in *Political and Social Writings* (1988) Vol 2

——(1964–65) 'Marxism and revolutionary theory', reprinted in the *Imaginary Institution of Society* (1987)

——(1975a) 'The social imaginary and the institution', reprinted in *The Imaginary Institution of Society* (1987)

——(1975b) 'An interview with C. Castoriadis' *Telos* 23

——(1978–79) 'The social regime in Russia' *Telos* 38

——(1980–81) 'Facing the war' *Telos* 46

——(1981) 'From ecology to autonomy' *Thesis Eleven* 3

——(1982) 'The crisis of Western societies' *Telos* 53

——(1983a) 'The destinies of totalitarianism' *Salmagundi* 60

——(1983b) 'The Greek *polis* and the creation of democracy', reprinted in *Philosophy, Politics, Autonomy* (1991)

——(1984a) *Crossroads in the Labyrinth* Brighton, Harvester; Boston, MIT

——(1984b) 'Marx today' *Thesis Eleven* 8

——(1985) 'The first institution of society and second-order institutions' *Free Associations* 1988, 12

——(1987a) *The Imaginary Institution of Society* Cambridge, Polity; Boston, MIT

——(1987b) 'The movements of the sixties' *Thesis Eleven* 18/19

——(1988a) 'The Gorbachev interlude' *Thesis Eleven* 20

——(1988b) 'Individual, society, rationality, history', reprinted in *Philosophy, Politics, Autonomy* (1991)

——(1988c) *Political and Social Writings* Vols 1 and 2 (Vol 3 forthcoming), Minnesota, Minnesota University Press

——(1989) 'The state of the subject today' *Thesis Eleven* 24

——(1990) 'Does the idea of revolution still make sense?' *Thesis Eleven* 26

——(1991) *Philosophy, Politics, Autonomy* Oxford, Oxford University Press

Secondary Sources

Arnason, J. (1989) 'Culture and imaginary significations' *Thesis Eleven* 22

Busino, G. (1989)(ed.) *Autonomie et autotransformation de la société* Geneva, Droz: a recent volume of Castoriadis criticism (with 'Fait et à faire', Castoriadis' reply to these and other criticisms) originally published in *Revue Européenne des Science Sociales* 86 (1989)

Habermas, J. (1987) 'Excursus on Cornelius Castoriadis: the imaginary institution', in *The Philosophical Discourse Of Modernity* Boston MIT Press

Hirsh, A. (1981) 'Castoriadis and *Socialisme ou Barbarie*', in *The French New Left: An Intellectual History from Sartre to Gorz* Boston, South End Press

Honneth, A. (1986) 'Rescuing the revolution with an ontology: on Cornelius Castoriadis's theory of society' *Thesis Eleven* 14

Howard, D. (1988) 'Ontology and the political project' and 'Cornelius Castoriadis: ontology as political', in *The Marxian Legacy* second edition, London, Macmillan

Joas, H. (1989) 'Institutionalization as a creative process: the sociological importance of Cornelius Castoriadis's political philosophy' *American Journal of Sociology* 94 (5)

Rorty, R. (1988) 'Unger, Castoriadis, and the romance of a national future' *Northwestern University Law Review* 82 (2)

Rundell, J. (1989) 'From the shores of reason to the horizon of meaning: Some remarks on Habermas' and Castoriadis' theories of culture' *Thesis Eleven* 22

Singer, B. (1979) 'The early Castoriadis: socialism, barbarism and the bureaucratic thread' *Canadian Journal of Political and Social Theory* 3

——(1980) 'The later Castoriadis: institutions under interrogation' *Canadian Journal of Political and Social Theory* 4

Thompson, J. B. (1982) 'Ideology and the social imaginary' *Theory and Society*

6

Jacques Derrida

Jacques Derrida was born of Sephardic Jewish parents in El-Biar, near Algiers, in 1930. At nineteen he went to France for military service. About this time he started to read Jean-Paul Sartre, the leading French intellectual of the day, and was thereby introduced to the writings of Maurice Blanchot, Georges Bataille and Francis Ponge which, unlike Sartre's own texts, have positively informed his work. He studied at the École Normale Supérieure ('Ulm'), and numbers Maurice de Gandillac and Jean Hyppolite amongst his teachers. At 'Ulm' Derrida examined the European philosophical tradition (especially Hegel, Husserl and Heidegger), while also reading widely in modern literature, Marxism and psychoanalysis. In 1956–57 he went to Harvard University on a scholarship. On returning to France, he registered to write a thesis on the 'The ideality of the literary object'. It was to be directed by Hyppolite but it was abandoned when his ideas about inscription took shape. In the 1960s he taught for a while at the Sorbonne and was associated with the avant-garde journal *Tel Quel.*

During the period 1967–84 he was maître-assistant in philosophy at the École Normale Supérieure, although he also made extended visits to American universities, particularly Johns Hopkins and Yale. In 1974 he was instrumental in establishing the Groupe de recherche sur l'enseignement de la philosophie (GREPH) which effectively resisted government attempts to limit the teaching of philosophy. In 1981 he was appointed as a director of the Collége International de Philosophie. He defended his thèse d'état in 1980, based on his more conventional published work. Derrida is currently professor of philosophy at the École des Hautes Études en Sciences Sociales, Paris, but also holds visiting professorships at the University of California, Irvine, and at Cornell University.

The name of Jacques Derrida is inextricably linked to one word, *deconstruction*, and a brief analysis of how that word arises in his writings is perhaps the best way to approach them. 'Deconstruction' translates two German words used by Martin Heidegger in *Being and Time* (1927): *Destruktion* and *Abbau*. For Heidegger, the crucial philosophical question, that of the meaning of 'being', has been forgotten by the Western tradition and needs to be properly restated. The history of philosophy is to be understood as the history of various concealments of 'being'. All the familiar sites of philosophy—Plato's doctrine of the Forms, Descartes's *cogito*, Hegel's elaboration of Spirit, and so forth— have one thing in common, for they all mark failures to think 'being' in the right way. This tradition is metaphysical, even when it appears not to be so, because on Heidegger's understanding metaphysics arises from an uncritical identification of two distinctions—between 'being' and beings, and ground and the grounded—and the Western tradition regards 'being' as the ground of beings. Now this tradition is not to be abandoned or nullified, Heidegger assures us. We grow out of this tradition, and cannot readily disassociate ourselves from it. The task is to loosen its structures so that we can examine it carefully and so reformulate the question of 'being' more rigorously. It is this delicate process of loosening or unbuilding a tradition to which Heidegger's words *Destruktion* and *Abbau* refer, and which Derrida's word 'deconstruction' tries to capture.

The noun 'déconstruction' and the verb 'déconstruire' were already in use as technical terms by French grammarians when Derrida began to use them. The grammarians wished to disclose the laws of sentence construction, to find out how sentences work in different circumstances. In their sense of the verb, to deconstruct verse is to transpose it into prose and, by suppressing metre and rhyme, display the laws of poetic composition. The great French dictionary, the *Littré*, points out mechanical senses of the verb. 'To deconstruct', it first tells us, is 'to disassemble the parts of a whole. To deconstruct a machine in order to transport it elsewhere'. Far from being alien to Derrida's interest, these linguistic and mechanical connotations were of considerable use to him. For the dominant discourse of the time in France was structuralism, which drew strength from linguistics, and an emphasis on de-structuring allowed him to engage in a dialogue with structuralism while departing from it. One of the more startling claims that Derrida makes about structuralism is that it is metaphysical. At first blush, nothing could seem more odd. Lévi-Strauss was not alone in thinking that structuralism provided an escape from the familiar and, for him, limited paths of philosophy. Yet Derrida's claim allows us to see the scope and strength of his style of analysis.

Structuralism reaches its limit, Derrida argues, in failing to think the 'structurality of structure'. Like all earlier thought about structures, this new movement never comes to terms with the paradoxical role of the centre: 'it has always been thought', Derrida explains, 'that the center, which is by definition unique, constituted that very thing within a structure which while governing the structure, escapes structurality' (1978b: 279). 'This is why', he continues, 'classical thought concerning structure could say that the center is, paradoxically, *within* the structure and *outside it*'. Traditionally, then, centres have been used to ground structures. Yet if we think through the implications of the paradox, we begin to realise that the grounding has been illusory. Nietzsche, Freud and Heidegger (to name just three), have led us to think that 'there was no center, that the center could not be thought in the form of a present-being, that the center has no natural site, that it was not a fixed focus but a function, a sort of nonlocus in which an infinite number of sign-substitutions came into play' (p. 280). To accept this, as Derrida urges us to do, is to agree that there are no theoretical limits to signification.

I will give some substance to this last point in a moment. Before though, I would like to place Derrida's account of structuralism in the wider context of his work. A good deal of Derrida's writing can be divided into two sorts of essays. On the one hand, he reads texts by a range of modern thinkers–Austin, Foucault, Heidegger, Husserl, Lacan, Lévinas, Lévi-Strauss and Saussure—and shows that, although they appear to break with the metaphysical tradition, they nonetheless confirm it at a deep level. The structuralists believed themselves to have found an exit from metaphysics, but ironically enough it led them back to where they started. On the other hand, he examines texts by the most stringent of metaphysicians—Plato and Hegel, for instance—and shows that their texts are not all of a piece: while they undoubtedly make metaphysical claims, they also provide the means to unsettle those same claims. So while Derrida contends that there is only one kind of metaphysics (what he calls, following Heidegger, 'the metaphysics of presence'), he is not tied to the view that metaphysics forms a closed unity. Quite the opposite, in fact: there is no unbroken line separating metaphysics from non-metaphysics; it is never true to say that a text is wholly metaphysical or completely eludes metaphysical categories.

This caveat should be kept in mind when considering Derrida's well-known ambit claim about interpretation. 'There are two interpretations of interpretation', he tell us (p. 292). 'The one seeks to decipher, dreams of deciphering a truth or an origin' while the other 'affirms play and tries to pass beyond man and humanism'. We could certainly call the former a metaphysical interpretation, and the latter a non-metaphysical interpretation; but it does not follow from this, as is often believed, that Derrida is commending a free play of subjective interpretation. On the contrary, the two modes of reading are always interlaced. For Derrida, interpretations are not true or false, but strong or weak; they are not chosen by the subject but impose themselves upon him or her. When reading a text we are always negotiating a field of conflicting forces which precedes the reader's subjectivity.

Rather than being interested in the subject, as was the preceding generation of French philosophers, Derrida is intrigued by the notion of the other. The subject, he claims, is not an entity which precedes language; rather, it is always and already inscribed in language. This conviction does not allow us to disregard the subject, though, for there are always traces and effects of subjectivity in any writing or act of reading. They have point and force, and they must be taken into account in any rigorous analysis (as must authorial intention, for that matter); but neither a subject nor an authorial intention can wholly determine the meaning of a text. Here as elsewhere, the first lesson of deconstruction is that no text can be totalised without a supplement of signification: there is always something left out, an aspect or dimension of the text which is reduced, bypassed, suppressed or repressed. Derrida's wish is to remain open and responsive to that otherness. Quite clearly, what counts as 'other' will vary from case to case. In one instance it may be class politics or questions of gender; in another instance, figural language or even typography. All the same, Derrida is principally concerned with that which is utterly foreign to the Western philosophical tradition, a mode of otherness he calls *différance*.

In a rich and lucid interview with Richard Kearney, Derrida succinctly sums up his varied studies:

> My central question is: from what site or non-site (*non-lieu*) can
> philosophy as such appear to itself as other than itself, so that it can
> interrogate and reflect upon itself in an original manner? Such a non-site
> or alterity would be radically irreducible to philosophy. But the problem is
> that such a non-site cannot be defined or situated by means of
> philosophical language (Kearney 1984: 108).

Derrida's nickname for this 'non-site' is *différance*. In order to find an entrance, however precarious, to this 'non-site' Derrida searches the margins of philosophical discourse: those moments when Plato or Austin disparage writing, or when Kant discusses the frames of paintings. Marginal or fringe cases, Derrida holds, 'always constitute the most certain and most decisive indices wherever essential conditions are to be grasped' (1988: 70). Literature and art offer passageways (sometimes crooked and dark ones, to be sure) to that 'non-site'. When reading Francis Ponge's prose poems, Derrida fastens onto his proper name and signature; faced with Paul Celan's lyrics, he examines the ways in which they are dated; while the affirmation 'yes' provides him with a guiding thread for reading Joyce's *Ulysses*.

These borderline cases allow Derrida to uncover oddities and deferrals in the texts which are usually bypassed by more traditional readers; and they lead, as directly as anything ever can, to an awareness of the strange workings of *différance*. The notion of *différance* works in two registers. One glimpses it, first of all, in writing (as opposed to speech) which, by dint of its resistance to immediate comprehension, appears to keep full understanding forever at bay. Literary texts offer the clearest example of a range of possible interpretations which compete for our attention and approbation. This is not because of their semantic density or syntactic complexity, but because they explore and expose the limits of linguistic and conceptual activity. Writing provides us with a spyhole from which we can glimpse archi-writing, a generalised pattern of difference and deferral which, Derrida argues, constitutes the condition of possibility for any writing or talking. Thus *différance* works at a phenomenal level (ordinary writing, such as on this page) and at a transcendental level (the condition of possibility for any communication, written or spoken). The two levels are not rigidly segregated, and much of Derrida's works consists of tracing how texts negotiate their passage from one level to the other and back again. What gives Derrida's texts, especially the later ones, the appearance of a mystical quality is that *différance* in its trancendental sense is ineffable and indescribable.

The political significance of Derrida's writing is often hotly debated, and no wonder, since his rethinking of the categories of thought pose problems for all right and left orthodoxies. Although deconstruction has been put to work in a variety of local political contexts, Derrida's own stance over particular issues—apartheid, education, the state of Israel, nuclear disarmament—is perhaps best described as 'open Marxism', with the proviso that the adjective is at least as important as the noun.

BIBLIOGRAPHY

Primary sources

Derrida, J. (1973) *Speech and Phenomena: And Other Essays on Husserl's Theory of Signs* Trans. and introd. by David B. Allison. Preface by Newton Garver. Evanston, Northwestern University Press

——(1976) *Of Grammatology* Trans. and introd. by Gayatri Chakravorty Spivak. Baltimore, Johns Hopkins University Press

——(1978a) *Edmund Husserl's 'Origin of Geometry': An Introduction* Trans. and preface by John P. Leavey, Jr. Ed. David B. Allison. Stony Brook, N.Y., Nicolas Hays

——(1978b) *Writing and Difference* Trans. and introd. by Alan Bass. London, Routledge & Kegan Paul

——(1979) *Spurs: Nietzsche's Styles/Éperons: Les Styles de Nietzsche* Introd. by Stefano Agosti. Chicago, The University of Chicago Press

——(1980) *The Archeology of the Frivolous: Reading Condillac* Trans. and introd. by John P. Leavey, Jr. Pittsburg, Duquesne University Press

——(1981a) *Dissemination* Trans. and introd. by Barbara Johnson. London, The Athlone Press

——(1981b) *Positions* Trans. by Alan Bass. Chicago, The University of Chicago Press
——(1982) *Margins of Philosophy* Trans. by Alan Bass. Chicago, The University of Chicago Press
——(1984) *Signéponge/Signsponge* Trans. by Richard Rand. New York, Columbia University Press
——(1985) *The Ear of the Other: Otobiography, Transference, Translation* Trans. by Peggy Kamuf. Ed. Christie V. McDonald. New York, Schocken Books
——(1986a) *Glas* Trans. by John P. Leavey, Jr. and Richard Rand. Lincoln, University of Nebraska Press
——(1986b) *Memories: For Paul de Man* The Wellek Library Lectures. Trans. by Cecile Lindsay et al. New York, Columbia University Press
——(1986c) *Parages* Paris, Galilée
——(1986d) *Schibboleth: Pour Paul Celan* Paris, Galilée
——(1987a) *The Post Card: From Socrates to Freud and Beyond* Trans. by Alan Bass. Chicago, The University of Chicago Press
——(1987b) *Psyché: Inventions de l'autre* Paris, Galilée
——(1987c) *The Truth in Painting* Trans. by Geoff Bennington and Ian McLeod. Chicago, The University of Chicago Press
——(1987d) *Ulysse Gramophone: Deux mots pour Joyce* Paris, Galilée
——(1988) *Limited Inc* Trans. by Samuel Weber and Jeffrey Mehlman. Evanston, North-Western University Press
——(1989) *Of Spirit: Heidegger and the Question* Trans. by Geoffrey Bennington and Rachel Bowlby, Chicago, The University of Chicago Press

Secondary sources

Culler, J. (1982) *On Deconstruction: Theory and Criticism after Structuralism* Ithaca, N.Y., Cornell University Press
Gasché, R. (1986) *The Tain of the Mirror: Derrida and the Philosophy of Reflection* Cambridge, Mass., Harvard University Press
Hart K. (1989) *The Trespass of the Sign: Deconstruction, Theology and Philosophy* Cambridge, Cambridge University Press
Kearney, R. (1984) 'Deconstruction and the other', in R. Kearney *Dialogues with Contemporary Continental Thinkers: The Phenomenological Heritage* Manchester, Manchester University Press
Lamont, M. (1987) 'How to become a dominant French philosopher: the case of Jacques Derrida' *American Journal of Sociology* 93(3): 584–622
Norris, C. (1987) *Derrida* London, Fontana
Ryan, M. (1982) *Marxism and Deconstruction: A Critical Articulation* Baltimore, The Johns Hopkins University Press

7

Louis Dumont

Louis Dumont has written copiously in social theory; has stimulated his colleagues throughout the world with his provocative and well documented writing; is no more difficult to read than Lévi-Strauss or Bourdieu and is, like them, a gifted interpreter of the Durkheimian heritage; has theorised precisely about ideology, and about the ideological impact of the idea of *homo aequalis* in particular, at least as cogently as any of his compatriots; but does not appear alongside them in most social theory collections, not even those dealing with 'structuralism'. He is rarely mentioned outside gatherings of 'Indianists'. Fittingly, the prime theorist of the ideology of individualism, and rebel against the individuation of knowledge, has not become an icon of intellectual individualism and been accorded the status of intellectual hero.

True to the tradition of Durkheim and Mauss and like his more feted professorial colleague at the Institutes des Hautes Etudes, Pierre Bourdieu, he theorises about his own society informed by the experience of intensively studying another, combining 'sociology' and 'ethnology' as integral to the development of an effective social theory. From the study of provincial French festivals he moved to the study of kinship and caste in India and from there back to France to the ideology of equality and individualism. We will follow the logic of his theoretical quest by turning first to India and his *Homo Hierarchicus* (1967b and 1980).

Dumont came to ethnology/anthropology when he joined the Musée de L'Homme in 1936, in particular the Musée des Arts et Traditions Populaires. While working at the Musée performing essentially clerical tasks, he began his studies under Marcel Mauss. Captured by the Germans during World War II, Dumont spent the rest of the war as a prisoner in a factory in Hamburg. There he studied Sanskrit. In this enterprise as in the whole of his career as an anthropologist/sociologist, he was emulating Mauss. But whereas for Mauss, as for Mauss' uncle and mentor Durkheim, the sociological task has been to analyse existing available ethnological material to test and expand theorising about society, the postwar crop of French anthropologists set out to collect material themselves, to engage in the experience of fieldwork as the British and Americans had done since early in the century. Dumont's prewar plans to follow up Mauss' work with field research in Melanesia were transformed and he prepared to do field work in India. After the war he resumed work at the Musée and his studies. He completed his work on a French provincial festival (see Dumont 1951) and also studied Tamil and Hindi. In 1948 he set out to do fieldwork among Brahmins in south India (1948–50) for his doctorate. This field research was followed soon after by further field experience in northern India (1954 and 1957–58), again among Brahmins but in the context of a multi-caste village.

Dumont's initial contributions to the anthropological literature via his doctorate fed into existing vibrant debates about kinship and marriage. Taking up issues raised by his compatriot Lévi-Strauss in *The Elementary Structures of Kinship*, Dumont provided vital ethnographically based analyses of marriage alliance. His debates with the British anthropologist Radcliffe-Brown in *Man* (Dumont 1953a and b) reinforced the value of emergent structuralism as a theoretical approach and unlike Lévi-Strauss, who was dismissed by some as dependent on available and inadequate secondary sources, Dumont challenged structural functionalist interpretations via first-hand ethnography. During this period Dumont established close links with elements of British anthropology when he took up the lectureship in Indian anthropology at Oxford University formerly held by Srinivas, occupying the position from 1951 to 1955, then returning to France to take up his position at the Institute des Hautes Etudes. He was later to forge similar links with American anthropology through an ongoing association with the University of Chicago.

His doctoral dissertation on south Indian kinship was published in monographic form in French (1957a) but the audience was specialised and an English edition of his monograph was not to appear until 1986. But while at Oxford he began to explore wider issues in Indian anthropology, embarking on a search for a structural model which would provide for a pan-Indian understanding of the Hindu caste system in all its bewildering variety. The vehicle for these explorations was an English language journal published in France and founded for this very purpose, *Contributions to Indian Sociology*, the first number appearing in 1957 under the joint editorship of Dumont and the Oxford anthropologist David Pocock, who had conducted field research in Gujarat in western India.

From the beginning it was clear that the venture was ambitious and that the search was to extend well beyond the confines of ethnographic specialisation that Anglo-American anthropologists were used to. Not only did Dumont seek to establish a coherent social theory that accounted for the unity and the diversity of Indian society, a true 'sociology of India', but this enterprise was itself oriented eventually beyond India to provide for a more coherent understanding of the unity and diversity of Western society (see 'The caste system and its implications: reflections of a social anthropologist', Appendix A to Dumont 1980). But first to the slow but sure birth of *Homo Hierarchicus* (Dumont 1980).

Dumont set the scene for his theoretical confrontation with caste and the hierarchical consciousness that lay behind it with a thorough review of the work on caste by the French social historian of Mauss' generation, Celestin Bougle. True to the Durkheimian tradition, Bougle, in his explorations into the caste system, had attempted to 'hit the bedrock' of the caste system, to find the underlying 'tendencies' that gave rise to 'caste' behaviour and thus served, to use a later terminology, to 'reproduce' the caste system. Bougle identified three 'tendencies' or 'elements' at the heart of the caste system: hierarchy, associated with the gradation of status; repulsion, associated with rules ensuring separation; and interdependence, associated with the division of labour through hereditary specialisation. 'The force which animates the whole system of the Hindu world is', wrote Bougle, 'a force of repulsion which keeps the various bodies separate' (*Contributions* 2: 24). Bougle, wrote Dumont, 'leaves us at the end with three elements of which the integrating principle is yet to be found' (*Contributions* 2: 42).

Dumont sought to go beyond the identification of 'tendencies' to the construction of a coherent relational model of caste ideology of the kind outlined by Lévi-Strauss in his essay on 'social structure' (1963). This dynamic model sought not only fundamental ideological principles but the consciousness/conscience that bound them together: a deep structure that underlay the myriad transformations through time and space. It was a *structural model* that sought not only the unity in the diversity of Indian caste but served to judge when apparent variations of the caste system were in fact fundamentally different, when they could not be understood as transformations of the same underlying structure as that which was the bedrock of the Indian Hindu system (see Dumont 1980: 201ff.). Dumont thus integrated Bougle's three elements into a structural model as 'organizing principles' which must be related to form a structure, a model of the whole. By the time of writing *Homo Hierarchicus* Dumont was able to conclude:

> The three 'principles' rest on a fundamental conception and are reducible to a single true principle, namely the opposition of the pure and the impure. This opposition underlies hierarchy, which is the superiority of the pure to the impure, underlies separation because the pure and the impure must be kept separate, and underlies the division of labour because pure

and impure occupations must likewise be kept separate. *The whole is founded on the necessary and hierarchical coexistence of the two opposites.* (Dumont 1980: 43).

This structural model of caste as ideology encapsulates the basic qualities of the caste consciousness, revealing the parameters according to which caste Hindus evaluate themselves, others and the world around them. Dumont's structuralist perspective found unity in diversity and form in apparent rigidity, whereas anthropologists such as Bailey had denied that there was a unity within the diversity of India's caste system. They had also seen the variety of possible rankings within the 'middle ranges' of caste systems as evidence of caste being a response to economic and political pressures, regarding the consistent ranking of the Brahmin castes at the top and the untouchable castes at the bottom as a 'peculiar rigidity'. For Dumont, the extremes, Brahmin and Untouchable, explain the form of the caste hierarchy, embodying the fundamental opposition and hierarchisation of the pure and the impure. The 'middle ranges' between the two extremes have a consistent though not necessarily linear structure as each caste evaluates its position vis-a-vis other castes in terms of the opposition and hierarchisation of the pure and the impure as applied to its and others' characteristics (they eat meat/we are vegetarian; they keep donkeys/we do not keep donkeys, given that the animal world is also evaluated in purity/pollution terms; and so on).

Dumont's model is based on a very particular understanding of the concept of *hierarchy*:

> I believe that hierarchy is not, essentially, a chain of superimposed commands, nor even a chain of beings of decreasing dignity, nor yet a taxonomic tree, but a relation that can succinctly be called 'the encompassing of the contrary' (Dumont 1980: 239).

> This hierarchical relation is, very generally, that between a whole (or a set) and an element of this whole (or set): the element belongs to the set and is in this sense consubstantial or identical with it; at the same time, the element is distinct from the set or stands in opposition to it. This is what I mean by the expression 'the encompassing of the contrary' (p. 240).

Dumont himself admits that his attempts to understand the Hindu caste system were constantly inadequate until the nature of hierarchy and its significance had penetrated his consciousness. He, like other Western scholars, had failed to appreciate the subsumption of differences and resultant oppositions and inequalities within and to the whole. The Western individualistic consciousness not only isolates people one from the other and fails to appreciate their shared socialness, but even when academics admit to the existence of the social and set out to study 'social facts', they constantly isolate the different elements studied from each other, setting them up in opposition to each other and failing to place them within the whole that explains their *relationships* of opposition, that *defines the quality of their difference.*

Thus, as Dumont points out, in the hands of Western sociologists hierarchy becomes social stratification: the linear, vertical representations of unequal but separate parts. The form, the unity, the whole are lost. The inequality cannot be explained, only described, for the explanation lies at the level of the whole. By denying the hierarchical relationship within our own society we succumb to egalitarian and individualistic ideology, condoning/reproducing discrimination on the basis of differences—racial discrimination, sexual discrimination, the discriminations that lie at the heart of totalitarianism—denying our own essential participation in the construction and evaluation of difference as members of a hierarchised whole. *Hierarchy thus becomes a concept which explains not only the valorised in Hindu society, but the unvalorised and denied in Western society.*

While debates continue about whether Dumont got it right or not, Dumont's discussion of the caste system revolutionised the way caste was understood and drew Indian studies back into mainstream social theory. The intensely 'micro' focus of so many village studies which implicitly represented Indian sociology as a collection of specialised ethnographies was challenged and enriched by Dumont's convicton that an encompassing theory was not only possible but ethnographically valid. Here again was grand theory of the kind of the 'great' sociologists like Weber had engaged in and, like Weber, Dumont did not theorise with a view to understanding India alone.

The painstaking work that filled the pages of nine issues of *Contributions to Indian Sociology* between 1957 and 1966 culminated in the book *Homo Hierarchicus* (Dumont 1980), which not only presented his work on the caste system in full but which made it clear from the start that the study was but the foundation stone for a long-term exploration of Western ideologies. A thorough understanding of *homo hierarchicus* was presented as the key to an understanding of *homo aequalis.* As Durkheim's *Elementary Forms of the Religious Life* used the ethnography of other societies to gain access to an understanding of his own capitalist society; as Mauss' study of *The Gift* sought to reveal the reasons behind the ills that plagued his own society; as Bourdieu's work on the acephalous Kabyle gave rise to the fundamentals for his theory of practice which revealed the hidden cultural agenda of our education system and the art world; so, too, was the *Homo Hierarchicus* the vehicle for Dumont's return to the sociology of his own society.

Dumont thus constructs a model against which to begin his explorations of Western ideology (Dumont 1980: 223). Particularly high on the agenda is a pursuit of the way extant communalities and inequalities are accommodated to the egalitarian and individualistic consciousness in the

West. Earlier he had pointed out that '... the "rational" society ... recognizing only the individual, i.e. seeing universality, or reason, only in the particular man, places itself under the standard of equality and is unaware of itself as a hierarchized whole. In a sense, the "leap from history into freedom" has already been made, and we live in a realized Utopia' (1980: 261). The inequalities and the subordination of individuals to categorical identities such as those based on race or ethnicity are accommodated via 'discrimination', with those deemed the same and inferior being classified as 'equal but different—different biologically, different culturally. The experience of inequality offers minimal challenge to the ideological domination of individualised egalitarianism. Apart from an identification with the nation, the Westerner retains an asocial and individuated consciousness, the hierarchical aspects of his/ her surroundings remaining beneath the 'threshold of consciousness'. In the hierarchical society of India, the individual appeared as a valorised element only in the form of the individual outside the world, the renouncer, the *sadhu*, posing no threat to the hierarchical consciousness within everyday life. In the West the sense of communal identity receives no such valorisation among those who reproduce the dominant ideology.

The books *From Mandeville to Marx* (1977) and *Essays on Individualism* (1986b) trace the development of this hegemonic domination of individualism in its essential relationship to the ideological domination of the economic over all other aspects of social life. *Homo aequalis* is also *homo oeconomicus*, the domination of the economic in capitalist societies a domination of the consciousness by the ideology of economic rationality which in turn leads to the subordination of all other aspects of social behaviour to the economy. So while Marx is recognised by Dumont as providing the most comprehensive analysis of the workings of capitalism, Marx's view of the economy as the prime mover in the historical process, as the 'base' to the 'superstructure' of ideology, polity and judiciary, is, according to Dumont, an ideological commitment to economism and individualism, evidence of Marx's failure to transcend the ideologies of his own society. In Dumont's scheme of the social process, of the shaping of history, the ideological *encompasses* all other aspects of thought and practice.

While *From Mandeville to Marx* concentrates on the emergence of *homo oeconomicus*, his *Essays on Individualism* provides a deeper historical and comparative analysis of the emergence of individualism as integral to modernity, the 'modern ideology' (equally applicable to the so-called 'postmodern') in which identity is ultimately reducible to ego, to individual self, unlike the non-modern where identity is contextual, non-unitary. Via these comparative explorations into the ethnography of perceptions of the individual through space and time, pointing to the unity at the heart of national variants of individualism throughout Europe in contrast to the fundamental difference between Western and

non-Western, modern and non-modern, perceptions, Dumont contributes vital material to the current so-called poststructuralist debates
about the construction of subjectivity. The terminology is different. He
does not write of 'logocentrism' or 'phallogocentrism' or of 'essentialism', but once you have read his work it is impossible not to include his
substantiated insights into the Western capitalist consciousness in discussions of the construction of subjectivity. Also, long before the current wave of articles on 'writing culture' discussed the ethnographic
fictions that resulted from the representations of others in our terms
(see, for example, Clifford and Marcus 1986), Dumont criticised the
Anglo-American view of caste as a distortion that resulted from the
overvaluing of what in the Indian context are secondary, determined,
residual aspects of the social process, namely the economico-political; in
other words, from a failure to transcend their own ideological valuing of
the economic. Dumont thus consciously treads the knife edge between
contrary ideologies, conscious of both but not directed by either.

Criticism of Dumont's work (Madan 1971) has focused on three
problems: firstly, on his concentration on 'sacred' texts (whether those of
the Hindu religion or those of the 'religions' of science and economics)
rather than on the ethnographic record. These criticisms fail to appreciate that Dumont sees these sacred texts as vital source material for
evidence of the consolidated and 'encompassing' discourses which he
has experienced in their everyday expressions during long and painstaking fieldwork. Criticisms have also focused on his view of ideology's role
in the historical process, not so much as a 'base' (he does not simply
turn the Marxian model upside down), but as a mantle encompassing
the social process. These are valid and important criticisms, but they
rarely appreciate the vital and indeed revolutionary nature of his use of
the concept 'to encompass' (*englober*), especially in relation to his rejection of a linear conception of the relationship between various elements
in the social process. Finally, his use of a structuralist perspective has
been criticised. These criticisms are familiar to anyone who has read the
dialogues between Lévi-Strauss and his Anglo-American critics
(Maybury-Lewis 1960; Lévi-Strauss 1960). On the whole they fail to
grapple with structuralism's attempt to come to grips with the seemingly
ineffable socialness that binds us together in all our diversity (see Bailey
1959; Dumont and Pocock 1959). These criticisms do indeed often
reveal weaknesses but they by no means cancel out the importance of his
analyses.

Hero he may not have become on any large scale. He may not appear
even where one would assume he would, among the bibliographies of
those dealing with the nature of modernity, or ideology, or the individual. But that is due to the vagaries of the intellectual field (see Bourdieu
1971 and 1988), to the ideologically bound nature of intellectual evaluations that Dumont himself is as aware of as anyone. Hopefully, as

Dumont approaches his eightieth birthday, this chapter will lead more and more students to discover a dedicated, sincere and humble social theorist, unsung, but worthy of a place with the best.

BIBLIOGRAPHY

Primary Sources

Dumont, L. (1950) 'Kinship and alliance among the Pramalai Kallar' *Eastern Anthropologist* IV (1)

——(1951) *La Tarasque: Essai de Description d'un Fait Local d'un Point de Vue Ethnographique* Paris, Gallimard

——(1953a) 'Dravidian kinship terminology' *Man* LIII

——(1953b) 'Dravidian kinship terminology as an expression of marriage' *Man* LIII

——(1953c) 'Definition structurale d'un dieu populaire tamoul: Aiyenar le maitre' *Journal Asiatique* CCXLI (translated in *Contributions to Indian Sociology* 3, 1959)

——(1957a) *Une Sous-Caste de L'Inde du Sud. Organization Sociale et Religion des Pramalai Kallar* The Hague, Mouton

——(1957b) *Hierarchy and Marriage Alliance in South Indian Kinship* London, Royal Anthropological Institute, Occasional Paper 12

——(1964) *La Civilisation Indienne et Nous: Equisse de Sociologie Comparee* Paris, A. Colin

——(1967a) 'Caste: A phenomenon of social structure or an aspect of Indian culture?', in A. de Rueck and J. Knight (eds) *Caste and Race: Comparative Approaches* London, J. and A. Churchill

——(1967b) *Homo Hierarchicus: Essai sur le Systeme des Castes* Paris, Gallimard

——(1967c) 'The individual as an impediment to sociological comparison in Indian history', in V. B. Singh and Baljit Singh (eds) *Social and Economic Change: Essays in Honour of D. P. Mukherji* Bombay, Allied Publishers

——(1970a) *Religion, Politics and History in India: Collected Papers in Indian Sociology* Mouton, Paris

——(1970b) 'Marriott's review of Dumont's *Homo Hierarchicus*: a comment' *American Anthropologist* LXXII(2)

——(1971a) *Introduction a Deux Theories d'Anthropologie Sociale: Groupes de Filiation et Alliance de Mariage* Paris, Mouton

——(1971b) 'On putative hierarchy and some allergies to it' *Contributions to Indian Sociology* New Series (not edited by Dumont & Pocock) 5

——(1971c) 'Religion, politics and society in the individualistic universe' *Proceedings of the Royal Anthropological Institute for 1970*

——(1975a) *Dravidein et Kariera. L'Alliance de Mariage dans l'Inde et l'Australie* The Hague, Mouton

——(1975b) 'The emancipation of economics from morality: Mandeville's fable of the bees' *Social Sciences Information* XIV(1)

——(1975c) 'On the comparative understanding of non-modern civilizations' *Daedulus* CIV

——(1975d) 'Preface to the French edition of [E. E. Evans-Pritchard's] *The Nuer*', in J. H. M. Beattie and R. G. Lienhardt (eds) *Studies in Social Anthropology* Oxford, Clarendon Press (French edition 1968)

——(1977) *From Mandeville to Marx: The Genesis and Triumph of Economic Ideology* University of Chicago Press, Chicago

——(1980) *Homo Hierarchicus: The Caste System and Its Implications* University of Chicago Press, Chicago

——(1983) *Affinity as a Value: Marriage Alliance in South India, with Comparative Essays on Australia* University of Chicago Press, Chicago

——(1986a) *A South Indian Subcaste: Social Organization and Religion of the Pramalai Kallar* Oxford University Press, Delhi

——(1986b) *Essays on Individualism: Modern Ideology in Anthropological Perspective* University of Chicago Press, Chicago

——(1986c) 'Collective identities and universalist ideology: the actual interplay' *Theory, Culture and Society* 3(3)

——(1988) *Introduction a Deux Theories d'Anthropologie Sociale: Groupes de Filiation et Alliance de Mariage* Paris, Ecole des Hautes Etudes en Sciences Sociales

——and Pocock, D. (1959) 'For a sociology of India: a rejoinder to Dr Bailey' *Contributions to Indian Sociology* 4

Secondary Sources

Bailey, F. G. (1959) 'For a sociology of India?' *Contributions to Indian Sociology* 3

Bourdieu, P. (1971) 'Intellectual field and creative project', in M. Young (ed.) *Knowledge and Control* London, Collier Macmillan

——(1988) *Homo Academicus* Cambridge, Polity Press

Clifford, J. and Marcus, G. (1986) (eds) *Writing Culture* Berkeley, University of California Press

Contributions to Indian Sociology 1–9, 1957–1966, Paris, Mouton & Co

Current Anthropology VII(3) 1966, contained a 'CA book review' of Dumont 1957a and b involving commentary by a range of anthropologists and a precis and reply to comments by Dumont

Lévi-Strauss, C. (1960) 'On manipulated sociological models' *Bijdragen tot de Taal* CXVI(1)

——(1963) *Structural Anthropology* Vol 1, London, Allen Lane

Madan, T. N. (1971) (ed.) 'Review symposium on *Homo Hierarchicus*' (includes a reply by Dumont) *Contributions to Indian Sociology* New Series 5 Delhi, Vikas

——(ed.) (1982) *Way of Life: King, Householder, Renouncer: Essays in Honour of Louis Dumont* Vikas, New Delhi

Maybury-Lewis, D. (1960) 'The anaysis of dual organizations: a methodological critique' *Bijdragen tot de Taal* CXVI(1)

8

Emile Durkheim

Emile Durkheim (1858–1917) is generally regarded as one of the key figures in the development of sociology as an academic discipline. His intellectual project was concerned with two central problems. The first was the autonomy of the social as a distinctive level of reality which could not be reduced to the psychological properties of individuals but required explanation in its own terms. The second was the crisis of modernity—the rupture of traditional social ties by industrialisation, the Enlightenment, and individualism. The two were inextricably linked for Durkheim, who believed that the problems generated by the collapse of traditional order would only be solved on the basis of scientific understanding of how societies worked. If the laws governing the natural world could be discovered through empirical observation, so too could the laws governing the social world. In Durkheim's view the crisis of the age gave the enterprise particular urgency. 'Science', he argued, 'can help us adjust ourselves, determining the ideal toward which we are heading confusedly' for '. . . in furnishing us the law of variations through which moral health has already passed, [it] permits us to anticipate those coming into being, which the new order of things demands' (Durkheim 1893: 34).

Durkheim's was a relatively uneventful life marked by academic success and a happy marriage, which does not make him a promising subject for biography. Born on 15 April 1858 in Epinal in the eastern French province of Lorraine, he grew up in an orthodox Jewish family and community, the son of a rabbi. If his decision to pursue a career in secular rather than religious scholarship signalled the preference for modernity over tradition which would characterise his thought, the conditions of his father's approval were equally prophetic—'being serious and working hard' (Lukes 1975: 41). By all accounts, Durkheim was a man of unrelenting seriousness whose punishing work schedule left little time for pleasure and damaged his physical and mental health (pp. 99–100).

After completing his studies in Paris, in 1882, Durkheim spent several years teaching philosophy in Lycees. In 1887, he was appointed to teach courses in sociology and education in the Faculty of Letters at the University of Bordeaux. In the same year, he married Louise Dreyfus, who devoted the rest of her life to supporting his scholarly work, taking full responsibility for the household and their two children, copying manuscripts, correcting proofs, and sharing the editorial administration of the *Année Sociologique*, which he founded in 1898. During his fifteen years at Bordeaux, he published three of the works for which he is best known—*The Division of Labor in Society* (1893), *The Rules of Sociological Method* (1895) and *Suicide* (1897)—in addition to his study of Montesquieu, numerous articles, and the first five volumes of the *Année Sociologique*. He also lectured on a vast range of subjects, participated in university administration, and was actively involved in working for educational reform. Little wonder that he 'worked according to a rigid timetable', talking to his family 'at mealtimes, but not afterwards' (Lukes 1975: 99).

Durkheim's scholarly reputation and the increasing legitimacy of the social sciences were confirmed by his promotion to a chair at Bordeaux in 1896, but the ultimate recognition—an invitation to teach at the Sorbonne—was withheld until 1902. Even then, his appointment was in pedagogy rather than social sciences, and he was at the Sorbonne for eleven years before the word sociology was added to his title. Thus while Durkheim's intellectual project was carried out within the academy, its legitimacy was only fully acknowledged towards the end of his career. With the outbreak of war in 1914, the focus of Durkheim's writing and public activity shifted to questions of its historical causes, and to issues of national morality (Giddens 1978: 216–33; Lukes 1975: 547–59). Health—already impaired by overwork—deteriorated rapidly after the death of his son at the front, in 1916. Durkheim died in November 1917, at the age of 59.

Throughout his work, Durkheim argued for a radically social view of human behaviour as shaped by social structure and culture. In *The Division of Labor in Society*, for example, he drew on historical evidence to demonstrate that the individualism which conservative thinkers held responsible for the breakdown of social order was itself a social product, found only in complex societies based on the division of labour. In *Suicide*, he used statistics to demonstrate that suicide rates varied with changes in social solidarity, and concluded that the apparently private act of taking one's own life was in fact a response to social forces. A social explanation of religion was advanced in *The Elementary Forms of the Religious Life* (1915), in which he argued that the sense of awe and reverence with which people respond to 'the sacred' is in fact an expression of their absolute dependence on society.

Durkheim's argument on the social construction of the subject has its clearest formulation in *The Rules of Sociological Method*, in which he staked his claim for sociology as a legitimate field of inquiry whose object of study was the 'social fact', which could not be explained in terms of individual psychology. 'Social facts', he argued, are 'external to the individual' and 'endowed with coercive power':

> When I fulfil my obligations as brother, husband, or citizen, when I execute my contracts, I perform duties which are defined, externally to myself and my acts, in law and in custom. Even if they conform to my own sentiments and I feel their reality subjectively, such reality is still objective, for I did not create them; I merely inherited them through my education ... The system of signs I use to express my thought, the system of currency I employ to pay my debts, the instruments of credit I utilise in my commercial relations, the practices followed in my profession, etc. function independently of my own use of them. And these statements can be repeated for each member of society. Here, then, are ways of acting, thinking, and feeling that present the noteworthy property of existing outside individual consciousness (1895: 1).

Durkheim argued that society was not 'a mere sum of individuals', and that 'the system formed by their association represents a specific reality which has its own characteristics' (p. 103). For example, a political party or a church, while composed of individual members, has a structure, a history, a way of understanding the world and an institutional culture that cannot be explained in terms of individual psychology. 'If we begin with the individual', Durkheim maintained, 'we shall be able to understand nothing of what takes place in the group' (p. 104). He utterly rejected the idea that society had its origins in a social contract between individuals, arguing that 'in the entire course of social evolution there has not been a single time when individuals determined by careful deliberation whether or not they would enter into the collective life, or into one collective life rather than another' (p. 105). Society—the principle of association—comes first, he argued, and 'since it infinitely surpasses the individual in time as well as in space, it is in a position to impose upon him [sic] ways of acting and thinking' (p. 102).

Durkheim argued that sociologists must put aside their social prejudices and preconceptions and assume the same state of mind as physicists or chemists in relation to the natural world (p. xv). It should not be assumed from this, however, that he was either politically conservative or indifferent to social problems. He was committed to social reform, but thought that reform based on anything less than scientific understanding of social reality was misconceived. In Durkheim's view, sociology's objectivity was a precondition for its usefulness rather than an end in itself. His commitment to a sociology which is practical rather than merely speculative is clearly stated in the Preface to *The*

Division of Labor in Society, his first major work: 'Although we set out primarily to study reality, it does not follow that we have no wish to improve it; we should judge our researches to have no worth at all if they were to have only a speculative interest' (1893: 33). Almost one hundred years later, the text in question has been incorporated into the sociological canon, read not for the light it might cast on what Durkheim calls 'practical problems', but because it forms part of the intellectual tradition into which we seek entry when we define ourselves as students of sociology. It is, in other words, impossible for us to read *The Division of Labor in Society* except as a 'classic', and while Durkheim might take satisfaction from the implied fulfilment of his aspirations for the establishment of sociology as a discipline, his disappointment at its manifest failure to provide solutions to the problems he identified would likely be profound.

Durkheim's thesis in *The Division of Labor in Society* is a defence of modernity. Rejecting the view that industrialisation necessarily leads to a breakdown in social order, he argued that the declining authority of traditional moral beliefs was not an indication of social disintegration but of social change, a historical shift from a form of social order based on shared belief and tight communal control (*mechanical solidarity*) to one based on the mutual interdependence of relatively autonomous individuals (*organic solidarity*). He characterised the 'mechanical solidarity' of traditional societies as dependent on the 'likeness' of its members, whose common life circumstances made for shared beliefs and values. Under conditions of mechanical solidarity, he argued, 'individuality is nil', for the 'individual conscience . . . is . . . dependent upon the collective type and follows all of its movements' (p. 130). The 'organic solidarity' produced by the division of labour, on the other hand, depends on individual difference—the difference which develops with occupational specialisation. Specialisation, he argued, creates the conditions for the development of personal difference, opening up spheres of action which are not subject to collective control. At the same time, however, it increases dependence on society, for with occupational specialisation the exchange of services becomes a condition of survival.

The problem with Durkheim's thesis was that the increased solidarity that he associated with the division of labour was not to be found in any actually existing industrial society. In what might be seen as a glaring failure to abide by his own methodological prescriptions, he held to his preconception of the solidarity that 'should' be produced by the division of labour, and classified its actual consequences as 'abnormal'. He identified two main causes of this 'abnormality'. The first was 'anomie', the absence of a 'body of rules' appropriate to the changing circumstances of economic life', which left markets unregulated and workers without any sense of social purpose. The second was structured inequality: the existence of social classes which reproduced privilege from one generation to the next." Durkheim's social ideal was meritocratic and he argued that the 'spontaneous' division of labour on which organic solidarity was based could only occur if society was 'constituted in such a way that social inequalities exactly express natural inequalities' (p. 377). He therefore made social justice—defined in terms of reward for merit—a precondition for organic solidarity, arguing that the division of labour could not be spontaneous 'if one class of society is obliged, in order to live, to take any price for its services, while another can abstain from such action thanks to resources at its disposal which, however, are not necessarily due to any social superiority' (p. 384).

There is, as Gouldner (Durkheim 1928: xxvi) observed, a 'surprising' convergence with Marx in Durkheim's argument that the exploitation inherent in the 'forced' division of labour generates class conflict and precludes social solidarity. Durkheim did not see Marxism as providing adequate solutions, however. In his view, the problems associated with the transition to modernity would be solved by neither revolution nor conservative reaction, but by social science. The problem with socialism, he argued, was that its conclusions and predictions were based on inadequate scientific understanding of existing social reality (1928: 6).

Equally dismissive of socialism's laissez faire opponents on the grounds that their claims were not based on 'scientifically induced' laws but on 'a prizing of individual autonomy, a love of order', and 'a fear of novelty' (1928: 7), Durkheim is best read not as a 'conservative', but as a technocratic reformer. Much of the secondary literature in English, based as it is on a conservative appropriation of his work as primarily concerned with the 'problem of order' on the one hand (Parsons 1949) or a left–romantic rejection of his preference for reform over revolution on the other (Zeitlin 1968), screens out what Pearce (1989) has recently called 'the radical Durkheim'. Durkheim's central problem was not the ahistorical question of how social order is possible, but the historically specific one of how a modern industrial society, in which the traditional ties that bound individual to society have been weakened, might provide its members with a sense of social purpose and belonging. This is not, as is often claimed, an inherently 'conservative' question, but one which must equally be addressed by socialists. While Durkheim undoubtedly underestimated the extent to which the conflicting interests of labour and capital limited the possibility of social reform under capitalism, it is equally true that Marxist theory, prior to Gramsci, ignored the extent to which the creation of a new social order was not just a question of changing the relations of production, but of changing consciousness.

While Durkheim stands beside Marx and Weber as a classic thinker whose work is known to most sociologists, his influence on Australian sociology is less apparent, and there are few obvious contenders for membership of a 'Durkheimian school'. There are a number of probable reasons for this. One is the outmoded organicism of his thought, which precludes an adequate analysis of power by assuming that 'what gives unity to organised societies ... as to all organisms, is the spontaneous consensus of parts' (1893: 360). Another is the fact that sociology was introduced into Australian universities in the 1960s, when prevailing intellectual fashion showed little sympathy for either his views on scientific method or the anti-utopian implications of his argument on the need for social constraint. However, while his uncritical positivism is no more acceptable now than it was in the 1960s, his arguments on anomie have undeniable contemporary resonance, and, as Pearce (1989: 159) has demonstrated, he has much to contribute to the discussion on the characteristics of a feasible democratic socialist society.

BIBLIOGRAPHY

Primary Sources

Durkheim, E. (1893) *The Division of Labor in Society* Trans. by George Simpson. New York, Free Press, 1964
——(1895) *The Rules of Sociological Method* Eighth edition. Edited by George E. G. Catlin. The Free Press, New York, 1964
——(1897) *Suicide* Ed. by George Simpson. London, Routledge & Kegan Paul, 1970 (Paperback edition)
——(1915) *The Elementary Forms of the Religious Life* New York, The Free Press, 1965
——(1928) *Socialism and Saint-Simon* Ed. and introd. by Alvin Gouldner. London, Routledge & Kegan Paul, 1958
——(1957) *Professional Ethics and Civic Morals* London, Routlege & Kegan Paul
——(1972) *Selected Writings* Ed., trans. and introd. by Anthony Giddens. Cambridge, Cambridge University Press

Secondary sources

Coser, L. A. (1971) *Masters of Sociological Thought* New York, Harcourt Brace Jovanovich
Giddens, A. (1978) *Durkheim* Glasgow, Fontana/Collins
Lukes, S. (1975) *Emile Durkheim: His Life and Work* Harmondsworth, Penguin Books
Parsons, T. (1949) *The Structure of Social Action* Glencoe, Free Press
Pearce, F. (1989) *The Radical Durkheim* London, Unwin Hyman
Zeitlin, I. (1968) *Ideology and the Development of Sociological Theory* Englewood Cliffs, Prentice-Hall

9

STEPHEN MENNELL

Norbert Elias

Norbert Elias (1897–1990) is best known for his theory of 'civilising processes', although his writings are wide-ranging and amount to a quite distinctive perspective on the discipline of sociology as a whole—a perspective sometimes known as 'figurational sociology' (Elias came to prefer *process-sociology*). The only book in which Elias attempted to make a programatic statement of his vision of sociology as a discipline is *What is Sociology?* (1970). The fullest secondary account to date of Elias' sociology as a whole is to be found in Mennell (1989). Recognition of Elias as a major sociological thinker came to him remarkably late in his long life. All but one of his dozen or more books, and nearly all his countless articles, were published after he reached normal retirement age.

Elias was born of Jewish parents in Breslau, Germany, now the Polish city of Wroclaw. After service on the Western Front in World War I, he read medicine and philosophy at Breslau University. He took his doctorate in philosophy in 1922. Turning to sociology, he moved first to Heidelberg and worked with Alfred Weber (Max Weber's younger brother), and then in 1929 to Frankfurt as academic assistant to Karl Mannheim. The university department of sociology which they ran was lodged in rented rooms in the basement of the wealthy, independent Institut für Sozialforschung, the 'Frankfurt School', headed by Max Horkheimer.

Like so many other German scholars, Elias fled into exile after Hitler came to power, first to Paris and then in 1935 to England. There he completed *Über den Prozess der Zivilisation* (1939), his masterpiece later known in English as *The Civilising Process*. It was published obscurely in Switzerland and was scarcely noticed until its reissue in 1969. Meanwhile, Elias had taught at the University of Leicester (1954–62), and then as Professor at the University of Ghana (1962–65). At Leicester, he helped build up a large and influential department of sociology, where junior colleagues included Anthony Giddens. Elias had a strong continuing influence on the research of Eric Dunning and others in Leicester (see Elias and Dunning 1986), on several sociologists in Germany, and especially on the 'Amsterdam School' around Johan Goudsblom, Abram de Swaan, Cas Wouters and others in the Netherlands (see Mennell 1989: chs 5, 6 and 10). Something of Elias' problematic can also be detected in Giddens' work, especially the attempt to bring together micro- and macro-sociology (or, in Giddens' terms, 'structure' and 'agency'), though their approaches are quite different.

CIVILISATION AND THE HUMAN SELF-IMAGE

Elias always considered himself a *sociologist*, not a 'social theorist', and had a low estimate of the potential contribution of philosophical reflection to the understanding of human society if it were divorced from the empirical investigation of human social interdependence. The origins of this attitude can be traced right back to his 1922 doctoral thesis in philosophy, which occasioned a dispute with his supervisor Richard Hönigswald about the merits of Kant's philosophy. Ever afterwards, Elias argued that the whole central tradition of modern Western epistemology, from Descartes through Kant to twentieth-century phenomenology, was misconceived. It was based on asking how a single, *adult*, human mind can know what it knows. Elias called this the model of *homo clausus*, the 'closed person', and found it in much of modern sociology (1939, I: 245–63, 1970: 119ff.; Mennell 1989: 188–93). He argued that we must instead think in terms of *homines aperti*, 'open people', and in particular of 'long lines of generations of people' building up the stock of human knowledge. His crucial point, however, was that the image of *homo clausus* corresponded to a *mode of self-experience* that was not a human universal but was a social product, particularly of European society from the Renaissance onwards.

Elias wrote his first book, which we now know as *The Court Society*, in the Frankfurt years, but it was not published in any form until 1969. It is a sociological study of aristocratic society in France in the century and a half before the Revolution. The reign of Louis XIV (1643–1715) was particularly crucial in completing the process of the 'taming of warriors' and transforming them into courtiers devoid of independent military power and increasingly the creatures of the king. Elias argued that the taming of warriors was a process of significance not just in European history but in the development of human societies generally, and that it had been relatively neglected by sociologists. The courtly nobility were a 'two-front stratum' (Simmel's phrase), grouped between the king and the rich bourgeoisie. Elias shows how much of what seems to us the bizarre detail of court ritual can be understood as mechanisms through which the king could manipulate courtiers through tiny expressions of favour and disfavour. The 'ethos of rank' became all-pervasive. He shows, for example, how rank determined the courtiers' expenditure, quite regardless of their *income* and as a result, many became impoverished. In an important corrective to the common assumption that bourgeois economic rationality or 'instrumental rationality' is the characteristic and even unique form of Western rationality, Elias contends that although the 'extravagance' of courtiers appears 'irrational' from a bourgeois point of view, it was a manifestation of a 'court-rationality' which itself involved a high degree of restraint of short-term effects for longer-term objectives; it was a form of rationality in which prestige and rank rather than capital and income, were made calculable as instruments of power.

Courtiers had to develop an extraordinary sensitivity to the status and importance that could be attributed to a person on the basis of fine nuances of bearing, speech, manners and appearance. Observing, dealing with, relating to or avoiding people became an art in itself. And self-observation was inextricably bound up in that: great self-control was required. To later sociologists reared on Erving Goffman, that may seem a universal characteristic of human society. In some degree it is—there is no zero-point, as Elias was fond of remarking in this and many other contexts—but Elias argued that the *extent* to which this sensitivity was developed in court society through the competitive struggle for prestige with vital interests at stake, was exceptional.

The courtly ethos of self-control, Elias argues, is reflected in the literature, drama and even in the French formal gardens of the period. But, above all, it is seen in the philosophy of Descartes and his successors. The image of the person as *homo clausus* so evident in 'Cogito ergo sum' is not just a philosophical idea but also the characteristic mode of self-experience that had been developing in Europe since the Renaissance and the Reformation. Elias saw his demonstration of the part played by court society in the development of this mode of self-experience as a supplement to, not necessarily contradictory to, Weber's parallel account in *The Protestant Ethic and the Spirit of Capitalism*. What was needed was a more comprehensive theory of the development of the modern self-image and mode of self-experience, and that is what Elias set out to provide in *The Civilising Process* and his later writings.

In this complex *magnum opus*, Elias speaks of civilising processes on two levels. The first is the individual level, and is rather uncontroversial. Infants and children have to acquire through learning the adult standards of behaviour and feeling prevalent in their society; to speak of this as a civilising process is more or less to use another term for 'socialisation', and ever since Freud and Piaget, there has been little dispute that this process possesses structure and sequence. The second level is more controversial. Where did these standards come from? They have not always existed, nor always been the same. Elias argues it is possible to identify long-term civilising processes in the shaping of standards of behaviour and feeling over many generations within particular cultures. Again, the idea that these standards *change* is not controversial; the controversy is about whether the changes take the form of structured processes of change with a discernible, though unplanned, *direction* over time.

The two volumes of *The Civilising Process* often strike new readers as being about quite different subjects: the first dealing with the history of manners in Western Europe from the late Middle Ages to the Victorian period, the second advancing a detailed model of the process of state formation, again in Europe, since the Dark Ages. The basic idea, and the basic link between the two halves, is that there is a connection between the long-term structural development of societies and long-term changes in people's social character or typical personality make-up (what Bourdieu would later call their social *habitus*—which was in fact the word Elias used in German in 1939). In other words, as the structure of societies becomes more complex, manners, culture and personality also change in a particular and discernible direction, first among elite groups, then gradually more widely. This is worked out with great subtlety for Western Europe since the Middle Ages.

Elias began the first volume of *The Civilising Process* by reviewing the accretion of evaluative meanings around the notion of 'civilisation'. The word was derived from *civilité*, the term used by courtiers to denote their own ways of behaving, but by the nineteenth century it had come to have a single general function: as a badge of the West's sense of superiority:

> ... this concept expresses the self-consciousness of the West ... It sums up everything in which Western society of the last two or three centuries believes itself superior to earlier societies or 'more primitive' contemporary ones. By this term, Western society seeks to describe what constitutes its special character and what it is proud of: the level of *its* technology, the nature of *its* manners, the development of *its* scientific knowledge or view of the world, and much more (1939, I: 3–4)

By the nineteenth century, the ways people in the West used the *word* civilisation showed that they had largely forgotten the *process* of civilisation. Confident of the superiority of their own now seemingly inherent and eternal standards, they wished only to 'civilise' the natives of the lands they were now colonising (or the lower orders of their own societies). They lost awareness that their own ancestors had undergone a learning process, a civilising process through which they *acquired* the characteristics now perceived as marks of an imagined *innate* superiority.

In order to retrieve an awareness of this forgotten process from the European past, Elias studied the development of social standards governing eating, blowing the nose, spitting, urinating and defecating, undressing and sleeping. The reason for investigating these most 'natural' or 'animalic' facets of behaviour was that these are things that by their biological constitution all human beings have to do in any society, culture or age. Moreover, human infants are born in more or less the same emotional and physical condition at all times and places, and in every society they have to learn how to handle these matters. Therefore, if the way they are handled changes over time, it stands out rather clearly.

Elias' principal sources were French, German, Italian and English manners books from the Middle Ages to the mid-nineteenth century. In earlier centuries these basic matters of behaviour—discussion of which would later cause embarrassment, or at least the humorous sensation of a taboo having been broken—were spoken of openly and frankly, without shame. Then gradually, from the Renaissance, a long-term trend becomes apparent towards greater demands on emotional management in adults: the child has further to travel, so to speak, to attain the adult standard. Codes of behaviour become more differentiated, and thresholds of shame and embarrassment advance. Many things become hidden behind the scenes of social life—and also repressed behind the scenes of conscious mental life, too.

Elias produces evidence to show that this long-term civilising process cannot be explained away by rising levels of material prosperity or by advances in scientific knowledge of health and hygiene. Moreover, a similar civilising curve can also be discerned in the development of social standards of self-restraint over resort to the use of *violence*. The explanation is found in the dynamic of social interdependencies. Over a period of many centuries in Europe, chains of social interdependence have grown longer and people have become more subject to more multipolar social constraints. In other words, 'more people are forced more often to pay more attention to more other people' (Goudsblom 1989: 722). In the course of this process, the *balance* of the controls by which individual people steer their conduct shifts from the preponderance of external constraints (*Fremdzwänge*—constraints *by other people*) towards more internalised self-constraints (*Selbstzwänge*). Here the influence of Freud on Elias is evident. But it is not just a matter of *more* self-restraint: rather, the balance tilts towards self-constraint being more *automatic*, more *even* (volatility of mood becomes less than in medieval times), and more *all-embracing* (standards apply more equally in public and private, and to all other people irrespective of rank etc.)

In the second volume, Elias puts forward a detailed theory of state formation in Europe, implicitly beginning from Weber's definition of the state as an organisation which successfully upholds a claim to binding rule-making over a territory, by virtue of commanding a monopoly of the legitimate use of violence, but Elias is more interested in the process through which a monopoly of the means of violence—and taxation—is established and extended. That innocent addition, *taxation*, is significant. Elias insisted that Marxist attempts to accord causal primacy to economic 'factors' or 'forces' or 'modes of production' was misleading. The means of production, the means of protection (including attack), and the means of orientation could not be reduced to each other; moreover, during the period of which Elias was talking, the means of violence and the means of production were simply inextricable.

Elias does not put all his causal eggs in the state formation basket. State formation, he argues, is only one process interweaving with others to enmesh individuals in increasingly complex webs of interdependence. It interweaves with the division of labour, the growth of trade, towns, the use of money and administrative apparatuses, and increasing population in a spiral process. Internal pacification of territory facilitates trade, which facilitates the growth of towns and division of labour and generates taxes which support larger administrative and military organisations, which in turn facilitate the internal pacification of larger territories, and so on: a cumulative process experienced as a compelling force by people caught up in it. Furthermore, this has long-term effects on people's habitus:

> . . . if in a particular region, the power of central authority grows, if over a larger or smaller area people are *forced* to live at peace with one another, the moulding of the effects and the standards of the demands made upon emotional management are very gradually changed as well (1939, I: 201, my emphasis; translation modified to reflect Elias' later terminology).

According to Elias, the gradually higher standards of habitual self-restraint engendered in people contribute in turn to the upward spiral—being necessary, for example, to the formation of gradually more effective and calculable administration.

LATER EXTENSIONS

The theory of civilising processes has provoked much scholarly debate (see Mennell 1989: ch. 10). Meanwhile, Elias extended his original thesis in many directions. *Time: An Essay* (1984) represents a major extension of the theory of civilising processes to the history of humanity as a whole. 'Time', argues Elias, refers not to any object or substance but to the human social *activity* of *timing*. This activity rests on the human biologically endowed capacity for memory and synthesis, for making connections through the use of symbols. More than any other creatures, humans are orientated by the experience not of each individual but also of long chains of generations, gradually improving and extending the human means of orientation. It is simply a means of using symbols to connect two or more sequences of changes—physical, biological or social—using one as a frame of reference for the others. But it is not just 'subjective'; it has evolved through experience in a long intergenerational learning process. The social need for timing was much less acute and pervasive in earlier societies than in the more highly organised modern industrial states. Increased differentiation and integration of social functions mean that in modern societies many long chains of interdependence intersect within the individual, requiring constant awareness of time in the coordination of numerous activities. There has developed a particularly complex system of self-regulation and an acute individual sensibility with regard to time. The individualisation of social time-control thus bears all the hallmarks of a civilising process.

Elias developed a sophisticated sociogenetic theory of knowledge and the sciences (see Mennell 1989, chs 7–8). In the perspective of the development of human knowledge over the whole history of the species, the 'double-bind' relationship between the dangers people faced and the fears they experienced posed formidable initial obstacles to an escape from emotionally charged, fantasy-laden and 'involved' knowledge. Escape can never be complete, but control over social dangers and fears has lagged behind that over natural forces, and the social sciences remain *relatively* less autonomous and 'detached' than the natural sciences. Elias argues that the predominant form of explanation gradually changes across the spectrum from the physical through the biological to the social sciences, with law-like theories becoming less important. The aim of the social scientist should be to construct 'process-theories' in various dimensions—the dimensions of space, time and *experience*. As always for Elias, his own substantive sociological investigations stand as exemplars of the pursuit of process theories resting on an image of humankind as 'open people'.

BIBLIOGRAPHY

Primary sources

Elias, N. (1939) *The Civilising Process* Vol I: *The History of Manners* Oxford, Basil Blackwell, 1978; Vol II: *State Formation and Civilisation* [Title of USA edition is *Power and Civility*] Oxford, Basil Blackwell, 1982

——(1965) (with John L. Scotson) *The Established and the Outsiders: A Sociological Enquiry into Community Problems* London, Frank Cass

——(1969) *The Court Society* Oxford, Basil Blackwell, 1983

——(1970) *What is Sociology?* London, Hutchinsons, 1978

——(1984) *Time: An Essay* Oxford, Basil Blackwell, forthcoming 1991

——(1985a) *The Loneliness of the Dying* Oxford, Basil Blackwell

——(1985b) *Humana Conditio: Beobachtungen zur Entwicklung der Menschheit am 40. Jahrestag eines Kriegsendes (8 Mai 1985)* Frankfurt, Suhrkamp

——(1986) (with Eric Dunning) *Quest for Excitement: Sport and Leisure in the Civilising Process* Oxford, Basil Blackwell

——(1987a) *Involvement and Detachment* Oxford, Basil Blackwell

——(1987b) *Los der Menschen: Gedichte/Nachdichtungen* [Elias' poems] Frankfurt, Suhrkamp

——(1987c) *The Society of Individuals* Oxford, Basil Blackwell, forthcoming 1991

——(1989) *Studien über die Deutschen* Frankfurt, Suhrkamp

——(1990) *The Symbol Theory* London, Sage

Secondary sources

Bogner, A. (1987) 'Elias and the Frankfurt School' *Theory, Culture and Society* 4 (2–3): 249–85

Goffman, E. (1961) *Asylums* Garden City, NY, Doubleday Anchor

——(1963) *Behaviour in Public Places* New York, Free Press

Goudsblom, J. (1989) 'Stijlen en beschavingen' *De Gids* 152: 720–2

Mennell, S. (1989) *Norbert Elias: Civilisation and the Human Self-Image* Oxford, Basil Blackwell

PAUL RAYMOND HARRISON

10

Michel Foucault

The work of Michel Foucault (1926–1984) is a philosophical contribution to the theory of truth. However, his work stands at an oblique angle to the mainstream philosophical universe in its attempt to effect a series of radical *decentrings*. Instead of a theory of constitutive subjectivity, Foucault explores firstly the discursive practices and then the forms of power which constitute the subject. Instead of a logical theory of truth, Foucault develops a theory of the regimes of truth and then a theory of the relationship between truth and power. Instead of a rationalist theory of history, Foucault gives us a history marked either by discursive discontinuities or forms of power–knowledge. These decentrings constitute nothing less than a philosophical anti-humanism. The intellectual origins of his thought are primarily locatable, therefore, in the re-readings of Western philosophy and the criticisms of its anthropocentrism which were carried out in the thought of Nietzsche and Heidegger.

ITINERARIES

Foucault's work can also be seen as a contribution to the theory of culture in social theory. Firstly, the objects of his study—asylums, clinics, prisons—shift the focus of the study of domination far away from the analysis of class and the economic base. Secondly, culture is not thematised as belonging to the merely representational realm as it is in a simple-minded Marxism. Thirdly, culture is not looked upon as a spiritual totality as it is in historicism. Fourthly, although Foucault is by no means a functionalist, he does operate with a concept of society and culture which implicitly recognises the differentiated character of both society and culture in modernity. In many respects, therefore, Foucault's work is a contribution to a *culturalist reading of modernity*. More specifically, the early work on discursive practices is an attempt at a theory of the internal coherence not so much of culture as a totality, but of domains or formation-specific cultures of a discursive kind. However, such a perspective must be tempered by the recognition of the importance of power in the middle period of Foucault's work.

The notion of power enters Foucault's work as an answer to the riddle of how and why discursive formations change. The autonomy accorded to culture due to the internal coherence of discursive formations is vitiated with the shift of accent to the 'power relation' as the most important axis. This makes knowledge the site of strategies, struggles and conflicts for control. Foucault's notion of 'disciplinary power' must, therefore, be read as an attempt at a *power-theoretical reading of modernity*. Once again Foucault is very far away from the concentration on the 'production relation' typical of Marxism. It is in this period that Foucault's work seems to draw near Weber's or, at least, certain readings of Weber's work.

In the final period of Foucault's work there is a recognition of the limitations of a power-theoretical framework and he makes an attempt to supplement it with another kind of archaeology. This time it is a question of an archaeology of problematisations and not of knowledge; an archaeology that he wishes to pursue simultaneously with a genealogy of the practices of the self. This leads to a more *hermeneutical reading of modernity*.

THE ARCHAEOLOGY OF DISCURSIVE PRACTICES

Foucault's early work is centrally concerned with the culture of modernity. If we take modernity as beginning in the sixteenth and seventeenth centuries, then Foucault's work can be seen as a critical reflection on the difference between pre-modern and modern cultural forms. In *Madness and Civilization* (1961) Foucault begins his 'archaeology of the silence of the madman' in a world in which the madman had become a presence with the retreat of the leper; and madness was replacing leprosy as the 'already there' of death.

According to Foucault, the madman's 'liminal position' in the middle ages was made visible by his social expulsion onto 'ships of fools'. The madman's embarkation both excludes him from the city, pushes him to its limits, and also opens up a passage from the city to the limits or, more precisely, from reason to madness. In this context the Renaissance performs the crucial role of preparing the ground for the classical experience of madness by gradually incorporating madness within reason in order to control it. Renaissance humanism both liberates the voice of the madman and controls it by bringing madness within the 'universe of discourse'; however, it is only in the classical period that the madman is reduced to silence through his confinement in hospitals.

In the *Birth of the Clinic* (1963) Foucault undertakes an 'archaeology of the medical gaze'. What concerns him here is the shift from a conception of medicine focused on health which left room for the patient to be his own physician in the eighteenth century, to a conception of medicine focused on normality where the body of the patient is subject to the sovereign gaze of the doctor in the clinical setting of the modern hospital. In both books Foucault is working on the constitution of new domains of rationality—the science of psychology and the science of modern medicine—and the domains of finitude to which they correspond: madness and death.

In *The Order of Things: An Archaeology of the Human Sciences* (1966), three new domains of finitude concern Foucault: life, labour, and language. Foucault works with the notion of *episteme* or 'epistemological field' which governs the conditions of possible knowledge. There are, according to Foucault, three differing *epistemes* which succeed one another: that of the Renaissance, the Classical period, and the nineteenth century. What separates the Classical period from the nineteenth century is that the former still maintains a relationship to the infinite whereas the latter constitutes an analytic of finitude. In this context man becomes 'a strange empirico-transcendental double' because he is both what knowledge is about and the condition of all possible knowledge. The book ends, therefore, with the discussion of trends in modern thought, notably psychoanalysis and ethnology, which are leading to a decentring of man from his privileged position. The erasure of man, as Foucault envisages it, is not something to bewail as it will make possible new spaces for thought. Here again, the philosophical anti-humanism of Nietzsche and Heidegger makes itself present.

In all three studies the term *archaeology* is prominent. In *The Archaeology of Knowledge* (1969) Foucault tries to make clear the methodological presuppositions behind his early works. His approach is to stress the autonomy of discourse or discursive formations and the rules or regularities which constitute them. This approach excludes from view the question of the genesis of discourses and concentrates on the problem of their rules of formation.

THE GENEALOGY OF THE WILL TO KNOWLEDGE

The notion of a genealogy dates from the time of Foucault's inaugural address published in English as the *Discourse on Language* (1971; 1972). Here the notion appears to complement the analysis of the system-like aspect of discourses with an analysis of how they are formed. However, genealogy soon begins to replace archaeology. The radical decentring nature of his thought is not forsaken. As Foucault makes clear in his key essay, 'Nietzsche, Genealogy, History', an analysis of the effective formation of discourses is not a search for an origin (1971; 1977). Rather, the task of a genealogy of power is to analyse the descent of knowledge.

According to Foucault, Nietzsche's distinction between origin and descent is a distinction between the presentation of history as the unfolding of an idea and as a purely contingent phenomenon. Furthermore, Foucault uses the Nietzschean notion of emergence to show that modes of knowledge are inextricably tied to the eruption of forces. Hence, Foucault arrives at the couplet power–knowledge: a couplet which dramatically expresses both the tying down of discourse into relations of force and power, and the productive capacity of power to give rise to discourses.

The most famous study of this period is *Discipline and Punish* (1975). Once again modernity is in question as the decisive break is between the Classical period and the nineteenth century. Foucault charts the emergence of a 'disciplinary society' out of a society dominated by the 'spectacle of the scaffold'. The two different forms of societies are dominated by two very differing forms of power. The juridico-political concept of sovereignty in pre-modern society makes public execution into the restoration of damaged sovereignty. In modernity the new forms of 'generalised punishment' stem from a new form of capillary power which reaches into every part of the social body, but which is most strikingly illustrated in the Panopticon of Bentham. At the methodological level, the problem is that we still think of power in politico-juridical terms and, as a consequence, we are unable to understand the productivity of power, but instead conceptualise it as something negative or interdictory. Hence, the motto of the new microphysics of power, which charts the dispersal of power, is the affirmation of the need to cut off the Kings's head. We cannot think the new type of normalising society with old concepts of power.

It was during this period that Foucault began to rethink the role of the intellectual. In a sense the old notion of the universal intellectual was like the notion of the sovereign, as they both made claims to totality. As the adversary of the sovereign, the universal intellectual in effect operated within the same juridico-political field. The notion of the specific intellectual is the counterpart to the notion of capillary power. The specific intellectual intervenes at a specific site in order to wage a struggle against the local uses of power. This idea is another registration of the validity of the idea of functional differentiation in modern society.

The first volume of the *History of Sexuality* (1976; 1978) and its proposed sequels also belong to this period. Foucault's attack on the repressive hypothesis is a consequence of his new idea of power. Instead of conceiving of modernity as involving the prohibition of sex, Foucault conceives of modernity as involving its deployment, its putting into discourse. Hence, our task is to say no to this 'sex-king'. The proposed sequels were to examine the various aspects of this investment in the sexual aspect of human life. Here he introduces the notion of bio-power. However, the sequels were not to be, as Foucault once more exercised his right not to remain the same.

THE ARCHAEOLOGY OF PROBLEMATISATIONS AND THE GENEALOGY OF PRACTICES

In the *Use of Pleasures* (1984a) and the *Care of the Self* (1984b) there is a return to archaeology, but this time Foucault is after an archaeology of problematisations and not of discourses. Instead of concentrating on the internal rules or regularities of discursive formations, Foucault is now concerned with the relationship between man and world. Foucault is interested in the way that 'human beings "problematise" what they are, what they do and the world in which they live'. This opening up of archaeology to 'problematisations' represents a more *hermeneutical turn* in his thinking about culture. Hence, the concern of these two books is with ethical problematisations in the worlds of antiquity and late antiquity. However, Foucault has not abandoned the genealogical dimension as he is still concerned to provide us with a genealogy of the practices of the self. In these books Foucault returns, albeit in a modified form, to the kind of complementary style of analysis he promised in his inaugural address. Both archaeology and genealogy are put into the service of the analysis of the doctrinal and practical aspects of the 'aesthetic of existence' in antiquity and its transformation in late antiquity.

The new series was to be completed with a study of Christianity, which, although already written, was not revised by Foucault and has not been published. All three books are understood by Foucault as contributions to the investigation of the 'mode of subjectivation' which inhabits a particular social formation in order to elucidate the 'man of desire' which Foucault understands as the key component of the contemporary 'mode of subjectivation'. Hence, despite the change of program, Foucault remains interested in the central question as to how Western man came to invest so much of himself in the question of his sexuality.

AN ONTOLOGY OF THE PRESENT

Foucault's work on archives can deceive. His central concern was with the present and the processes of rationalisation which have led to our present. Hence, his concern with our relationship to madness; the construction of the body in the new setting of the medical clinic; the birth of the human sciences in the nineteenth century; our false pride in our new humanistic penology; and the modern 'man of desire's' obsession with the 'sex-king'. His thought, as Habermas rightly put it, was an arrow aimed at the heart of the present.

BIBLIOGRAPHY

Primary sources

Foucault, M. (1961) *Madness and Civilization: A History of Insanity in the Age of Reason* New York, Vintage Books, 1965
——(1963) *The Birth of the Clinic: An Archaeology of Medical Perception* New York, Vintage Books, 1973
——(1966) *The Order of Things: An Archaeology of the Human Sciences* New York, Vintage Books, 1970
——(1969) *The Archaeology of Knowledge* New York, Harper and Row, 1972
——(1971) *Language, Counter-Memory, Practice: Selected Essays and Interviews* Ed. D. F. Bouchard. Ithaca, Cornell UP, 1977
——(1975) *Discipline and Punish: The Birth of the Prison* London, Allen Lane, 1977
——(1980) *Power/Knowledge. Selected Interviews and Other Writings 1972-1977* Ed. C. Gordon. New York, Pantheon Books
——(1980) *The History of Sexuality*: Vol 1: *An Introduction* New York, Vintage Books
——(1984a) *The History of Sexuality* Vol 2: *The Use of Pleasure* New York, Vintage Books, 1985
——(1984b) *The History of Sexuality* Vol 3: *The Care of the Self* New York, Vintage Books, 1986
——(1988) *Politics, Philosophy, Culture: Interviews and Other Writings 1977-1984* Ed. L. D. Kritzman. New York and London, Routledge

Secondary sources

Hoy, D. C. (1986) *Foucault: A Critical Reader* Oxford, Basil Blackwell
Morris, P. and Patton, P. (1979) *Michel Foucault: Power, Truth, Strategy* Sydney, Feral Press

11

The Frankfurt School

The term 'critical theory' has come to be associated with the diverse body of work which emerged out of the Frankfurt Institute of Social Research, a privately funded organisation that was established in Germany in 1923 by a group of Left intellectuals. The 'Frankfurt School' of critical theory began to assume its distinctive, though by no means uniform, features after Max Horkheimer became director in 1931. Under the auspices of a multidisciplinary program, Horkheimer headed an array of thinkers working in the areas of philosophy, sociology, psychology, literary criticism, musicology, economics, political science and law.

Aside from Horkheimer, the key figures who contributed in one or several of these fields were Theodor W. Adorno, Herbert Marcuse, Leo Lowenthal, Erich Fromm, Otto Kirchheimer, Franz Neumann, Friedrich Pollock and, on the periphery of the 'inner circle', Walter Benjamin. This group is now customarily referred to as the 'first generation' of the Frankfurt School while the more contemporary work of Jürgen Habermas, Albrecht Wellmer, Oskar Negt, Claus Offe, Alfred Schmidt and Klaus Eder is sometimes referred to as emanating from the 'second generation'.

Such a lineage is, in a way, misleading if only because of the reproblematisation of the notion of critical theory by the second generation. Moreover, recourse to the label of a Frankfurt *School* of thought can be equally misleading in regard to both generations: the heterogeneity of the work of individuals does not always coalesce into an interdependent enterprise. Nevertheless, there are several major themes that can be said to characterise the approach of the first generation, even if these themes ultimately converge in on the work of perhaps the most well-known of this generation: Horkheimer, Adorno and Marcuse.

In addition, these themes underwent certain transformations as the Institute's circumstances became bound up in the changing historical situation. On Hitler's rise to power, the Institute—most of its members were Jewish and 'Marxists'—was relocated from Frankfurt to Columbia University in New York in 1934. During World War II, Adorno and Horkheimer went to Los Angeles while Marcuse, Lowenthal, Neumann and others worked for the US government in Washington. After the war, although Adorno, Horkheimer and Pollock returned to the Federal Republic, others stayed on in the US, going on to become influential teachers or, as in Fromm's case, a leading member of the American Neo-Freudian school.

Apart from this geographical dislocation and the intellectual 'parting of ways' of several of the members of the Frankfurt 'circle' during this period, the experience of Nazism and of American 'mass culture' had profound effects on the formulation of critical theory, especially that of Adorno and Horkheimer. By the time the Frankfurt School of critical theory began to make a significant impact on the English-speaking world, the theoretical evaluation of these experiences had been thoroughly digested into the theory. One consequence of this was that what became two of the key texts accorded status by the English-speaking world in the 1960s and 1970s—Marcuse's *One Dimensional Man* (1964) and Adorno's and Horkheimer's *Dialectic of Enlightenment* (1973a)— were so imbued with the historical experience of the 1940s (and, in Marcuse's case, of the US in the 1950s) that the theory relinquished one of its key methodological insights and became caught in a historical vortex. The suggestion here of a theoretical foreclosure into a historically frozen moment raises matters concerning the notion of 'critique' and the nature of theory formation in the work of the Frankfurt theorists.

The notion of 'critical theory' has its antecedents in the German philosophical tradition and, in particular, the critical philosophy of Kant. In his late philosophy, Kant set out to analyse the conditions and limits of the rational faculties in their pure-theoretical and practical-ethical dimensions using reason itself. 'Critique' in the Kantian sense is enacted in the demonstration of the principles of reason which in Kant's view are located transcendentally and immanently. In humanity's relationship to nature we become rational beings by employing the categories of the understanding (and thus realise the possibility of objective knowledge). In the world of moral experience we become rational by employing the maxims of practical reason in a consistent and universal manner.

Two lines of thought can be traced out of this Kantian notion of critique. The first of these is linked to the nineteenth century's growing attention to historical research and reflection, and finds its most notable realisation in the work of Weber. This line of thought involved a Neo-Kantian attempt to stretch the transcendental approach across the socio-cultural horizon, thus making history the central focus of critical self-reflection. While this injection of the historical dimension broadened the parameters of objective knowledge onto the cultural level (in the widest sense), the procedure also brought with it the postulate of the monadic subject: the philosophical 'I' (whose 'transcendental' posture created the distance for critical self-reflection). This set up the dichotomies of fact and value, formal and substantive rationality, and so on. Nevertheless, the expansion of the 'philosophical' agenda onto the historico-philosophical plane was to be taken up by several key figures who had an early influence on the Frankfurt theorists, namely Hans Cornelius, Husserl, Heidegger and, above all, Georg Lukács.

The second line of thought also involves the infusion of a historical dimension and has its beginnings in Hegel's critique of Kant. Hegel undercuts the Kantian antinomies and, in particular, the distinction between the noumenal and phenomenal, by incorporating critical self-reflexivity into the processes of rational thought such that the Kantian categories of reason are submitted to the historical context. The transcendental posture is dethroned through its dialectical reintegration with the phenomenological conditions of its own generation, thereby creating the possibility for reason to critically scrutinise its rational ordering of the world. The Hegelian notion of critique therefore understands objective knowledge as the outcome of reason's critical self-reflective encounter with the world.

Marx's notion of ideology critique takes methodological sustenance from this procedure in its attempt to reveal the sociological interests that lay behind theoretical constructions. More than this, the phenomenological approach is mobilised to differentiate between false and critically sustainable theories of the world. Consequently, Marx's critique of political economy endeavours to simultaneously present an analysis of the economic system and a critique of the social relations generated in the commodity form. The sum total of social relations are theorised back into the economic system such that the critical theory of capitalism exhausts the social totality.

Georg Lukács develops this concept of totality in his formulation of an Hegelianised Marxism in *History and Class Consciousness* (1923). In this work—and in opposition to the prevailing mechanistic and scientistic versions of Marxism—Lukács attempted to articulate a Marxist historicism at a high level of abstraction while at the same time rejecting all generalising philosophical systems as 'reified'—a paradox that is collapsed into a conceptual mythology of the proletariat as the subject–object of history, thus privileging the 'proletarian standpoint' as the sole repository of 'truth'.

The concept of 'reification' is developed in this context by means of distilling Weber's analysis of rationalisation and Marx's concept of commodity fetishism: the tendency of modern rationalisation to penetrate to ever-deepening levels all aspects of social life is integrated with the tendency of capitalism to reduce all social relations to abstract exchange relations. The critique of bourgeois rationalism and culture is thus not regarded merely as epiphenomenal but integral to the ideology critique of capitalism. The critical reception of Lukács' Hegelian Marxism—especially the notions of totality and reification—was the single most important Marxist influence on the Frankfurt circle.

A brief sketch of the Frankfurt circle's appropriation of the critical tradition into Critical Theory can, at best, only synthetically reconstruct a theoretical path that in many ways is bound to gloss over the important differences between the various theorists. Nevertheless, a certain trajectory can be traced (even if it tends to be weighted towards the work of Horkheimer and his 'hidden' Marxist orthodoxy). In his inaugural lecture on the research project of the Institute, Horkheimer outlined the tasks of what he calls 'social philosophy'. The term indicates a concern with a theory of society that is developed out of a dialectical interplay between contemporary 'philosophical problematics' and empirical scientific research.

Horkheimer's conception is construed on a theoretical level in terms of a critical substantive theory of society as well as on a metatheoretical level in terms of a self-reflective treatment of theory and method. The guiding motivation is stated to be an interest in human destiny where individuals as social beings are contextualised in the social totality of material and spiritual culture. Unlike Mannheim's sociology of knowledge or Lukács' location of 'truth' in the proletarian standpoint, Horkheimer historically situates truth in the critical-dialectical interpretation of the socio-historical totality.

Until the mid-1930s, Horkheimer regarded the revelation of this immanent 'truth' as having possible explosive effects on the existing social reality, ascribing to social philosophy a major role in social critique and transformation. During this period the potential audience for this social critique was still seen as the labour movement. In the 1931 lecture, Horkheimer pinpoints what he considers to be the contemporary concretised version of the perennial philosophical problems:

> . . . the question of the connection between the economic life of society, the psychological development of its individuals and the changes within specific areas of culture to which belong not only the intellectual legacy of the sciences, art and religion, but also law, customs, fashion, public opinion, sports, entertainments, lifestyles, and so on (Bronner and Kellner 1989:33).

The fruits of the Institute's research in these areas as well as the changing historical circumstances of the 1930s—the defeat of the German workers' movement and the rise of fascism, the growing pessimism about the Soviet experience, and the hovering clouds of war—were to have profound effects on the formulation of critical theory.

The Institute's investigations in the areas identified by Horkheimer in 1931 would, during the course of the 1930s, take on new and leading directions. In the area of *political economy,* Pollock developed the thesis of state-monopoly capitalism. Initially formulated out of an analysis of the relationship between the economy and the Nazi state, the theory culminated in the claim that in post-liberal state capitalism—in either its authoritarian or democratic (Keynesian) form—the economy is subject to political direction (Arato and Gebhardt 1978: pp. 71–94). In the process, power, not profit, becomes the steering mechanism according to technical imperatives. An implication of this thesis is that the double-sidedness of the immanent critique of the economy (à la Marx and nineteenth-century entrepreneurial capitalism) becomes truncated, for its ability to contrast the reality (anarchy of production) with the ideal claim (rational economic organisation) is overtaken by the technical implementation of economic organisation. In the area of *social psychology,* the Institute adopted the enterprise of a Freud–Marx synthesis, initiated by Fromn (and Wilhelm Reich). In this synthesis there was an attempt to analyse the active and passive development of the individual psyche in relation to socioeconomic conditions.

Against the backdrop of the rise of fascism, the Institute's 1936 work *Studies in Authority and the Family* investigated the possible links between the patriarchal family's generation of authoritarian traits and the susceptibility of individuals to submerge themselves in fascism. The kernel of this analysis was that fascist mass psychology targeted the *id,* not for the sake of strengthening and developing the autonomous *ego,* but to weaken it, if not to obliterate it: what Adorno called 'psychoanalysis in reverse'. The processes of individual socialisation in the new era thus came to be understood not in terms of the ideal of the self-development of the individual and the reality of integration through individual economic self-preservation, but as a flattening-out of psychic life into individual vulnerability to administrative/authoritarian manipulation and the construction of false collectivity. In this light Horkheimer would argue that the role of the family was no longer just an internaliser of authority but also a realm in which forces of resistance to authority were engendered (1972: 277).

Parallel arguments emerge in the Frankfurt theorists' *cultural criticism.* Marcuse's 'The Affirmative Character of Culture' argues that in the culture of liberal capitalism there is a tension between the need for happiness and the misery of actual existence. Art's 'beautiful illusion' presented a critique of bad existence yet simultaneously asserted, in an affirmative mode, that a better life is only realisable by each individual in an abstract internal way (1972c: 122). However, under the conditions of monopoly capitalism this internal world of loneliness is turned inside out such that the 'illusion' of the culture industry—ephemeral gratification under the guise of the promise of happiness—is generalised onto an equally abstract, but external, collectivity. The need for happiness is falsely collapsed into the mass consumption of the culture industry's products, and thus the critical line between everyday existence and cultural reflection is erased.

In the area of cultural criticism, similar evaluations would lead Horkheimer and, even more so, Adorno to champion those autonomous works of art which critically incorporated fragments of the bad present into their form. The general theme which began to be drawn from these different areas, especially after 1940, was that the new social formation which had replaced liberal capitalism subsumed the 'two-dimensional' character of the latter—its vulnerability to an immanent critique of its ideal against the real—into a 'one-dimensional' society in which technological rationality veiled political-economic relations and where administrative and cultural manipulation and control reigned over the 'decline of the individual'.

During the 1930s the term 'critical theory' had generally been used as a code word for critical Marxism or a Hegelian Marxism. However, Horkheimer's explicit reference to the term in 'Traditional and Critical Theory (1972: pp. 188–243, 244–252) takes on a far greater significance. In what Dubiel called the 'materialist' period (1930–1937), the Frankfurt theorists already considered the formulation of a critical theory of society as being (contra Lukács) removed from proletarian class consciousness. But in the 'Critical Theory' essay Horkheimer makes this approach far more explicit and radicalises the argument: the critical theorist's interest in social emancipation expressed through the pursuit of a theoretically adequate social theory commits the theorist to a self-imposed marginalisation from even the addressees of the theory— the proletarian masses. A stronger interpretation of this thesis is that the critical theorist is the 'subject' of the critical theory of society and bears the burden of opposing the status quo.

Underpinning this re-situation of critical theory was its understanding of the new social formations, and in particular the new conditions of the political steering of the economy and the accompanying forms of socialisation. Under these conditions of social integration through atomisation from above, the empirical 'standpoint' of the proletariat was seen to have been absorbed into an undifferentiated, though still stratified, mass society of the status quo. The turn to psychoanalysis was an attempt to explain the disappearance of proletarian class consciousness as potentially oppositional. Nevertheless, during the period between 1937 and 1940, the task of critical theory was still considered to be the critical analysis of the dynamics of the new society and to uncover its ideological forms.

From 1940 onwards, this task began to take on a new flavour. In the 'End of Reason' (Arato and Gebhardt 1978: 26–48), Horkheimer signals what would become essential elements of the 'critique of instrumental reason' elaborated upon in the *Dialectic of Enlightenment* (Adorno and Horkheimer, 1973a). In particular, Horkheimer presents the argument that the new forms of domination of the historical epoch found their ideological justification in the claims of technical efficiency. The 'fetish' of technological rationality had displaced traditional and bourgeois ideals as the ideological veil of society. In this form, the domination of man over man is now coupled with the new theme of man's domination over nature.

The rational central plan is no longer regarded as a positive step in human emancipation but as an instrument of authoritarian regimes (including the Soviet model). These shifts mark a departure from the classical Marxist tenets of the progressive character of humanity's instrumental control over nature and of the rational ordering of the economy. Yet this new critique initially remained in the tradition of a Marxian immanent critique of politics to the extent that it attempted to unmask the ideological fetish—technological rationality—of society in order to expose its dynamics.

In the *Dialectic of Enlightenment*, Adorno and Horkheimer consolidate these themes generalising the critique of politics into a critique of culture. The key assumption brought into this wider critique is that state capitalist culture is inextricably one of manipulation and control, totally penetrating social and psychic structures—the very reason why the proletariat as revolutionary subject was jettisoned. This assumption leads the critique into an acceptance of the new social formation's own ideological caricature—technical efficiency—in an unproblematical manner, that is, without consideration of crisis tendencies. Left bereft of a key to social transformation by its own demolition of the Marxist philosophy of history (yet still bearing its burden), the critique of instrumental reason endeavours to ground itself in a speculative philosophy of history that transgresses the whole of Western civilisation.

The political experiences of fascism, of Soviet totalitarianism, and of American mass culture, now consumed into the critique of instrumental reason, are swept up into a history of the growing domination of the 'concept' in the West. The Enlightenment's struggle against myth is confronted with the Enlightenment myth of inevitable progress whereby the increasing control of external nature is necessarily accompanied by the increasing domination of internal nature. From pre-Homeric Greece through De Sade to the culture industry, the liberating promise of enlightenment inevitably recoils on itself into ever-new forms of heteronomy—the very dialectic of enlightenment. The debt to Nietzsche is made explicit by Adorno and Horkheimer. Under the duress of this acute pessimism, social emancipation is put into abeyance shorn of any historical or utopian reference. The 'totally administered society' exiles the critical theorist into social hibernation where critical self-reflection on the autonomous art-work and critical philosophy is the only mode of resistance.

In *One Dimensional Man*, Marcuse ventures into a macrological analysis of the totally administered affluent society in search of oppositional tendencies using the criterion of marginalisation. However, by the time this work was published, the very dimension left unthematised in the critique of instrumental reason—the possible crisis tendencies of the system's steering mechanisms—as well as new problems of social integration, were beginning to emerge. It was with an eye to these developments that the 'second generation' of critical theorists embarked upon a new critical theory of society with an emancipatory intent. In conclusion, the eclipse of the 'older' critical theory into a pessimistic philosophy of history can be seen, with historical hindsight, to be not merely a theoretical foreclosure into a historically frozen moment but simultaneously an inability to unload crucial components of its Marxist heritage, notably the postulate that the 'proletariat' is *the* 'revolutionary subject' of capitalism. The subsequent mapping of its decline by the critical theorists could not but lead into profound despair.

BIBLIOGRAPHY

Adorno T.W. (1967) *Prisms* London, Neville Spearman
——(1967) *Philosophy of Modern Music* London, Sheed & Ward
——(1969) *The Authoritarian Personality* New York, Norton
——(1976) The *Positivist Dispute in German Sociology* London, Heinemann
——and Horkheimer (1973a) *Dialectic of Enlightenment* London, Allen Lane
——(1973b) *Introduction to the Sociology of Music* New York, Routledge & Kegan Paul
——(1973c) *Negative Dialectics* London, Routledge & Kegan Paul
——(1974) *Minima Moralia* London, New Left Books
——(1981) *In Search of Wagner* London, New Left Book
——(1982) *Against Epistemology* Oxford, Basil Blackwell
——(1984) *Aesthetic Theory* London, Routledge & Kegan Paul
Arato, A. and Breines, P. (1979) *The Young Lukács and the Origins of Western Marxism* London, Pluto
——and Gebhardt, E. (1978) (eds) *The Essential Frankfurt School Reader* Oxford, Basil Blackwell
Benhabib, S. (1986) *Critique, Norm and Utopia* New York, Columbia U.P.
Bloch, E. et al. (1977) *Aesthetics and Politics* London, Verso
Breines, P. (1972) (ed.) *Critical Interruptions* New York, Herder & Herder
Bronner, S. and Kellner, D. (1989) (eds) *Critical Theory and Society: A Reader* London, Routledge
Buck-Morss, S. (1977) *The Origin of Negative Dialectics* Hassocks, Sussex, Harvester
Dubiel, H. (1985) *Theory and Politics* Cambridge, Mass., MIT

Funk, R. (1982) *Erich Fromm: The Courage To Be Human* New York, Continuum
Held, D. (1980) *Introduction to Critical Theory* London, Hutchinson
Horkheimer, M. (1972) *Critical Theory* New York, Seabury
——(1974a) *Critique of Instrumental Reason* New York, Seabury
——(1974b) *Eclipse of Reason* New York, Seabury
——(1978) *Dawn and Decline* New York, Seabury
Jay, M. (1973) *The Dialectical Imagination* Boston, Little Brown
—— (1984a) *Adorno* Cambridge, Mass. Harvard U.P.
——(1984b) *Marxism and Totality* Berkeley, University of California
——(1986) *Permanent Exiles* New York, Columbia University
Kellner, D. (1984) *Herbert Marcuse and the Crisis of Marxism* Berkeley, Free Press
Lind, P. (1985) *Marcuse and Freedom* London, Croom Helm
Lunn, E. (1982) *Marxism and Modernism* Berkeley, University of California
Marcuse, H. (1955) *Reason and Revolution* London, Routledge & Kegan Paul
——(1958) *Soviet Marxism* London, Routledge & Kegan Paul
——(1969) *An Essay on Liberation* Boston, Beacon
——(1970) *Five Lectures* Boston, Beacon
——(1972a) *Counterrevolution and Revolt* London, Allen Lane
——(1972b) *Eros and Civilisation* London, Abacus
——(1972c) *Negations* Harmondsworth, Penguin
——(1972d) *Studies in Critical Philosophy* London, New Left Books
——(1978) *The Aesthetic Dimension* Boston, Beacon
——(1987) *Hegel's Ontology and Theory of Historicity* Cambridge, Mass., MIT
Nagele, R. (1988) (ed.) *Benjamin's Ground* Detroit, Wayne State U.P.
Pippon, R. et al. (1988) (eds) *Marcuse: Critical Theory and the Promise of Utopia* South Hadley, Mass., Bergin & Garvey
Roberts, J. (1983) *Walter Benjamin* Atlantic Highlands, N.J., Humanities
Rose, G. (1978) *The Melancholy Science* London, Macmillan
Schoolman, M. (1980) *The Imaginary Witness* New York, Free
Smith, G. (1988) (ed.) *On Walter Benjamin* Cambridge, Mass., MIT
——(1989) *Benjamin* Chicago, University of Chicago
Telos 45, Fall 1980, special issue on Leo Lowenthal
Wolin, R. *Walter Benjamin: An Aesthetic of Redemption* New York, Columbia U.P.
Wolff, K.H. and Moore, Barrington Jr. (1967) (eds) *The Critical Spirit* Boston, Beacon

12

French Feminisms

French feminisms are diverse writings on questions of sexual difference by women associated with recent French intellectual and political movements. They have come to be grouped together through the various alliances and dialogues they sustain with, and against, psychoanalysis (Freud, Lacan), deconstruction (Derrida) and post-Saussurean linguistics (Kristeva). They can also emerge as distinct for feminism through the marked difference in their writing practices from that of most Anglo-American feminists. Indeed many French theorists of sexual difference maintain a principled 'anti-feminism' (Spivak 1981) in order to signal their distance from that Anglo-American approach which has been favoured for the position 'feminist'.

Those whose work has generated the most interest in Australian networks include Hélène Cixous, Christine Delphy, Luce Irigaray and Michèle Le Doeuff. The work of others, individual and collaborative, can be traced through the bibliographical references at the end of the chapter.

In 1980 the anthology *New French Feminisms* by Elaine Marks and Isabelle de Courtivron gave some taste of this material to a wider English-speaking audience. Their selection of translations has become a textbook in women's studies courses, used to furnish examples of feminist 'theorists of difference' as compared to either the equal rights feminists or the 'identity politics' writers associated with Anglo-American feminism. The distinction is widely used to point out the difference of philosophical resources available to French- and English-speaking feminist critics, which has come to feature significantly in their exchange. Spivak notes that while these cultural characterisations have 'French' and 'Anglo-American' set up as categories in opposition, together occupying the whole field of feminism, a focus on *the other woman*—her example is women in the Third World—discloses that difference as superficial (Spivak 1981: 179).

'Identity politics' describes writing which invokes a sense of belonging, finally and unambiguously, to an oppressed group, for example realising the truth of one's being as a woman, as black or lesbian (Weeks 1985: 185–210). In contrast 'high' French feminism ('theorists of difference') involves neither a search for identity nor a search for equality. It challenges sexism, the systematic privileging of *man* over *woman*, but not on the grounds of any essence which woman partakes of. Thus it appeals neither to an *essential human nature*, common to men and women (assumed by liberal or 'equal rights' feminism, and much of socialist feminism) nor to an *essential feminine nature*, which one might identify with and argue the higher merits of (assumed by radical feminism). In their rejection of these paradigms of the feminist project, French feminists contribute to an *anti-humanist* critical movement in Europe.

Humanism is that mode of thought which posits a human essence (reason, feeling, experience) in place of the divine one, as the secure grounding of knowledge and history. Anti-humanism takes this secularisation of European thought further and challenges all notions of the human which presuppose a transcendental self, or one still modelled on the positive idea of God: a self which is enduring, unified and fully present to consciousness; one which claims to possess its singularity, its self-sameness, prior to and beyond its relations with others. This construction of the human (privileging *self* over *other, identity* over *difference)* is seen as complicit with the symbolic system which underlies Western forms of domination, including sexism. The editors of *New French Feminisms* associate the writings in their collection with a broad anti-humanism, and with the political and intellectual events which have led to its characteristic rethinking of the possibilities and terms of resistance. These events include the student-led revolt of May 1968 in France, in which many French feminists participated. Thus they say that French feminist writings are not to be understood *diachronically*, as part of a progressive history of French feminism, but rather *synchronically*, in relation to these upheavals which continue both to shape and rupture critical thinking in contemporary France (Marks and de Courtivron 1980: 30). Anti-humanist lines of thought have opened up the analytic systems of Marxism, psychoanalysis, phenomenology, existentialism, and structuralism to new ways of intervening in the cultural reproduction of capitalism.

French feminist writing is enabled by the European current of these critical traditions as much as it contributes its own re-evaluations of their systems. The extent of engagement in each of these theoretical frameworks varies, of course, with different women; in their relation to the psychoanalytic model, those, such as Hélène Cixous, associated with the group *Psychoanalyse et Politique* (1968; the group which controls the publishing house *editions des femmes* and the name *MLF,* the Women's Liberation Movement acronym given by the press to diverse groups of activist women in France—see Kaufmann-McCall 1983; Duchen 1987) differ greatly from someone like Catherine Clément or the women, such as Monique Wittig, of *Féministes révolutionnaires*. All these women, however, sustain some commitment to Marxist perspectives on capitalist culture (while taking the freedom to pursue unorthodoxies), with those of the *Tel Quel* group most outspoken against France's own imperialist developments. Some women, notably Julia Kristeva and Marguerite Duras, also sustain allegiances to the literary avant-garde and to dissident art practices.

Simone de Beauvoir can be considered a figure to whom all French feminists owe some debt, for introducing the question of a differently sexed body into the philosophical arena of French politics. She took up the phenomenological scheme of self/other relations—put to such extensive use in existentialist strategies of analysis as a model of male/female relations in the symbolic domain—declaring, in 1949, that woman is the Other. Another historic de Beauvoir statement was that 'one is not born, but rather becomes, a woman' (de Beauvoir 1953: 9). Both the social construction of femininity and its symbolic significance as otherness and negativity have become starting points of French feminist inquiry.

One becomes a woman through being incorporated into a binary symbolic order. This is a system wherein one term, for example *man, mind, reason,* is given a positive value through being positioned as primary (more essential) in relation to an opposing term, which is negatively coded—*woman, body, passion.* The positive term is primary also in the sense of being first, originary—both *origin* as starting point, and *original* as singular—giving the theology of *self* over *other(s)*. If the anti-humanist argument is that neither term (man *nor* woman, reason *nor* feeling), is essential in the story of our becoming human, the feminist (also deconstructivist) argument against dualisms is that neither term can contain the radical *difference* at play between them. This is a multiplicity of differences, a heterogeneity which exceeds the simple structure of an opposition; it is radical because in a binary system it enables the negative, 'feminine' term to become *duplicitous*, subversive. The system which looks to downplay this difference, as a defence against all that is disconcerting in the idea of femininity, is said to be *phallocentric*, where what is privileged at the centre comes to resemble, in its morphology, the erect penis. This is the Unique as that which 'stands alone'—that which does not depend upon its difference from an absence, the hidden, labyrinthine form of woman, in order to signify its singular presence as 'man'.

French feminist strategies of writing seek to disrupt this symbolic order and its normative effect on social relations on several fronts. One is to set up exchanges with the major corpuses of Western knowledge, both texts which are taken to found it (e.g. Plato, Freud) and those which push at its limits (Nietzsche, Joyce). Another is to rewrite the category 'woman': to take what the mythology of femininity in turn threatens and promises, and fashion it to new possibilities of 'becoming'. This is to be women *whatever that might be* rather than getting stuck in any determination of what woman *is*. And finally another strategy, the most telling in some respects, is to turn the material practice of writing itself to an engagement in the argument against phallocentricity.

In the effort to gesture towards something other than the singular to which everything gets reduced—words, desires, the heterogeneity within and among people—French women writers deploy devices of ambiguity and indeterminacy of meaning, effects usually reserved for the writing of poetry. Their writing is often made up of fragments defying a linear progression of sense. The pleasures of reading are understood to be differentiated as much as are bodies and their pleasures, along sexual lines. A play of meaning which is never closed off and which does not oppose the real and the imaginary, truth and fiction, is thought to be the writing of woman's pleasure.

The combination of theory, fantasy, and innovative wordcraft in many French feminist texts often does not translate well, however, and an enigmatic style can be frustrating to those who are unfamiliar with the critical dynamics in which they are often engaged. It should be noted that not all French feminists write in a 'plural style', seeking to provoke excesses and abysses of meaning. Some choose a plain prose, in reaction at times to a perceived 'will to power' involved in the elaborate theoretical manoeuvres or clever word games favoured by groups of male intellectuals (e.g. Clément 1987). These women tend to be less well-known outside of France, though the style and approach of their texts more closely resembles feminist writing in English; perhaps, as Toril Moi suggests, they have been seen as 'lacking in exotic difference' (Moi 1987: 6). Though a distinction in writing practices is widely taken to mark a division between French and Anglo-American feminism, it is important not to reproduce this schema uncritically. To reduce the many differences at work within 'French feminism' to a defining key, in order to sustain some categorical dualism, would be to acquiesce—on the account of many of these women—in one of the major symbolic determinations of Western culture.

HELENE CIXOUS

Hélène Cixous is best known outside of France for her early work, particularly 'The Laugh of the Medusa' translated in the journal *Signs* in 1976. In this essay she takes up questions raised by French novelist Annie Leclerc, in her groundbreaking 1974 text *Parole de Femme*, on the possibility of a feminine language; and like Leclerc, she offered them in a lyrical celebration of woman's specificity, the difference her body 'speaks': 'Text: my body—shot through with streams of song . . . (body? bodies?), no more describable than god, the soul, or the Other; that part of you that leaves a space between yourself and urges you to inscribe in language your woman's style' (1976c: 882). A feminine writing practice, she claims, will never be definable. It is to be found in spaces which cannot be enclosed under the dominion of the Father—in excess, in the in-between, and in an interminable exchange between one and other. The woman's writing is akin to laughter ('it is the rhyth-me that laughs you') and to the 'mother' ('She writes in white ink'—Cixous 1976c: 881)). The fear of finding the worst (for men)—that women *aren't* castrated versions of themselves—has kept us from looking for her. But, she says, 'You only have to look at the Medusa straight on to see her. And she's not deadly. She's beautiful and she's laughing' (1976c: 885).

Cixous was associated with the *Psych et Po* group until the early 1980s. Like others in that organisation she is primarily committed in her writing to challenging the symbolic law of Western culture. While she uses the psychic categories of Freudian theory to disclose the phallocentric order of the symbolic, she accuses psychoanalytic rhetoric (including that of Lacan) of collusion with that order, and calls for a flight into a female imaginary. She was among those to argue against 'feminism' (in its platform of 'equal rights'—equal access to masculinist modes of being, structures of power), but she upholds allegiances within the women's movement in France, and with the American radicalesbians to a limited extent (see Stambolian and Marks 1979: 74–5). Her writing is closely allied to the deconstructive writing of Derrida. They are comparable in their concern with the texts of Nietzsche, Bataille and Blanchot, for example, and often share a similar analytic focus (on the dynamics of oppositions, the *propre*, Hegel's *Aufhebung*). Other figures featured in Cixous' texts are the writers Lewis Carroll, James Joyce, Shakespeare, Blake, Hoffman, Kleist, Poe, Rimbaud and Lautréamont; and from myth, ancient and modern, the figures Penthesilea, Cleopatra, and Dora. She has written one novel, *Angst* (1985a).

Cixous reports a change in her thinking since the mid-1970s (Strombolian and Marks 1979: 70), by which date most of her work best known in Anglo-American circles had been already published. Besides 'The Laugh of the Medusa', significant amongst this early work was *La Jeune Née* (1975), a collaboration with Catherine Clément, translated into English as *The Newly Born Woman* (1985b). It is notable for its articulation of the differences between the two writers, explored in the third section entitled 'Exchange'. The first section, 'The Guilty One' by Clément, is an analysis of the mythology of woman as sorceress and hysteric. The second part by Hélène Cixous is called 'Sorties: Out and Out: Attacks/Ways Out/Forays'. It contains writing of a deconstructivist bent, elaborating the complicities between the systems of logocentrism (Derrida) and phallocentrism. The British critic Annette

Kuhn describes the more recent writings of Cixous as marking a break in that they succeed more in practising rather than beckoning towards an alternative textuality. She describes the image of the orange in *Vivre L'orange* (1979a) as an emblem of this writing of Cixous: The orange's juiciness, sensuousness, texture, and brightness are present in the writing itself, which is as tactile as the fruit being held and weighed in the hands. The sound association with Oran, the writer's birthplace, implies a return to sources, but the shape of the orange, the O, tells us that the route will not be a linear one. The shape also suggests the roundness of femininity, the shape and weight of a breast, a full and positive sign of sexual difference to replace the Lacanian Lack (Kuhn 1981: 38–9).

CHRISTINE DELPHY

Christine Delphy can be thought of in many ways as an exception to the rule of 'French Feminism'—that is, to the most popular understanding (amongst Anglo-Americans) of French women's writing on sexual difference. Her writing style is not highly enigmatic or overlayered with combinations of possible meanings. She does not focus on 'the body' and its excesses as the privileged site from which to 'read' or 'write' feminine otherness. She does not position herself with recourse to a psychoanalytic lexicon, even as she argues against its claims. And lastly, she embraces the term 'feminist' without hesitation. Indeed, her 1976 essay 'Protofeminism and antifeminism' (1984), written against Annie Leclerc's 1974 book *Parole de Femme*, condemns those women who, she says, cast off the very movement to which they owe their own accomplishment. Leclerc's text, and those of others aligned with the group *Psych et Po*, are reproached as 'protofeminist', as taking their starting point from the moment of individual rather than collective revolt; making their *end* point, she claims, a proclamation of the end of feminist struggle. '*Proto*feminism promoted as *post*-feminism and becoming militant', she declares, 'is *anti*feminism' (1984: 209).

Delphy's work can be likened to that of socialist feminists in the English-speaking world, and it is within these circles that she is most renowned in Australia. She emphasises historical, economic and social determinants in the analysis of women's oppression, calling for a 'materialist' feminism. She argues for a broad understanding of materialism which she says is not to be subsumed under a scientific Marxist analysis of capitalism. Her most controversial assertion and claim to notoriety beyond the borders of France is that women constitute a class. A debate with Michèle Barrett and Mary McIntosh was set up with their critique of her position appearing in *Feminist Review* (January 1979) and her reply to that journal in 1980 (for an altered version, see Delphy 1984: 154–81); others have also entered the fray (Moi 1987: 13, n.8). Much of her campaign is against idealism and its corollary, the intellectual orthodoxies generated within political movements. She challenges what she sees as the ideological dangers in the thinking of those 'on her side'— that is, those women who also seek to mobilise resistance against capitalism or the psychoanalytic enclosure, for example—just as vigorously as she challenges her outright enemies. She targets that 'disciplining' of knowledges which works to subject the materiality each takes up as its object of study—the condition of women, for example—to the idealist 'laws' of its own privileged assumptions (1984: 213).

Delphy works as a sociologist; many of her essays cover issues related to the family, its significance and structure, and marriage, particularly its contractual role in securing the woman's labour for the 'master's' household. If Clausewitz is famed for his statement 'politics is the continuation of war by other means', Delphy should be remembered for her analysis of divorce as the continuation of marriage by other means (1984: 99).

Simone de Beauvoir has described Christine Delphy as 'France's most exciting feminist theorist' (1984: 7). Delphy has worked closely with de Beauvoir, particularly during the early 1970s. Both women helped to found the 1977 journal *Questions Féministes*.

LUCE IRIGARAY

The writing of Luce Irigaray is allied to that of Hélène Cixous and very different from Christine Delphy's. Indeed, Irigaray has been the principal target of the *Questions Féministes* critique (launched by Monique Plaza and sustained by Delphy), against what the journal's editors state is an over-engagement in philosophical and psychoanalytic discourse by their fellow French feminists (Moi 1987: 6). Irigaray is a trained Lacanian psychoanalyst and is well seasoned in the discipline of philosophy. Far from being taken in by the doctrines of philosophy and psychoanalysis, however, Irigaray undertakes not only to criticise but to move on from their programs, to sink their major thrusts, as it were, under the currents of her woman's 'textuality'.

Irigaray shares with Cixous a delight in inscribing what she sees as the promise of femininity in the materiality of writing, its 'performative' capabilities. The myriad pleasures of meaning production are not to be exhausted by full stops and the orderly procession of syntax. If her phrases do reach the status of sentences they may yet be 'unfinished'— ambiguous, catacombed, ringing with the clamour of many voices. She adopts different styles for different moments in her thinking and for the diverse bodies of theory addressed in her work (Grosz 1989: 101, 240). For all the playfulness of her writing it is rigorous in its craft and in its explorations in critical theory. This rigour, however, goes hand in hand with a resistance, inscribed in the texts, to the building up of any system which would lend her thought to totalisation. There is thus no proper philosophy or controlling framework of propositions able to be abstracted from the irreducible dynamics of Irigaray's textual practices.

With Cixous, Irigaray's mode of thought can be described as utopian. She rejects the larger story given by psychoanalysis of the system of relations it claims to retrace in individual histories, that the privileged position of the phallus in the symbolic system of the human psyche is a necessary condition for sociality. Instead she foreshadows non-hierarchical, utopian patterns of exchange, imagined between one another at a psychic level, as an alternative to this patriarchal symbolic order. These relations are 'yet to come'; and so as better to focus on and mobilise them in a process of infinite 'becoming', Irigaray argues in *Divine Woman* for a dream of *godly* femininity. 'What we need', she writes, 'we who are sexed according to our genre, is a God to share, a verb to share and become. Defined as the mother-substance, often obscure, even occult, of the verb of men, we need our *subject*, our *noun*, our *verb*, our *predicates*; our elementary sentence, our base rhythm, our morphological identity, our generic incarnation, our genealogy' (1986a: 11).

The imaginary relations aspired to in a God of the feminine genre may be articulated from the perception of otherness that woman already embodies, however. Alongside the Lacanian elaboration of Freud on the privilege sustained by the phallus—Lacan depicts the values of transcendental unity and presence ('something to see') in the morphology of the erect penis—Irigaray poses a metaphor drawn from the morphology of woman. Quite other values from those of the male God, from the system of binarism which works to reduce heterogeneity to sameness, to the One and Only, are invoked in the image of a woman's labia or 'two lips'. 'Woman', she writes, '. . . is in touch with herself by herself and in herself . . . without the necessity of a mediation and prior to any possible distinction between activity and passivity. Woman "touches herself" all the time, moreover without anyone being able to forbid her to do so for her sex is made up of two lips which embrace each other continuously. Thus, in herself, she is already two—but indivisible into ones—which affect, are affected by, are attached to each other' (1978: 162).

Besides the 'larger story' of psychoanalysis, Irigaray challenges the more particular stories and hypotheses it enlists in its account of the passage to normal human subjectivity. She targets the Oedipal myth especially, for its work in directing the transformation of a presumed initial sameness of girls and boys into a binary opposition (Grosz 1989: 108). The inscribed masculinity of drives and the negative conception of femininity as 'lack' are also scorned by Irigaray, notably in her sustained critique of Freud and Lacan in *Speculum of the Other Woman* (1985a). A further dialogue Irigaray enters into with psychoanalytic discourse is on the question of the mother–daughter relationship, in a lyrical piece entitled 'One does not move without the other' (1982).

Irigaray exposes not only the 'phallic economy' operative within psychoanalysis but also that controlling the affairs of Western societies more generally. In an approach which should be unorthodox enough for Delphy, she takes up the ideas of Marx on commodity production in order to describe relations between men and women. Underlining the masculine indication in the word 'homosexual', she insinuates into it the French word *homme* (man) to argue that we are placed in a *hommosexual* culture. Women, she claims, are the 'goods' exchanged between men in order to conduct their affairs between themselves, between men only. 'It is out of the question for [women]', she says, 'to go to "market" on their own, enjoy their own worth among themselves . . .' (1985b: 196). She advocates a withdrawal from the mediating labour of this economic-symbolic relation into a more autonomous encounter with each other. Some interpret this as a call to lesbian experience; in her later texts, though, she is more concerned with the possibility of inscribing ways for the irreducible polarities of sexual difference to be renegotiated more positively (Grosz 1989: 148).

As part of her deconstructive engagement with the major texts of Western philosophy, Irigaray has proposed a four-volume work (as yet untranslated) written to parallel the elements of earth, air, fire and water. These are *Amante Marine* (on Nietzsche, explored through 'water', 1980), *Passions élémentaires* ('earth': on the possibility of love between the sexes, 1982), *L'Oubli de L'Air* (on Heidegger and the breath of spirit, 1983), and a planned fourth text, perhaps on Marx in terms of fire (of technology, of desire (see Irigaray 1981: 44)). Among other figures Irigaray addresses in her texts are Levinas and Feuerbach, Lévi Strauss and René Girard. Along with Cixous, she finds Freud's Dora and Lewis Carroll's Alice characters of great interest.

Some of Irigaray's texts have been published by *des femmes* but of her affiliations with other feminists she declares: 'I refuse to be limited by the boundaries of just one group in the Women's Liberation Movement' (1977: 68–9).

MICHÈLE LE DOEUFF

If Irigaray resists being pinned down as to her position within French feminism, Michèle Le Doeuff presents a body of texts in which the question (either of her relation to feminism or to some textual 'feminine') is hardly marked—though one might, on another level, argue that it is marked on every page (Morris 1988: 76). Her work displays few signs of affiliation or disaffiliation with any of the major groupings of French women writers on sexual difference. She takes Irigaray to task for dismissing philosophy wholesale, but her project is not set against those who would discover in philosophy an antithesis to 'woman', to what it casts and casts out as feminine. Her work explores what she calls the 'imaginary' of philosophy, the images, myths and 'old wives' tales' it relies on, but maligns, in its pursuit of true knowledge.

Where Le Doeuff differs from other French feminists is that she has no wish to disrupt or abandon philosophical writing. For her, rationality is too valuable a claim for it to be given up to the masculine designs put upon its project. She insists on continuing to take up positions within the discipline—even if for philosophy, as she says, 'woman is an internal enemy' (1977: 7). But because of this determination to reaffirm philosophy *and* the difference her femininity signifies, Le Doeuff must continually confront problems not only of her own sex in relation to philosophy, but also that of women's relation to the 'feminine' Other philosophy engenders—questions also taken on by Cixous, Irigaray and others. Without dreaming the utopia of an autonomous femininity in a different kind of textual practice, Le Doeuff shares their concern with questions of sexual difference, writing positions, and feminist politics. She addresses these concerns both explicitly, for example in her essay 'Women and Philosophy' (1977), and implicitly, in her engagement with positions from which to speak about the production of philosophy.

The Australian critic Meaghan Morris notes that it is perhaps more in her *disengagement* from critical positions that Le Doeuff is able to offer feminists an alternative practice to traditional philosophy (Morris 1988: 77). This, in Le Doeuff's analyses, is philosophy subject to a misogynist fantasy, wherein the initiate is required to call up and renounce, as so much feminine seduction, the spectre of the indefinite: a 'disciplining' of the self to unachievable standards of knowledge certainty and completion. The essay form Le Doeuff prefers allows her movement from one perspective to another to show a thought in process. Her commitment to the positions she takes up is determined by their '*sufficiency to their tasks*' (Morris 1988: 73). It is a pragmatism which insists that the resulting gaps and disparities remain in place in order to resist the pressure to totalise her thinking, and so reduce the horizons opened at the unfolding of her various questions. Morris calls this model of theoretical practice 'operative reasoning', after Le Doeuff's own phrasing in relation to de Beauvoir, of 'operative philosophy': the resources of philosophy put to work for feminist politics.

Essays in Le Doeuff's collection entitled *Recherches sur L'Imaginaire Philosophique* (1980) dip into the writings of Descartes, Galileo, Kant, Plato, Rousseau and others, exploring the images and 'hearsay' enlisted at moments in their deliberations. Because regulating and overriding survey work is not carried out by Le Doeuff on the scene at large, the concept of an *imaginary* is not definitively formalised; nor even is the precise concept *image*. Her own image for the philosophical imaginary is that of the discipline's own 'shameful face'. It needs but is unable to embrace the mythopoetic dimension of human imaginings; for all its ontological rigours, philosophy is ever a process of 'thinking-in-images'.

In her various accounts of *logos* overcoming *mythos*, psychoanalytic significances or relations between the symbolic and the imaginary (Lacan) are mobilised alongside the more metaphysical and rhetorical import of the real (literal meaning, The Word as sacred truth, objectivity, reason) versus the imaginary (the figurative, the deceptive realm of images, subjectivity, emotion).

Importantly, Le Doeuff claims *'There is not just* one *reason,* one *imaginary'* (Morris 1988: 79). We are not locked into a static system which cannot be challenged and transformed through critical practices. Influenced by the work of Foucault, Le Doeuff insists on tracing the multifold historical dynamics involved in any genealogy of philosophy. She is critical of those theorists (particularly the New Philosophers) who bracket all philosophical discourse under the name of some monolithic monster ('Western metaphysics', 'Logocentrism'). For her, the hegemony ('Corporate' power) currently enjoyed by a certain 'style of imagination' is bound to make way for other styles as it is led to admit—finding itself incapable of realising its own myths—that knowledge is always partial.

Woman is not *necessarily* that negative-coded Other that philosophy must have (nothing to do with) in order to establish itself on its own claims, according to Le Doeuff; but she does embody the paradigm within the Greek-derived history of the discipline. Elizabeth Grosz reads a 1981 Le Doeuff essay, translated as 'Pierre Roussel's chiasmas', to show how the philosophical metaphor of woman can be 'literalised' in medical-scientific discourse on her body, as an image legitimating certain forms of knowledge; in this case, moral ideology (Grosz 1989: 219–24). That Other upon whom the scandal of image-dependence is projected can also be the child, the idiot, the crowd, and so on; 'people who live on legends' (Le Doeuff 1980: 14–15). Le Doeuff traces the intertextuality at play as philosophers struggle to establish the truth of their proposals. A particular image or metaphor (for example, the island of truth in Bacon and Kant) can migrate across texts, to be reactivated, and reworked, in a process she likens to 'giving a nod and a wink' to earlier investments in the battle against indeterminacy.

As part of her interest in the historical effects of philosophy and the mythic closure of knowledge, Le Doeuff has also made a study of 'real' women, the institutional conditions of women's involvement in the discipline. In 'Women and Philosophy' (1977), Le Doeuff argues that contrary to popular belief, women have been able to participate in the production of philosophical discourse (she cites, for example, Diotima, Hyppatia, Heloise, Christine de Pisan, Queen Christina of Sweden). Their admittance to the fold, however, is conditional upon them taking up one of two roles: either as lovers, or faithful commentators, of some Great Man. Another essay, on de Beauvoir and her relation to Sartre (1979), seeks to show how the misogynist moments in a philosophical framework—here, the famous 'holes and slime' image of women's bodies, in Sartre's existentialist account of self and other—can be out-manoeuvred in a feminist appropriation of the discourse in which they figure.

A third essay, 'Utopias: Scholarly' (1982) deals with an aspect of utopian thought (following on from Le Doeuff's earlier textual readings of More, Bacon and Campanella on utopias) that works to serve the interests of 'the school', of pedagogy. Here the influence of Bachelard (*The Formation of the Scholarly Mind*) is clearly marked. She writes: 'We know that for Nietzsche the categorical imperative is a hypothetical imperative whose hypothesis has been forgotten. We can likewise suppose that the imperative "you must teach" is presented to the teaching conscience as a categorical imperative insofar as this conscience has "forgotten" the origin of the imperative, which is categorical or corporate' (1982: 457).

Michèle Le Doeuff is only recently gaining a sizeable readership in Australia, due in part to her inclusion in Grosz's popular book *Sexual Subversions* (1989). Her most recent contributions to a genealogy of philosophy concentrate on scientific discovery and the writings of Francis Bacon.

Other French feminisms influential in Australian circles include that of Kristeva. She has a more direct focus on the textuality or materiality of texts than Le Doeuff. She also sets out her position in relation to feminist movements more systematically, in her article 'Women's Time' (1981). Here three feminist generations are specified: one characterised by a feminist desire to be the same as men (de Beauvoir is positioned here); one striving after difference, or an autonomous femininity (represented by Cixous, Irigaray); and one which seeks to move beyond all identities (Kristeva situates herself among this generation). Not all feminists accept the tacit progressivism of this schema, of course; Spivak for one is highly critical of Kristeva for the position she takes up in relation to other women in her 1977 text *About Chinese Women* (Spivak 1981: 157–62).

Readers might also like to look into the writings of Catherine Clément (*The Weary Sons of Freud* as well as *The Newly Born Woman*); or the more Derridean theorist Sarah Kofman (whose text *The Enigma of Woman* can be read as a sustained attempt to refute Irigaray on Freud in *Speculum*); or again, the more literary figures Marguerite Duras (*The Lover*, her film *Indiasong*) and Monique Wittig (*Les Guerillères, The Lesbian Body*). All have had some impact on local textual production: in the fields of writing, both academic and literary, and art and filmic practices.

BIBLIOGRAPHY

Primary sources

Cixous, H. (1976a) *The Exile of James Joyce* London, John Calder
——(1976b) 'Interview with Hélène Cixous' *Sub-Stance* 13
——(1976c) 'The Laugh of the Medusa' *Signs: Journal of Women in Culture and Society* 1 (4)
——(1979a) *Vivre L'Orange* (written in French and English) Paris, Editions des Femmes
——(1979b) 'Rethinking differences' (interview), in G. Stambolian and E. Marks (eds) *Homosexualities and French Literature:Cultural Contexts/Critical Texts* Ithaca and London, Cornell University Press
——(1980) 'Poetry is/and (the) political' *Bread and Roses* 2 (1)
——(1981) 'Castration or decapitation?' *Signs: Journal of Women in Culture and Society* 7 (1)
——(1982) 'Introduction to Lewis Carroll's *Through the Looking-Glass* and *The Hunting of the Snark*' (trans. by Marie Maclean) *New Literary History* 13
——(1985a) *Angst* London, John Calder
——(1985b) (with Catherine Clément) *The Newly Born Woman* Minneapolis, University of Minnesota Press
Delphy, C. (1977) *The Main Enemy: A Materialist Analysis of Women's Oppression* London, Hutchinson
——(1970) 'The main enemy' (1970), *Feminist Issues* 1, 1
——(1980) 'Women's liberation: the tenth year' (trans. by C. Duchen), in C. Duchen (ed.) *French Connections: Voices from the Women's Movement in France* London, Hutchinson, 1987
——(1984) *Close to Home: A Materialist Analysis of Women's Oppression.* Trans. by Diana Leonard. London, Hutchinson
Irigaray, L. (1977) 'Women's exile' (trans. by Couze Venn) *Ideology and Consciousness* 1
——(1978) 'That sex which is not one' (extracts trans. by R. Albury), in P. Foss and M. Morris (eds) *Language, Sexuality and Subversion* Darlington, NSW, Feral Publications
——(1980a) 'When our lips speak together' (trans. by Carolyn Burke) *Signs* 6 (1)
——(1980b) 'When the goods get together' (trans. by Claudia Reeder), in E. Marks and I. de Courtivron (eds) *New French Feminisms* Sussex, Harvester
——(1981) *Le corps—à corps avec la mère* Montreal, les Editions de la pleine lune
——(1982) 'One does not move without the other' (trans. by R. Braidotti) *Refractory Girl* March

——(1983a) 'An interview with Luce Irigaray, by Kiki Amsberg and Aake Steenhvis' (trans. by R. van Krieken) *Hecate* 9 (i) and (ii)

——(1983b) 'For centuries we've been living in the mother–son relation . . .' *Hecate* 9 (1) and (2)

——(1983c) 'Luce Irigaray, interviewed by Lucienne Serrano and Elaine Hoffman Baruch', in J. Tudd (ed.) *Women Writers Talking* New York, Holmes and Meier

——(1983d) 'Veiled lips' (passages from Irigaray's *Amante Marine: de Friedrich Nietzsche*, trans. by Sara Speidel) *Mississippi Review* 11 (3)

——(1985a) *Speculum of the Other Woman*. Trans. by Gillian C. Gill. Ithaca, Cornell University Press

——(1985b) *This Sex Which Is Not One*. Trans. by Catherine Porter with Carolyn Burke. Ithaca, Cornell University Press

——(1985c) 'Any theory of the "subject" has always been appropriated by the masculine' *Trivia* Winter

——(1985d) 'Is the subject of science sexed?' *Cultural Critique* 1

——(1986a) *Divine Women*. Trans. by Stephen Muecke. Sydney, Local Consumption Occasional Paper 8

——(1986b) 'The fecundity of the caress', in R.A. Cohen (ed.) *Face-to-Face with Levinas* New York, State University of NY Press

——(1986c) 'Women, the sacred and money' (trans. by Diana Knight and Margaret Whitford) *Paragraph* 8

——(1989) 'The gesture in psychoanalysis' (trans. by E. Guild), in Teresa Brennan (ed.) *Between Feminism and Psychoanalysis* London and New York, Routledge

Le Doeuff, M. (1977) 'Women and philosophy' *Radical Philosophy* 19

——(1979) 'Operative philosophy: Simone de Beauvoir and existentialism' *Ideology and Consciousness* 6

——(1980) *Recherches sur L'Imaginaire Philosophique* Paris, Payot

——(1981/2) 'Pierre Roussel's chiasmas' *Ideology and Consciousness* 9

——(1982) 'Utopias: scholarly' *Social Research* 49 (2) Summer

Secondary sources

Clément, C. (1987) *The Weary Sons of Freud*. Trans. by N. Ball. London, Verso

de Beauvoir, S. (1953) *The Second Sex*. Trans. by H.M. Parshley. London, Jonathan Cape

Duchen, C. (1987) (ed. and trans.) *French Connections: Voices from the Women's Movement in France* London, Hutchinson

Duras, M. (1986) *The Lover* trans. by B. Bray, London, Flamingo

Grosz, E. (1989) *Sexual Subversions* Sydney, Allen & Unwin

Kaufmann-McCall, D. (1983) 'Politics of difference: the women's movement in France from May 1968 to Mitterand' *Signs* 9

Kofman, S. (1986) *The Enigma of Woman: Woman in Freud's Writings* Urbana, University of Illinois Press

Kristeva, J. (1977) *About Chinese Women* London, Marion Boyars

——(1981) 'Women's time' *Signs* 7 (1)

Kuhn, A. (1981) 'Introduction to Cixous's "Castration or decapitation?" ' *Signs* 7 (1)

Leclerc, A. (1974) *Parole de Femme* Paris, Grasset

Marks, E. and de Courtivron, I. (1980) *New French Feminisms: An Anthology* Amherst, University of Massachusetts Press

Moi, T. (1987) *French Feminist Thought: A Reader* Oxford, Basil Blackwell

Morris, Meaghan (1988) *The Pirate's Fiancée: Feminism, Reading, Postmodernism* London, Verso

Spivak, G. C. (1981) 'French feminism in an international frame' *Yale French Studies* 62

Stambolian, G. and Marks, E. (1979) (eds) *Homosexualities and French Literature: Cultural Contexts/Critical Contexts* Ithaca and London, Cornell University Press

Weeks, J. (1985) *Sexuality and its Discontents* London, Routledge

Wittig, M. (1973) *Les Guerillères*. Trans. by David Le Vay. New York, Avon

——1975 *The Lesbian Body* trans. by David Le Vay. London, Owen

13

Sigmund Freud

Freud was not always a Freudian. Born in Austria in 1856, he trained as a neurologist. He commenced clinical practice in 1886 and in 1895 published *Studies on Hysteria* with his colleague, Joseph Breuer. Freud credits Breuer with having treated the first psychoanalytic patient, Anna O, who had dubbed this method, the 'talking cure'. The term psychoanalysis was first used by Freud in 1896.

Pioneers in a field of knowledge see the field in a new way. The questions they ask about what they see are quite different from those asked by their predecessors. Freud inaugurated a radically different way of understanding human existence. Like any theory, however, psychoanalysis is a construction—Freud even thought of it as a 'mythology'—and it does not form a monolithic system which can be understood as a unified whole. Freud attempted to understand the complex life of human beings both internally and externally. These complexities were impossible to codify into an all-inclusive system, and Freud's approach was basically exploratory and open. As a result, ideas from one period of his research were often different from those of others. As a pioneer in this field, Freud did not discover his basic ideas all at once. In his endeavour to find new methods of understanding the intricate fabric of human experience, he made many different starts and detours along the way. Freud's ideas have become a part of our common vocabulary with concepts such as the unconscious, repression, sublimation, defence, anxiety, ambivalence, and the Oedipus complex. The poet W. H. Auden could write that Freud today represents 'a whole climate of opinion under which we conduct our different lives'.

Freud made much of the resistance to psychoanalysis, to our self-knowledge; he believed that our narcissism had suffered three great blows. First, Copernicus had shown that the earth revolved around the sun rather than vice versa; second, Darwin demonstrated that human beings had descended from apes rather than angels. Psychoanalysis had inflicted the unkindest cut of all: the last thing humankind wanted to know was that the ego 'is not master in its own house' (1916–17: 285). From another perspective Marx had argued that people were products of social and class systems into which they were born. In all there is a general radical decentring of human beings from a position of sovereignty in the universe. Freud emphasises that even our desires are products of dynamic processes within ourselves of which we are unconscious. These unconscious desires are paramount and are often sexual in nature, relating to our childhood experiences.

Freud insisted that all human behaviour could be understood as meaningful or significant, and that these meanings are often unknown (consciously) to the individual because they are repressed. Freud also claimed that the most frequent repressed wishes and desires were sexual ones which are forbidden in our everyday conventional life, and for a variety of reasons are generally unacceptable to the conscious mind of the person who has them. They are excluded or repressed from consciousness and become 'unconscious'. In other words, because we do not want to acknowledge them and live with them in our conscious life, we attempt to disown them. But they nevertheless continue to exist 'unconsciously'.

The central term 'unconscious' has a technical meaning for Freud. The realm of the 'unconscious' should be distinguished from what Freud terms the 'preconscious', which includes ideas easily accessible to consciousness but not presently in it (a forgotten name, a forgotten memory of what I ate last night). Freud deliberately avoids the inexact term 'subconscious' which covers both the preconscious and unconscious mind. For him, the 'unconscious' consists of ideas, thoughts, feelings, fears, wishes, drives and representations that are permanently excluded from consciousness so that they cannot be directly recalled—indeed, their very existence is denied. For Freud, the conscious aspect of ourselves are importantly determined by the unconscious parts. Paradoxically, the most important part of me is the part I do not know! Freud even describes our thinking as operating through *primary and secondary processes:* the primary mode is unconscious while secondary processes are conscious and preconscious.

Psychoanalysis extended the area of scientific interest to the mind itself. Freud first used the term 'psychoanalysis' in an article in 1896, marking his abandonment of earlier therapeutic procedures, which included hypnosis, and his exclusive therapeutic use thereafter of what became the fundamental technique of psychoanalysis: *free association.* This technique involved patients saying whatever came into their minds, no matter how seemingly irrelevant, meaningless or unpalatable. Freud discovered that he could interpret and make sense of the data so obtained and that the relatively uncensored 'free associations' became meaningful when seen within a larger framework or context.

For Freud, 'free associations' are not really 'free'. They may appear to be haphazard, in the sense of their being unrelated to the rest of the talk and wishes of the patient, but they can be seen to be determined by unconscious influences. Thus psychoanalysis concentrates on understanding the more transparent derivation of the unconscious dimensions of ourselves as revealed in disguised form through dreams, myths, slips of the tongue, fantasies, etc.—all forms of experience which at first may appear to be irrational, random and trivial, but which in reality are full of significance.

Psychoanalysis is often viewed simply as a therapy. Freud was a medical practitioner as were many of his fellow psychoanalysts. Previously, mental disorders had been treated by doctors and psychiatrists (the general term 'psychiatry', first used in 1846, is derived from two Greek words meaning 'soul healing' and refers to the medical treatment of mental diseases). Freud did not want to deny the importance of organic and constitutional factors in the formation of mental illness. But he parted company with the organically oriented psychiatrists when he asserted that there were other factors involved in mental illness. According to Freud, psychoanalysis sought to find the *meaning* behind the experience of the mentally ill person, to make conscious the unconscious wishes, desires, motives, etc, that form the basis of mental illness. Organic or genetic factors may provide predispositions toward this kind of behaviour, but they are not necessarily the full explanation.

Freud regarded psychoanalysis as far more than a therapy; he considered psychoanalysis primarily to be a science or methodology. Indeed, Freud was most concerned that the therapy would not destroy the science or intellectual discipline of psychoanalysis. Psychoanalysis can be viewed in its several aspects:

1. A method of investigation which brings out the unconscious meaning of the words, actions, dreams, fantasies or, generally, the experience of a particular person or cultural product, such as a work of literature or myth. These unconscious meanings are normally inaccessible by other means.

2. A form of psychotherapy, or a method of helping neurotic people to learn about themselves and grow as a result of this learning-therapy.

3. A body of knowledge about the nature of human experience derived from the data provided by the psychoanalytic method of investigation and treatment.

4. A philosophical view of civilisation or culture based on the psychoanalytic view of the human psyche.

All the above aspects of psychoanalysis have at least this much in common: psychoanalysis is the study of the unconscious and how it relates to conscious phenomena. The focus or specific object of psychoanalysis is psychic reality, the inner world of fantasy, instead of the external world. This not to say that the outer world is unimportant, simply that it is not the specific concern of psychoanalysis. Psychoanalysis is interested in the relation of external to internal reality, but the emphasis in psychoanalysis is on the exploration of the role of the inner world of unconscious experience in our lives. This includes not only dreams, Freudian slips and neuroses, but also psychoanalytic aspects of culture which he explored in many works. These works include *Totem and Taboo* (1913), an anthropological study; *Group Psychology and the Analysis of the Ego* (1921); *The Future of an Illusion* (1927), a study of our need for religion; and *Civilization and Its Discontents* (1930).

I have already referred to the way in which we do not want to know about ourselves, particularly regarding the three blows to our narcissism. This involves the concept of *resistance*, whereby analysands obstruct gaining access to their unconscious. A related central concept of Freud is that of *transference*, whereby the patient transfers, or carries over, his or her attitudes to important figures deriving from childhood (mainly parents) into the analytic situation, and experiences and treats the analyst as though he or she were someone else, often a parental figure. For Freud, therefore, analytic therapy is no dry theoretical search for the origin of the patient's past traumas. It becomes an emotional experience from which patients learn about the way they relate to others.

For Freud, patients who experience their parents as diffident and rejecting will often treat the analyst as a diffident and rejecting parent. Similarly, somebody who has felt special throughout his or her life (e.g. has been treated as the most important child in the family) may think that he or she is the special patient of the analyst. However, the analyst will not respond in the same way as the patient experienced those significant others as responding—rather, the analyst will analyse what the patient says; the analyst will try to understand it and communicate it to the patient so that the patient will learn from it.

Transference—where a person treats another not only as who they are but, importantly, as though they were somebody else—occurs in most, if not all, relationships. But analytic therapy provides a special setting within which the patient can reflect and learn about it instead of acting it out. Learning about it might enhance the patient's choices, relieving symptoms or neurotic behaviour.

According to Freud, we are always involved in relationships. For him, individual psychology was simultaneously always social psychology. This is clear in his theory of *psycho-sexuality*, which is not a theory of biology but one that goes beyond it. Freud's theory of the *Oedipus Complex*, inspired by Sophocles' play, *Oedipus Rex*, involves loving and hostile feelings that the child has for his or her parents and plays a central role in the structuring of the personality and desire.

According to Freud (1920) our mental lives are governed by two basic principles: the *pleasure principle* and the *reality principle*. The pleasure principle aims at immediate satisfaction of our drives by the shortest route and avoiding unpleasure. It must be seen in close relation to the reality principle which modifies the pleasure principle and delays immediate satisfaction, engaging in detours demanded by accommodating to conditions imposed by the external world. Thus the reality principle is essential for the fulfilment of the goals of the pleasure principle since what is possible and the best way of achieving it need to be taken into account.

But Freud developed a further vital principle: the 'death drive' lay 'beyond the pleasure principle'. The two great driving principles in the universe were creation and destruction, life and death. A little later, Freud (1923) developed his well-known 'structural model' of the mind which described the mind as consisting of the id, ego and superego (the German should have been translated as 'it', 'I' and 'over-me'). Psychoanalysis was not ego-centred: the unconscious 'it' was, for Freud, fundamental. The task of psychoanalysis was the decentring of the ego, not adapting to it.

Nowhere is the conflict between the life and death drives more evident than in Freud's major work on contemporary culture, *Civilization and Its Discontents*. Freud focused on the uneasiness which he regarded as inevitably inherent in culture: 'it is impossible to overlook the extent to which civilization is built up upon a renunciation of instinct, how much it presupposes precisely the non-satisfaction ... of powerful instincts. This "cultural frustration" dominates the large field of social relationships between human beings' (1930: 97).

Freud had himself suggested the title of this work, *Das Unbehagen in der Kultur,* as *Man's Discomfort in Civilization* (1930: 60). The inevitable tension and conflict between the demands of the drives and the taming effects of civilisation meant constant disquiet which resulted from compromise. Our uneasiness is the price we pay for the advantages of civilisation which is built on the repression of our drives; we have 'exchanged a portion of our possibilities for happiness for a portion of security' (p. 115). Indeed, Freud wondered, was the whole effort really worth the trouble? (pp. 144–45).

But Freud's own culture could not even afford him a 'portion of security'. In 1938 the Nazis occupied his native Austria. He was able to leave Vienna in 1938 'to die in freedom' in London in 1939, less than three weeks after the outbreak of World War II.

BIBLIOGRAPHY

Primary sources

Freud's works can be found in *The Standard Edition of the Complete Psychological Works of Sigmund Freud* (SE). Trans. by James Strachey.

London, Hogarth Press and the Institute of Psycho-Analysis, 1955. The Pelican Freud Library contains his major work grouped into areas of interest rather than chronologically. A good introduction to Freud's general theory is supplied in his *Introductory Lectures on Psychoanalysis* (1915–17) and his *New Introductory Lectures on Psychoanalysis* (1933), Vols 2 and 3 of the Pelican Freud Library. His work on social theory in this series is in Volume 12, *Civilization, Society and Religion*. Of particular importance to this chapter are the following titles from the Hogarth Press series:

Freud, S. (1916–17) *Introductory Lectures on Psychoanalysis* Part III, SE XVI.

——(1920) *Beyond the Pleasure Principle* SE XVIII: 7–64

——(1923) *The Ego and the Id* SE XIX: 12–66

——(1930) *Civilization and Its Discontents* SE XXI: 59–145

Secondary sources

Bettelheim, B. (1983) *Freud and Man's Soul* New York, Knopf. Bettelheim claims that the real Freud has been distorted and medicalised by his descendants, especially in America.

Davies, A.F. (1980) *Skills, Outlooks and Passions* Cambridge, Cambridge University Press. An application of psychoanalytic ideas and findings to three ways of looking at politics: politics as work, politics as beliefs and politics as the play of emotions.

Jacoby, R. (1971) *Social Amnesia* Boston, Beacon Press. Jacoby investigates psychological thinking within its historical context and links it with contemporary society.

Jones, E. *The Life and Work of Sigmund Freud* (abridged) Harmondsworth, Penguin Books. The classic biography of Freud's life, times, personal and political struggles.

Kirsner, D. (1977) *The Schizoid World of Jean-Paul Sartre and R.D. Laing* Brisbane, University of Queensland Press. Viewed from a psychoanalytic perspective, Sartre and Laing are seen both as expressing and reacting to central problems of our time.

Kovel, J. (1983) *The Age of Desire: Reflections of a Radical Psychoanalyst* New York, Pantheon. A Marxist psychoanalyst discusses theory and case histories from both Marxist and psychoanalytic perspectives.

Little, G. (1985) *Political Ensembles* Melbourne, Oxford University Press. A reorganisation of psychoanalytic theory for studies in leadership and politics.

Marcuse, H. (1955) *Eros and Civilization* Boston, Beacon Press. An inquiry into the critical underpinnings of Freud's theory of civilisation.

Mitchell, J. (1975) *Psychoanalysis and Feminism* Harmondsworth, Penguin. An important feminist critique of Freud, Reich and Laing that repays careful reading.

Rieff, P. (1979) *Freud; The Mind of the Moralist* 3rd edn, London, University of Chicago Press. A Freudian social theorist discusses Freud's views on sexuality and domination.

14

Anthony Giddens

Anthony Giddens is a fellow of King's College and Professor of Sociology at the University of Cambridge. Over the past two decades he has published more than twenty books and established himself as a central thinker. Giddens' writings combine a detailed exegesis of the classics with a sensitivity to the issues at the forefront of contemporary social theory. He brings these concerns together under the rubric of an overarching project. This project involves identifying and criticising the shortcomings of traditional thought and developing a way of theorising issues that are obscured or ignored within that framework.

Giddens argues that social theory from the time of the classics to the 1960s has been characterised by a set of pre-theoretical assumptions that are unsuitable for the study of social life. Erstwhile thinkers tended to have a naturalist interpretation of social theory and relied heavily on positivist philosophy. This led to reductionist and essentialist forms of theorising. Giddens criticises the positivist tendency to view society as the expression of an underlying principle of identity and development. In this scheme the actor is reduced to a product of impersonal and determinate social forces. The reproduction of society is taken to be a mechanical outcome rather than an active and contingent process constituted by the activity of agents. Giddens points out that this approach employs a defective theory of action. It grants primacy to society over the actor and thus falls into the error of objectivism.

Despite the prominence of positivist philosophy, not all schools of thought in social theory subscribed to its tenets. Giddens argues that thinkers drawing on traditions like hermeneutics, ordinary language philosophy and phenomenology have avoided positivist assumptions and have contributed a great deal to an adequate conceptualisation of action. However, these interpretative schools of thought have focused almost exclusively on the active production of social life without developing any concept of structural analysis. Interpretative schools recognise that people make society but they fail to acknowledge that they do not do so under conditions of their own choosing. Giddens argues that such approaches lack an ability to account for either the causal conditions or the unintended consequences of action. Interpretative forms of thought grant primacy to the actor over society and thus lapse into subjectivism.

In light of the failure of traditional thought adequately to conceive of the nature of structure and action and the relation between them, Giddens concludes that social theory stands in need of reconstruction. He proposes to reconstruct social theory by way of a critical encounter with the three most important schools of social thought: interpretative sociology, functionalism and structuralism. He aims to retain the insights provided by these traditions and, at the same time, to find a way to overcome their deficiencies and transcend their irreconcilability. This involves a reconceptualisation of the concepts of action, structure and system in order to integrate them into a new theoretical approach. Giddens calls this new approach the 'theory of structuration'. Although he prefers to characterise his project as one of reconstruction rather than of synthesis, it is evident that the synthetic strategy figures largely in his work.

The reconceptualisation of the concepts of action, structure and system begins by granting analytical primacy to ongoing social practices. Thus social practices are taken to be the basis for the constitution of both the actor and society. Giddens' interpretation of the nature of social practices draws heavily on the philosophy of the later Wittgenstein. He argues that social practices must be understood as involving an intersection between saying and doing, or signification and action. This allows Giddens to emphasise the reflexive character of action and the knowledgeability of agents. To engage in social practices an actor has to know what he or she is doing, although this knowledge is largely tacit. Giddens maintains that knowing how to participate or how to 'go on' in the contexts of social life involves knowing how to follow a rule. This is essentially a practical knowledge. Giddens proposes that such knowledge is indicative of a practical consciousness that can be distinguished both from discursive consciousness and the unconscious.

The actor's participation in social practices on the basis of knowing how to follow a rule is what Giddens calls the recursive nature of social life. Giddens is aware that the explication of social life in terms of rules is a controversial move and, consequently, he takes great pains to clarify how he employs the notion of a rule. Rules in social life are not like the rules in a game such as chess. They are not isolated formulae, nor can they be defined in their own terms. Rather, Giddens' argument is that rules generate, or are the media of, social practices, but they do not exist apart from them. Moreover, there is no one-to-one correlation between 'a rule' and 'a practice'; practices are constituted in the context of overlapping and interconnected sets of rules. Finally, rules have two aspects that must be distinguished. On the one hand, they play a role in the constitution of meaning and, on the other, they relate to the sanctioning of modes of conduct.

Giddens' account of practices in terms of rules enables him to join a theory of action with structural explanation. This is achieved via a reconceptualisation of structure as the rules and resources which actors draw upon and reconstitute in processes of interaction. This formulation highlights the mutual dependence of structure and action. Structure makes action possible, it is the medium of action but, at the same time, it is reproduced only in and through action. Giddens refers to this as the 'duality of structure'. Structure cannot be identified with constraint nor can it be opposed to action: structure is both enabling and constraining; it is both the medium and outcome of action. As structure exists only at the moment of instantiations in action it cannot exist in space and time. Structure has only a 'virtual existence'.

Structures, as rules and resources, are properties of social systems but they are not to be confused with social systems. Social systems have structuring properties, they are more or less structured totalities but they are not structures in themselves. For Giddens, the concept of a social system should be employed in a purely descriptive manner. Social systems are social practices reproduced across space and time. They vary greatly as to their degree of internal unity and integration depending on the nature of their structuring properties. Giddens uses the concept of structuration to connect the concepts of structure and system. The structuration of a social system is the process whereby the structure properties of a system are drawn upon and reconstituted in the practices that constitute that system.

Giddens' reworking of the concepts of action, structure and system forms the basis of his theory of structuration. He progressively elaborates and refines the interconnections between these concepts. Conceiving of society as social practices reproduced across space and time avoids the objectivist error of granting society a predefined essence and reducing it to some underlying explanatory principle. Similarly, his concept of action portrays the actor as neither a determined object nor an unambiguously free subject. Giddens traces the way subjects make themselves through participation in ongoing social practices.

His concept of action points to the key role of power in social life. Giddens argues that power is a logical component of action where action is understood as an ability to 'make a difference'. This broad view of power as transformative capacity can be linked to the duality of structure to illustrate how power is routinely incorporated into social life. In processes of interaction actors draw upon resources which are structural elements of social systems. Asymmetrical access to these resources is the basis of power relations which exist as reproduced relations of autonomy and dependence.

Giddens stresses the need to come to terms with the temporal nature of social life. He argues that the interdependence of action and structure can be conceived only as a temporal relationship. This, in turn, suggests that change is always implicit in social interaction because every process of action is a new production, albeit in the context of what has gone before. It follows from this that the reproduction of social systems cannot be conceived in functionalist terms. In Giddens' view, social systems exist as reproduced practices and thus the concept of system presupposes that of reproduction. As reproduced practices, social system can have no needs of their own. Their reproduction is a contingent process based on the activity of actors.

Although structuration theory overcomes many of the deficiencies of traditional thought, it is an inadequate response to the tasks confronting contemporary social theory. Giddens' project of reconstruction and synthesis is an inherently conservative one. Making action and structure more accessible to each other is certainly an improvement but it does not help to breach the divide between them. Turning a dualism into a duality does not solve the problem. It is ironic that Giddens, one of the foremost critics of Parsons, should fail to see to what extent his own project is a continuation of the Parsonian legacy.

A closer examination of Giddens' strategy of reconstruction and synthesis reveals a strong scientistic bias in his thought. The process of synthesis involves the dismantling and reassembly of the logical structures of various theoretical perspectives and thus can occur only as epistemology. The very activity of synthesis requires separating the methodological from the substantive and granting priority to the methodological. This belief that theory can be refined independently of its object involves the hidden assumption that theory exists as ever better approximations to its object. The strategy of reconstruction and synthesis attempts to divorce theory from history and distort the relationship between the two. This amounts, finally, to a reification of theory.

Giddens' scientistic bias is also manifested in his theory of structuration. Structuration theory is not a theory in the usual sense of the term. Rather, as a child of a project of synthesis, it must be seen as a methodological apparatus separated from substantive concerns. Indeed, Giddens argues in the preface to his main account of structuration (1984) that he is concerned with the development of an 'approach' to the study of social life. In stressing the term 'approach' he wishes to emphasise that he is largely interested in the formulation of 'conceptual schemes that order and inform processes of inquiry into social life'. As a methodological apparatus structuration theory lacks the ability to generate substantive concepts. It is parasitic upon the work of other thinkers for this purpose. This accounts for the eclecticism of Giddens' writings and highlights the lack of originality in his own thought.

When confronted with important questions concerning the nature of the contemporary human condition, structuration theory is mute. It provides no interrogation of the world, no elucidation of emergent possibilities and limited conception of social theory as critique. Within its framework questions of ethics and political projects cannot even be asked. It is difficult to see structuration theory making any significant or original contribution to social theory. In Australia, at least, Giddens has been influential as a populariser of relatively unknown schools of thought rather than as a novel thinker in his own right. It would seem that Giddens' work is best regarded as a postscript to the predominant trends of social thought in the twentieth century.

BIBLIOGRAPHY

Primary Sources

Giddens, A. (1971a) *Capitalism and Modern Social Theory* Cambridge, Cambridge University Press
——(1971b) (ed.) *The Sociology of Suicide* London, Cass and Co
——(1972a) (ed.) *Emile Durkheim: Selected Writings* Cambridge, Cambridge University Press
——(1972b) *Politics and Sociology in the Thought of Max Weber* London, Macmillan
——(1973a) *The Class Structure of the Advanced Societies* London, Hutchinson
——(1973b) (ed.) *Positivism and Sociology* London, Heinemann
——(1976) *New Rules of Sociological Method* London, Hutchinson
——(1977) *Studies in Social and Political Theory* London, Hutchinson
——(1978) *Emile Durkheim* London, Fontana
——(1979) *Central Problems in Social Theory* London, Macmillan
——(1981) *A Contemporary Critique of Historical Materialism* London, Macmillan
——(1982) *Sociology: A Brief but Critical Introduction* London, Macmillan
——(1983) *Profiles and Critiques in Social Theory* London, Macmillan
——(1984) *The Constitution of Society* Cambridge, Polity Press
——(1985a) *The Nation-State and Violence* Cambridge, Polity Press
——(1985b) *Social Theory and Modern Sociology* Cambridge, Polity Press
——(1986) (ed.) *Durkheim on Politics and the State* Cambridge, Polity Press
——(1989) *Sociology* Cambridge, Polity Press
——(1990) *The Consequences of Modernity* Cambridge, Polity Press
——and Held, D. (1982) (eds) *Classes, Conflict and Power* London, Macmillan
——and Mackenzie, G. (1982) (eds) *Classes and the Division of Labour* Cambridge, Cambridge University Press
——and Stanworth, P. (1974) (eds) *Elites and Power in British Society* Cambridge, Cambridge University Press

——and Turner, J. (1987) (eds) *Social Theory Today* Cambridge, Polity Press

Secondary sources

Cohen, I. (1989) *Structuration Theory: Anthony Giddens and the Constitution of Social Life* London, Macmillan
Held, D. and Thompson, J. (1989) (eds) *Social Theory of Modern Societies: Anthony Giddens and His Critics* Cambridge, Cambridge University Press

15

Antonio Gramsci

Gramsci was concerned with how power was maintained in the modern state. As a Marxist who had lived through the defeats of the anticipated socialist revolution in Western Europe in 1918–23 and watched the organisations of the working-class and socialist movement smashed by fascism in the years 1922–37, he noted how strongly committed large sections of the population were to the modern state even at times of crisis, when they might have been expected to lose faith in it. When they did lose faith they had found their solution in fascism rather than socialism.

The two objects of his reflections when he wrote his celebrated *Prison Notebooks* (1927–37) were thus: why and how does the modern state enjoy this consensus in its rule among the majority of the populace, and why and how can a socialist ensure that this consensus is made into a new consensus in favour of socialist values? The answers were not to be found in the Marxist classics; Marx never got around to an examination of the modern state. Those to be found in the works of Lenin, the intellectual leader of the international communist movement to which Gramsci belongs, referred to a quite different sort of state from that which Gramsci was interested in (Gramsci 1975: 866). Gramsci thus had to develop a theory of the modern state on his own, using Labriola's, Sorel's and Croce's work. His distinctive and original contribution to social theory is this theory of politics—or how power works—in the modern state.

He typified this state as emerging at various dates in the second half of the nineteenth century, depending on the case. His examples were usually taken from the history of Italy, his own country. Viewed as a historical process its emergence was characterised by the intrusion of the institutions of state—executive, legislature, judiciary and so on—into the realm hitherto regarded as *private*, or outside the regulatory concerns of the state. The obliteration of the realm known to earlier commentators, both hegelian and liberal, as 'civil society'—where on the whole the economic and social life of the society was left to the rules elaborated in a continuous market of material and immaterial goods between individuals—was making the state practically coterminous with society itself. Fascism in its self-proclamation as the total or totalitarian state epitomised this process (Gramsci 1975: 1566-7).

The process of the increasing regulation of the market at all levels of social life from child-rearing practices and marriage, to schooling, to the organisation of work relations through trade unions, reordered the practices of society, or everyday life. It thus was a form of education which produced a citizen functional to the state (Gramsci 1975: 757, 1570-1). As it eliminated the kaleidoscope difference of the marketplace and produced more and more homogeneous and complementary 'citizen—individuals', people who conformed in their individual lives to more general socialised norms, it produced at the same time the democratic citizen on whose consensus in the system state power rested (Gramsci 1975: 757, 937). A system of rule based on produced or educated consensus in the state, Gramsci termed '*hegemonic*'. As a Marxist who believed that capitalism produced specific forms of contradiction, such a hegemonic system would, for Gramsci be in unceasing struggle to educate antagonistic opposition into conformity (Gramsci 1975: 801-2).

Opposition to such a state took at least two forms. Firstly, there was the opposition of pre-existing systems of community life which were interfered with by the modern state and secondly, there was the opposition of new sections of the community whose needs conflicted with the organised social world produced by the state. Hegemony could therefore never be '100%' (Gramsci 1975: 89-90, 329-32). Moreover, hegemony itself would blend force and consent depending on the situation, the end being the citizen who through self-discipline conformed to norms set by the state because the citizen saw that was the best way to survive and prosper in the world of structured practices created around him or her by the intrusion of public power into the private realm (Gramsci 1975: 763-4).

What interested Gramsci about the historical process of the evolution of the modern state was the way it educated the majority to consensus in its rule, which could not for a Marxist be more than a rule which held together a society in which capitalism was in dominance. It is important not to make too reductionist an analysis of the way Gramsci thought a constant (changing as the society changed) and yet unthreatening support of the system worked. This *passive revolution* which made the national people *the* source of power without threatening a society biased towards capitalism was different in different types of modern state. Gramsci distinguished between modern democratic, fascist and Stalinist variants of the modern state.

In the first, limits were posed to the tendency to establish a total hegemony by the location of the state in the world economic system. Where, as in Italy, this prevented a balanced modernisation, pre-modern modes of production tended to survive and reproduce social relations inimical to the modern state. A 'peasantry' which had private property was the majority of the population. Compromises had to be made with the traditional organisers of such societies, leaving them to run their worlds as they always had in return for their support of the democratic modern state. Thus 'three-class' societies continued to exist. The ideology of a rational liberal democracy co-existed uneasily with ideologies created by pre-modern semi-feudal social relations. The problem for a modernising state was that the majority pre-modern middle class might assert its right to rule, especially if the state became weak. This in fact happened with fascism, when what Gramsci called the 'Bandarlog', or monkey-people, occupied the public space left empty after the forces of the modern state and the proletarian new order had fought to a standstill in a rare crisis of hegemony brought on by a world war.

The *compromise* characteristic of hegemony was made vis-a-vis the emerging proletariat as the liberal state took on the role of the regulator of relations between capital and labour in accord with a criterion of distributive social justice—the beginnings of the welfare state (Bobbio 1983: 101ff.) On the other hand, fascism was characterised by the exclusion of the proletariat from hegemonic rule and its brutal repression was the basis for the survival of a society based on private property in the means of production through an alliance of the 'middle' (petite bourgeois and peasant) classes and the bourgeoisie proper. The combination of class interests in a *historic bloc* of different compositions led to the further question of how *compromise* was attained between classes who in the classical Marxist schema should be continually forced into antagonistic positions. In other words, how was the compromise made in *politics* maintained?

Gramsci understood that politics took place at the level of ideologies which themselves rested on the social organisation (Gramsci 1975: 445–6). What citizens would do would depend on their self-conception or world view, itself corresponding with the order of their real life. Such a world view would have to involve, he maintained, an organisation of both their life practices and, since there was no automatic determination by this everyday life, the way they thought those life practices. The organisers of such practices he called *intellectuals*. Because all human beings feel and think, i.e. intellectualise, Gramsci indentified the intellectuals as a particular social category by their practice of organising the practices of everyday life. Using the south of Italy as his model, he identified intellectuals from the previous mode of production as *traditional* and those of the capitalist mode of production as *organic*. The latter could be further broken down into *hegemonic* and *counter-hegemonic* intellectuals.

The task of both hegemonic and counter-hegemonic intellectuals was to organise and reorganise continuously the unconscious and conscious lived life of national-popular mass, the first to ensure that world views consistent with capitalism were accepted by all classes and the second to detach the proletariat from such views and establish a socialist world view. The former had clearly effected a compromise with the traditional intellectuals at the margins where the traditional and capitalist social structures met and where these had to be reconciled in an intellectual practice which ensured that any feeling of contradiction with the system did not become elaborated into a hostile world view (Gramsci 1969: 150–7; 1975: 1566).

Gramsci's theory of compromise/reconciliation is most interesting not where he focuses on the majority who are integrated into the system but where he theorises reconciliation at the margins where the small percentage which is not yet hegemonised is prevented in an organisational operation from becoming more than a small percentage. What is seen at these margins is a 'bizarre combination' of ideas in which the *good sense* which comes from lived experience is deviated into *commonsense,* or *popular wisdom* through its being blended in a particular way with the accepted understanding of the world coming from the organic intellectuals (Gramsci 1975: 89, 1579ff.) What takes place is the repression of a political language which reflects the felt needs of the unhegemonised in favour of one functional to the modern state and the value of labour. While this clearly has a disciplinary component in that it is inculcated through the schools, universities, church and so on, what Gramsci called science in the service of ignorance involved a much more sophisticated notion of power than that of repression of wrong ideas.

Given the order of society created by the modern state, the procedures and structures for its self-understanding (knowledge) had to be of a certain type. If any person refused to learn the languages they imposed (the language of science or philosophy), that person as a speaker of 'idiolalia' would not be understood by others and would thus be disempowered. The struggle between hegemonies was over the *form* or reasoned order of world views and not their content, or the facts which they made sense of (Gramsci 1975: 1400).

When writing that a counter-hegemony must start from the commonsense and religious views which arise from a non- or extra-hegemonic realm, he makes clear what the intellectuals of the bourgeois hegemony do to secure a certain *form* of understanding. He also indicates how a counter-hegemony cannot simply replicate that activity if is is to establish itself. Instead of making the popular knowledge which comes from experience coherent with high knowledge, the organic intellectuals of capitalism banish it through their intellectual practices to the realm of non-knowledge. Only authorised or expert knowledge is heard. The authorised system of reason then constitutes a vicious circle for those caught within it or who seek to challenge it. It runs as follows, at the highest level of abstraction:

1 An explanation for the way the world works is proposed and consequent solutions to existing problems are found.
2 These propositions are refined in a series of mediations until they are far from the reality which they described and exist only as 'philosophy'.
3 They are then verified by the 'elect minds' who are already defined by their sites in this process (experts with certain training).

The process is thus its own verification because it can prove that education and authority are the guarantees of the best judgement, by the obvious impossibility of referring back complicated propositions to the populace. This is a vicious circle because the appeal to practice (what the mass 'feels') for verification is proved impossible precisely by an appeal to practice which shows to commonsense its own critical insufficiency. Yet the object of the process is to exclude what it presupposes (Gramsci 1975: 451–2, 1396–1400).

The result is popular or democratic consensus in rule by the experts (usually bureaucrats) of the modern state whose structures are such that it is unreasonable to demand any alternative to expert rule. Indeed, it is 'unreasonable' since the structures of the modern state provide the only conditions for 'truth statements' within it. Gramsci therefore argues that the structures of the state must be changed in order for other truth statements to become real, i.e. taken up in a socialist counter-hegemony.

He argues against the Leninist notion that a revolution can start from a party or elite-led new enlightenment where 'twelve wise men' lead a hundred fools (Lenin 1902: 204–5). Rather he proposes a molecular transformation of the mass broken up as it is into the passivity of 'citizen-individuals', into an active direct democracy in which the corporate interests of different groups in society are articulated into an overall program for transformation by a 'collective intellectual', a party of huge dimensions which embodies the socialist *ethic*. His vision is not that of a proletarian party which, in accord with an *uncompromising* ethic based on privileging the proletariat, knows in advance what others will see later.

His frequent condemnations of bourgeois democracy—which led many authors to see him as totalitarian—are not condemnations of representative democracy—all that can exist in modern complex societies. Rather they condemn the insufficient political presence of the citizen and of representativity through decentralisation (Gramsci 1975: 1386–93, 1624–35; Davidson 1977: ch. 3). Instead, in the course of their self-organisation different social groups will attain identity through overcoming the disaggregation of society into individuals without a sense of social power. This psychological transformation will create the possibility for new 'truth statements': one set of these will be proposed by the party committed to socialism, and they will not be beaten before they start by the effects of the bourgeois hegemony.

BIBLIOGRAPHY

Bobbio, N. (1983) *Il futuro della democrazia* Turin, Einaudi
Cammett, J. (forthcoming) *Bibliografia Gramsciana* Rome, Riuniti. Contains a list of all work published in Australia.
Cozzens, P. (1977) *Twenty Years of Antonio Gramsci: A Bibliography of Gramsci and Gramsci Studies Published in English, 1957–77* London, Lawrence and Wishart
Davidson, A. (1977) *Antonio Gramsci: Towards an Intellectual Biography* London, Merlin
——(1984) 'Gramsci, the peasantry and popular culture' *Journal of Peasant Studies* XI (4)
Gramsci, A. (1969) *La Questione Meridionale* Rome, Riuniti
——(1975) *Quaderni del Carcere Edizione critica,* 4 vols. Ed. by V. Gerratana. Turin, Einaudi
Laclau, E. and Mouffe, C. (1985) *Hegemony and Socialist Strategy* London, Verso
Lenin, V. (1902) *What Is To Be Done* Moscow, FLPH 1952

16

Jürgen Habermas

Jürgen Habermas was born in Düsseldorf in 1929 and was Adorno's assistant between 1956 and 1959. In 1964 he became professor of philosophy at J. von Goethe University, Frankfurt. Between 1971 and 1981 he was director of the Max Planck Institute. Currently he is professor of philosophy at J. von Goethe University, Frankfurt (see Dews 1986).

Habermas' work is fuelled by a simple idea. In the context of 'a modernity at variance with itself' (Habermas 1987a: 396), he is preoccupied with the public and non-violent strength of the better argument, which he terms rational practical discourse. Everyone should be able to take a yes or no position to statements about the world and the way it is understood, whether or not they refer to the worlds of nature, of society or themselves (Habermas 1984: 70). He experiments with formulations and paradigms with which to ground this basic idea.

Habermas' notion of politics, at its most minimal and anthropological, simply means a non-violent inter-subjectivity in the making, where words—more strictly, sentences or speech acts—rather than rituals or weapons, are the form of social intercourse that counts. This utopian horizon remains the central obstinate and permanent feature which resonates throughout his work as a whole. The utopian horizon is thus freedom interpreted by him as democracy. This, in turn, is formulated as a rationally motivated and discursively redeemable consensus formation. It typifies him and his work as quintessentially belonging to the self-understanding of modernity, a self-understanding he constantly defends, criticises and reconstructs whether it be in *The Structural Transformation of the Public Sphere* (1961), *Toward a Rational Society* (1968–69), *Knowledge and Human Interests* (1972), his essays on the reconstruction of historical materialism (1976), *The Philosophical Discourse of Modernity* (1987) or his magnum opus, *The Theory of Communicative Action* (1984).

In the political dimension of Habermas' work, there is an appearance of urgency, a sense that the legacy of *practical reason*—that form of reason pertaining to questions of social norms and ethical practices, and how they are both formed, accounted for and judged—has been inadequately recognised as the fountainhead of modernity. In Habermas' view, it needs not so much to be redeemed, but defended and reconceptualised against those who think that practical reason has either become exhausted or is simply another formulation for the domination of rationality *sui generis*. And it is here that Habermas makes his argument again and again—the idea of reason that *at first sight* was invented by the Enlightenment philosophers is not synonymous with the project of calculating reason. It is *at first sight* because, for Habermas, the problem of defending rationality today is not only in its meaning, but also in how it is grounded—and by this he means how it refers to the self-constitution of the human species.

Three aspects of Habermas's project will be touched on here:

1 the socio-critical aspect, i.e. the emancipatory horizon of freedom,
2 interpretations of modernity, and
3 Habermas' formulations concerning the way in which humans constitute reality in the first place; his theory of communicative action, leaving to one side his theory of socio-cultural evolution (his evolutionary learning theory) which is internal to his notion of culture or world views as cultural interpretative systems.

In order to pursue his 'simple idea' Habermas moves simultaneously in two directions—sociological and philosophical. According to Habermas, any critical theory of society *should* address the substantive issues and dilemmas of (in this instance) modern societies, *as well as* have a reflexive attitude to its own theoretical categories. This reflexive attitude depends on a philosophical grounding of the project of (substantive) critique. This is Habermas' major charge against the first generation of the Frankfurt School, his often assumed predecessors although this assumption is open to dispute. His charge of one-dimensionality directed against his predecessors revolves around competing images of the modern world as well as competing interpretations of modern philosophy.

For Marcuse, Horkheimer and Adorno, modernity is typified, at the level of sociological analysis, as a capitalist cum bureaucratic system which transforms all patterns of social relations into objectified and commodified administered systems. Philosophically, this is rendered by them as the unfettered expansion of the Enlightenment's own interpretation and construction of reason as instrumental rationality. This expansion is the final assault of *ratio*, of identity thinking, upon an either unsuspecting or colluding humanity which rushes to control its inner and social worlds, as well as its external environment, under the auspices of any number of instrumentally constituted totalising administrative spheres. For Adorno, at least, the study of this is rooted in not only the Enlightenment's own historical experience and understanding (from Descartes to De Sade and Kant), but also in humankind's ultimate entrapment in identity thinking, typified by Odysseus' voyage out of myth, which mythologises enlightenment thought itself. According to Habermas, while Adorno (as well as Horkheimer and Marcuse) generated a critique of modern society from the ground of the deformations and transvaluations of enlightenment thinking, he was, because of his own *reading* of reason, largely immune to its meaning and grounding in any positive sense whatsoever.

On the philosophical level Habermas addresses this issue in terms of the form and content of reason. For Habermas, Kant's insight, if not his formulation of a subject (whether a monad or a species) who uses reason transcendentally, is fundamentally correct. Reason is divided into three distinct realms: one dealing with the categories of understanding through which humans organise their perception, understanding and knowledge of nature, termed by Kant pure reason (and has also been termed calculating reason); another termed practical reason, which as already stated deals with the domain of the social, its normativity; and one dealing with the criteria of taste, i.e. aesthetic judgment. Habermas imagines and thus reiterates Kant's interdiction against the post-Kantian, Hegelian collapse of humankind's attempts at self-constitution under a single ontological notion of reason, which Marx would later 're-invent' as labour, one-sidedly interpreted by him as the technical mastery of nature through the application of purposive rules.

The issue here is double-sided for Habermas; on the one hand he reformulates the monadic basis of subject-centred philosophy, while on the other he simultaneously recasts the transcendental basis of Kant's philosophy whilst maintaining that Kant's insight about the differentiation of reason into different domains was essentially correct. In *Knowledge and Human Interests* he argues that the notion of labour is both too restrictive, because it refers only to humankind's relation to nature, and too idealist, because it relies on an often hidden notion of a reconciliation of the subject (*qua* humankind *or* worker) with her/himself to fully articulate the project of freedom. For Habermas, the solution to both sides of the problem is taken in part from ordinary language philosophy, especially as it has developed from Wittgenstein.

Language implies inter-subjectivity; we objectify ourselves as social beings through language use and always in the context of other-boundedness. This turn towards linguistics, or more properly the recognition of the constitutive linguisticality of the social world, is not Habermas simply replicating the work of the ethnomethodologists and ordinary language philosophers. In the communicative practice of everyday life, language functions as the means for and the context by which social intercourse is established. But more than this, it is also the means through which social rules are learned, tested, unlearned and criticised as social problems. So, according to Habermas, whilst subjects partici-pate *permanently* in social interactions both constituted through and mediated by language, this language use is oriented to validity claims, both through its use *and*, as importantly, in the cultural horizons which lie underneath or arch over it. There is then, for Habermas, an intended relation between meaning, use and validation: in inter-subjective every-day communicative activity, the recognition of social norms imbedded in language and the rightness of those norms to the social context is constantly being recognised.

Sociologically Habermas contests the one-dimensionality of social critique by developing a counter-image of modernity. Modernity is typ-ified by a differentiation and development of the constellations of the three *modern* types of action complexes and institutional forms: science, morality and political legitimation, and aesthetics. This has an homolo-gous relation with the philosophical level, i.e. with the differentiation of the types of rationality appropriate to the formation of action/ knowledge in those three spheres: science is developed according to the principles of a cognitive construction of rationality, with its validation in terms of truth; political and legitimatory patterns of action and know-ledge develop and proceed according to the principles of moral-practical rationality with its validation in terms of normative rightness; modern aesthetics develops according to its own distinctive form of rationality, the expressive with its own form of validation, truthfulness.

Moreover, each form of differentiation accords, so Habermas argues, with the way in which humankind orients itself to the worlds that it creates—the external world of nature or systemic environments, which he terms *the system* and the world of inter-subjectively constituted sociality which he terms the *life-world* which encompasses everyday life in the mundane sense, political forms of consensus formation, as well as the world of inner subjectivity of desires, needs and fantasies which 'matches' homologously with aesthetic experience.

From *Legitimation Crisis* (1975) onwards Habermas formalised this distinction and differentiation between system and life-world and the perspectives which each embodies, embraces and develops. Social sys-tems, as they become more complex, differentiate themselves and become self-regulating according to their own media, or forms of self-regulation and self-reflexivity, constituted through either purposive/ cognitive or strategic knowledge and criteria of validity. The life-world thematises, as has been suggested, the normative structures (values and institutions) of a society. According to Habermas' schema, this 'inner life' of society does not belong to the system simply as an environment, as do other systems; rather it exists as a world *sui generis* and resists total absorption to the system's imperatives through socialised individuation and the interpretative capacities which persons and societies have to develop to ensure a coherent identity.

This distinction, and especially the life-world perspective, allows Habermas the critical leverage, he assumes, which the Frankfurt School denied itself. Programmatically, Habermas attempts to develop a critique (critical theory) of the deformations and unfettered expansions of instrumental and strategic rationalities whilst simultaneously providing the basis for this critique from the vantage point of redeeming the utopian horizon of modernity itself, located neither in the world or perspective of systems-orientated administrative affairs or capitalist commodification, nor in aesthetics, but in the moral-practical perspectives located in the life-world.

Hence we return to our opening theme. This outline indicates two things about the Habermasian project from the vantage point of his utopian horizon. Firstly, it indicates his commitment and interest in the public sphere. The notion of the public sphere was the initial point of departure for his reflections, and in many respects provides a continuing point of reference around the problem of political modernity as 'purely human' relations as well as provides a shift in perspective. In *The Structural Transformation of the Public Sphere* (1989) Habermas' theory of democracy involves the historical-philosophical working through of the separation of civil society from the state, and its formation as both a realm of (capitalistic) economic activity located in private property and as the public political sphere as public opinion formed by autonomous personalities. Habermas rightly argues that economic 'man' and 'citizen' stand as two differentiated and competing aspects of the modern world, aspects which have either been minimised or treated as derivatives of one or the other in political philosophy and social theory from Kant onwards. Habermas adds to his discussion about modernity the formation of the modern state from its absolutist form, to its form as a constitutional republic to its form as a social democratic welfare state in the twentieth century. In this framework the public sphere is diagnosed as having both shrunk and been absorbed by the state or the interests of capital.

In *The Theory of Communicative Action* (1984 and 1987b) the public sphere emerges through the perspective of his differentiated image of society with its paradoxes and pathologies in the relation between its system and life-world constituents. The relation between life-world and system constitutes the battleground between the dynamics of modernity, none of which are reducible to one another—capitalism, which is typified by strategic rationality and is systematised and secured through the media of money; the nation state, especially the welfare state, which is systematised and secured through the media of bureaucratic-administrative power; and democracy, which is formed rather than systematised through the dynamics (rather than secured media) of consensually orientated 'political will formations' that are anchored in the life-world.

Conflicts arise at the seam between system and life-world. The imperatives of the autonomous systems of either the market or the bureaucratic-administrative-welfare state can 'infiltrate' life-world contexts in a way that can assimilate the life-world to one or other of the system imperatives. This phenomena of 'the internal colonisation of the life-world' by the system results, so Habermas argues, in the 'cultural impoverishment and fragmentation of everyday consciousness' (1987b: 355). But this process of colonisation is not total, it is neither precipitous nor does it predecide the outcome. Rather there are only tendencies and contradictions because the life-world itself contains a permanent communicative potential through which protests and social movements are formed. The issue then becomes what type of potential is located in the life-world and its social movements. Critical theory can ask whether the communicative potential is traditionalising or modernising, that is post-traditional in that it refers to the universality of reason, as well as the forms of reason invoked. From the vantage point of conflict Habermas singles out the public political sphere, i.e. the democratic moment of modernity, as the central guiding focus for his theoretical/ philosophical endeavours. The problem he sets for himself is its *meaning* and *grounding*. And it is here that we can indicate the second aspect: in *The Structural Transformation of the Public Sphere* he is interested in examining and reconstructing the historical meanings of the idea of the public sphere; in *The Theory of Communicative Action* he is interested predominantly in its philosophical grounding.

Lurking between the meaning and the grounding is an almost Aristotlean moment in Habermas' project. One can intuit a sympathy for Aristotle's (and Arendt's) notion of politics as acting, as doing, as *praxis* and *poeisis*, as against technique, strategies and technical expertise. In establishing the *sensus communis*, the truth is *in* the agreement, in the activity of understanding and reaching consensus over the norms which are deployed. For Habermas this is essentially a practico-discursive affair in which, through argumentation, the social actors *expose* and make known the norms that are in use. Language 'is orientated to observing intersubjectively valid norms that link reciprocal expectations' (1979: 118). This provides the basis from which the rational content of communication is established. Rationality entails

> ... the moral-practical aspect of the responsibility of the acting subject and the justifiability of the action norms ... [to express] the truthfulness of intentional expressions and [...] the rightness of norms. In this sense, while language is always 'content sensitive' it presupposes a validity basis in which the participants at least implicitly raise and reciprocally recognise a consensus that makes communication possible.

The Theory of Communicative Action witnesses a shift in emphasis from universal pragmatics where the ideal speech situation functions as a normative horizon to the *activity* of discourse or argumentation itself. The rationality criteria of social action are located and made visible in the act of speaking itself. We are, for Habermas, not labouring animals or even ratiocinating animals or writing animals but speaking, interacting and potentially autonomous and democratic beings.

BIBLIOGRAPHY

Primary sources

Habermas, J. (1971) *Towards a Rational Society*. Trans. by Jeremy Shapiro. London, Heinemann
——(1972) *Knowledge and Human Interests*. Trans. by Jeremy Shapiro. London, Heinemann
——(1974) *Theory and Practice*. Trans. by John Viertel. London, Heinemann
——(1975) *Legitimation Crisis*. Trans. by Thomas McCarthy. Boston, Beacon Press
——(1979a) *Communication and the Evolution of Society*. Trans. by Thomas McCarthy. Boston, Beacon Press
——(1979b) 'History and Evolution' *Telos* 39
——(1983) *Philosophical-Political Profiles*. Trans. by Frederich Lawrence. Boston, The MIT Press
——(1984) *The Theory of Communicative Action* Vol I: *Reason and the Rationalisation of Society*. Trans. by Thomas McCarthy. Boston, Beacon Press
——(1987a) *The Philosophical Discourse of Modernity*. Trans. by Frederick Lawrence. Cambridge, Polity Press
——(1987b) *The Theory of Communicative Action* Vol II: *Lifeworld and System: A Critique of Functionalist Reason*. Trans. by Thomas McCarthy. Boston, Beacon Press
——(1988) *On the Logic of the Social Sciences*. Trans. by Shierry Weber Nicholsen and Jerry A. Stark. Cambridge, The MIT Press
——(1989) *The Structural Transformation of the Public Sphere*. Trans. by Thomas Burger with Frederick Lawrence. Cambridge, Polity Press

Secondary sources

Bernstein, R. J. (1985) (ed.) *Habermas and Modernity* Cambridge, Polity Press
Brand, A. (1990) *The Force of Reason: An Introduction to Habermas' Theory of Communicative Action* Sydney, Allen & Unwin
Dews, P. (1986) *Habermas: Autonomy and Solidarity* London, Verso

Honneth, A., McCarthy, T., Offe, C. and Wellmer, A. (1989) (eds) *Zwischenbetrachungen Im Prozeß der Aufklärung: Jürgen Habermas zum 60 Geburtstag* Frankfurt, Suhrkamp Verlag. See the essays in English by Martin Jay, Thomas McCarthy, Gajo Petrović, Seyla Benhabib, Richard Bernstein, Cornelius Castoriadis, Jean Cohen/ Andrew Arato and Charles Taylor.

Pusey, M. (1987) *Jürgen Habermas* London, Tavistock

Thompson, J. B. and Held, D. (1982) *Habermas: Critical Debates* London, Macmillan

17

Agnes Heller

Agnes Heller was born in Budapest, Hungary, in 1929. A student and close associate of Georg Lukács, she was Assistant and Associate Professor at the University of Budapest from 1955 to 1958. Removed from this post for participation in the 1956 revolution in Hungary, she subsequently became Chief Research Fellow at the Sociological Institute at the Hungarian Academy from 1963 to 1973. In 1973, she was dismissed from that post, for political reasons, and left Hungary, taking up a senior lectureship, later readership at La Trobe University, Melbourne. In 1985 she was appointed Professor of Philosophy and later Hannah Arendt Professor in the Graduate Faculty at the New School For Social Research in New York.

Heller's social theory focuses on five key themes: everyday life, culture, institutions, morality, and despotism.

EVERYDAY LIFE

Heller's work shares with the philosophy and aesthetics of Lukács one central attribute: critical disposition toward 'mere life'. Both cultural forms and morals represent, for Heller, different ways of transcending everyday life. The primary concern of everyday life, she argues, is self-preservation. To survive, each person must cultivate abilities and appropriate words, man-made things, and customs—the three constituents of the sphere of objectivation 'in itself', which is the backbone of everyday life and the social *a priori* of human experience. Every person must appropriate, and acquire competence in observing, the 'norms and rules' of the sphere of objectivation 'in itself'. To be 'grown up', to have competence in social life, is the end result of this process.

There is, however, little opportunity for persons in the everyday life-world to cultivate abilities or appropriate words, things, and customs beyond narrow confines. In everyday life, persons perform *heterogeneous* tasks so as to reproduce themselves; they cannot concentrate on a single task. This is true even when the life-world is internally differentiated and there is a social division of labor, say, between lord and serf. The heterogeneous nature of everyday activity is also reflected in the fact that there is no 'systematic' connection, or unity, between the tasks a person performs in daily life. There is no unity between, for example, taking a train, saying a prayer, making love, gardening, taking a drug etc. In order to carry out such diverse and unrelated tasks, the subject of everyday life has to develop the most heterogeneous propensities and abilities: manipulation, discussion, self-control, love, sensitivity, decision-making etc. The subject of everyday life is the *human being as a whole*.

CULTURE

Beyond everyday life is the sphere of objectivation 'for itself'. In advanced societies this sphere is internally differentiated—between the arts, sciences, religions, and philosophy. In *Everyday Life* (1984a), Heller offers a much broader conception of this sphere, so as to include politics, law, work, and morals. In later works, for example *The Power of Shame* (1985), this breadth of conception disappears.

The sphere of objectivation 'for itself':

1 provides human life with *meaning*, by establishing the unity of the heterogeneous 'norms and rules' of everyday life, and thereby it *legitimates* the social order.

2 absorbs and employs the *cultural surplus* produced in everyday life. Each subject appropriates the 'norms and rules' of the sphere of objectivation 'in itself' in different ways. Each person's experience of the life-world is unique; it goes beyond the shared understandings of that world. This experience cannot be adequately expressed in ordinary language. It can, however, be expressed in the language of the sacred, of art, etc. Personal experience which is subjective within the sphere of objectivation 'in itself' can be *objectified*—and can eventually become *inter-subjective*—if absorbed into the sphere of objectivation 'for itself'.

3 is *homogeneous*. All tasks, all actions, all 'norms and rules' within the cultural sphere are interrelated. While in everyday life taking a bus is a meaningful action independent of visiting a friend or going to school, taking holy communion is a meaningful action only in its interrelation with the whole body of Christian belief.

4 entails the *suspension of heterogeneous everyday activities*. When subjects 'ascend' to the cultural sphere, they concentrate all their faculties on one task. All their mental, spiritual, and manual abilities, developed and practised in pursuing several distinct activities in everyday life, are thus unified. The *whole human being* is the subject of the sphere of objectivation 'for itself'.

INSTITUTIONS

The 'whole human being' can be distinguished from the 'specialised human being'. The specialist operates neither in everyday life nor in the sphere of culture, but rather in the sphere of objectivation 'for and in itself'—or, more simply, in institutional settings. In modernity, routine science, bureaucracy and markets are central institutions. Institutional actors exhibit neither the heterogeneous orientation of the everyday actor, nor the all-round development of capacities typical of those who move in the cultural sphere. Rather, the institutional actor focuses on a restricted range of tasks for which he or she develops a specialised and narrow range of abilities.

The strength of modern institutions lies in their cognitive-procedural, rather than normative-legitimating dimension. Their capacity to legitimate (i.e. to provide life with meaning) is weak. They are good at accumulating techniques, producing 'instructions for use', harnessing and utilising the cognitive surplus of society (produced by 'revolutionary' science). The technical rules accumulated by institutions are fed back into everyday life, often in intrusive ways. Institutions are morally 'indifferent' in the sense that they do not produce values. What they do instead is to refine and extend the procedures and organisational methods by which values can be attained. The moral implications of this, of course, depend on the extent to which institutional actors are able, in practice, to orientate to values, and value-centred norms, *as well as* to technical rules. The loss of value orientation is, potentially, morally devastating.

MORALITY

In the everyday life-world, a condition of survival is learning to appropriate ready-made group norms. A person in the everyday life-world reasons—discriminates between good and bad—unreflectively, i.e. according to norms which are taken for granted. When persons 'act according to reason', they are repositories of the 'rationality of reason'. Historically, this was the only kind of rationality. Persons, thus, obeyed the authority of social custom. Disobedience of this authority was shameful; feelings of shame were elicited by the disapproval of the 'eye of the community'. In some, mainly recent, societies, reason can also judge the 'norms and rules' of society. Persons can question and test the validity of the 'norms and rules' of their social environment in the name of a few abstract norms (virtues, natural law) or universalised values (freedom, life chances) that they observe. In doing so, they 'act according to the rationality of intellect'.

The ground for the 'rationality of intellect' is laid with the emergence of *practical reason* or *morality*. Morality enables individuals to distance themselves from given social demands. As well as reacting to the authority of society, they listen to the authority of practical reason, their 'inner voice'. The disapproval of this authority elicits feelings of guilt. Individuals, in this manner, gain moral autonomy in relation to society. They begin, firstly, to apply, amplify, and interpret social norms relying on their practical reason. The rationality of practical reason is still at this stage the 'rationality of reason'. The development of practical reason is furthered by the appearance of *ideal* external authorities that can be counterposed to the authority of society. This is represented, in antiquity, by, firstly, the Judaic concept of God's law that justifies the righteous rejection of custom and community opinion and, secondly, the Socratic ideal city and the abstract norms (virtues) it embodies.

In modernity, a few universalised values (freedom, life chances, etc.) take on the role of ideal external authorities. Consequent upon the emergence of these universalised values, practical reason assumes the role of *ultimate arbiter* in practical questions. It is able to devalidate social norms and expectations—to question their justice, validity, etc.—in the name of the few abstract values that are 'beyond question' (work and intimacy in the case of the Protestant 'bad conscience'; freedom in the case of the legislative conscience; tolerance in the case of the sceptical conscience).

TOTALITARIANISM, CAPITALISM, NARCISSISM

Modernity also develops more pathological cases, where conscience becomes the *sole* arbiter of human conduct, or, in the case of totalitarianism, where practical reason is disowned.

The communist parties sought to 'totalise' society, eliminating social and political pluralism. In pursuit of this, the Party's aim was virtually to eliminate any 'conscience culture' in favour of a 'shame culture'. This was a program of de-enlightenment. The maxim 'think for yourself' was interred. The Party sought to extinguish moral autonomy and to substitute reflected application of norms by the individual with obedience to concrete behavioral patterns. The Party presented itself as the 'conscience' of the people; the supreme virtues of totalitarian regimes were loyalty and obedience to the Party. What was good was what was commanded by the Party leadership; there was no independent measure of good and evil, nor could such a measure be applied by the individual.

Where totalitarianism sought to extinguish conscience, other modern conditions have sought to overextend it and, in doing so, pervert it. When conscience emerges as the *sole* arbiter of conduct, it becomes either *calculative* or *narcissistic*. The narcissist is concerned entirely with self-realisation or self-reflection—and finds other persons indifferent and the outer world tedious. The narcissist exemplifies Nietzsche's 'good conscience'. The calculative conscience, on the other hand, is concerned entirely with its own success. The calculative conscience grows out of the 'bad conscience' of the Protestant ethic, yet at the same time radically transforms the Protestant conscience. The calculative conscience belongs to late rather than early capitalism. For it, worldly achievement is no longer a sign of grace, it is grace. The good is identified with success.

Ironically, the appearance of conscience as the sole arbiter of conduct leads, ultimately, to the emergence of new kinds of external authority— ones that are non-moral, even despotic. Into the moral vacuum created by the success orientation steps public opinion; conformance to public opinion replaces the observance of moral norms. The narcissist, on the other hand, deifies the individual who knows no limits—i.e. the 'superman'—and bows to the authority of the leader who acts without restraint, shame, or humanity.

BIBLIOGRAPHY

Primary sources

Heller, A. (1955) *Chernyshevsky's Ethical Views: the Problem of Rational Egoism* Budapest, Szikra

——(1966a) *Aristotelian Ethics and the Ethos of Antiquity* Budapest, Akadémiai Kiadó

——(1966b) *Social Role and Prejudice* Budapest, Akadémiai Kiadó

——(1969) *Value and History* Budapest, Kiadó

——(1973) *Towards A Marxist Theory Of Values* Carbondale, Southern Illinois University

——(1976) *The Theory Of Need In Marx* London, Allison and Busby

——(1978) *Renaissance Man* London, Routledge & Kegan Paul

——(1979a) *On Instincts* Assen, Van Gorcum

——(1979b) *A Theory of Feelings* Assen, Van Gorcum

——(1982) *A Theory of History* London, Routledge & Kegan Paul

——(1983a) *Dictatorship Over Needs* (with F. Fehér and G.Márkus) Oxford, Blackwell

——(1983b) *Hungary, 1956 Revisited* (with F. Fehér) London, George Allen and Unwin

——(1983c) (ed.) *Lukács Revalued* Oxford, Basil Blackwell

——(1984a) *Everyday Life* London, Routledge & Kegan Paul

——(1984b) *Radical Philosophy* Oxford, Basil Blackwell

——(1985) *The Power of Shame: a Rational Perspective* London, Routledge & Kegan Paul

——(1986a) *Eastern Left, Western left: Totalitarianism, Freedom and Democracy* (with F. Fehér) Cambridge, Polity

——(1986b) (ed.) *Reconstructing Aesthetics* (with F. Fehér) Oxford, Basil Blackwell

—(1987) *Beyond Justice* Oxford, Basil Blackwell
—(1988a) *General Ethics* Oxford, Basil Blackwell
—(1988b) *The Postmodern Political Condition* (with F. Fehér) Cambridge, Polity
—(1990a) *Can Modernity Survive?* Cambridge, Polity Press
—(1990b) *From Yalta to Glasnost* (with F. Fehér) Oxford, Blackwell
—(1990c) *A Philosophy of Morals* Oxford, Blackwell

Secondary sources

Arnason, J.P. (1984) 'Progress and pluralism: reflections on Agnes Heller's *A Theory of History*' *Praxis International* 3(4)
Benhabib, S. (1980) 'Review of Agnes Heller, *On Instincts* and *A Theory of Feelings*', *Telos* 44
Bernstein, R. (1987) 'Agnes Heller: philosophy, rational utopia, and praxis' *Thesis Eleven* 16
Boella, J. (1978) 'Radicalism and needs in Heller' *Telos* 37
Burnheim, J. (1991) (ed.) *Essays for Agnes Heller* Dordrecht, Reidel
Cohen, J. (1977) 'Review of Agnes Heller, *The Theory Of Need In Marx*, *Telos* (33)
Cooper, D. (1987) 'Agnes Heller and our needs' *Thesis Eleven* 16
Habermas, J. (1987) 'Excursus: Obsolescence of the Production Paradigm', in J. Habermas *The Philosophical Discourse of Modernity* Cambridge, Polity
Murphy, P. (1987) 'Freedom and happiness: the pathos of modernity in Agnes Heller' *Thesis Eleven* 16
—(1990) 'Radicalism and the spheres of value' *Thesis Eleven* 26
Robinson, G. (1990) 'The ethical dilemmas of modernity' *Thesis Eleven* 27
Vigorelli, A. (1987) 'Paradigm changes in critical theory: Agnes Heller's reconsideration of rationality' *Thesis Eleven* 16

18

Julia Kristeva

With the publication in 1990 of her *roman à clef*, *Les Samouraïs*, Julia Kristeva's status as an intellectual of repute in Paris begins to invite comparison with that of her mentor, Simone de Beauvoir. For, like de Beauvoir's *Mandarins*, *Les Samouraïs* is also a vivisection of the lives and loves of the Parisian intellectual avant-garde. This time, it is the generation after Sartre which takes centre stage. Kristeva, in short, is now well-known—at least in France. In Australia, by contrast, her name is still more familiar to those in feminist circles, although this is now changing.

Thus if Kristeva's intellectual trajectory is marked at its present moment in the 1990s by renown, and the turn to the more or less transparent prose of a realist, postmodern novel, at its beginning in the 1960s it is characterised by relative anonymity and the arcane language and mathematically inspired *semanalysis* of *Séméiotiké* (from the Greek, *semeîon* meaning distinctive mark, trace, index, etc.) (Kristeva 1969). What then are the salient features which make up the content of this trajectory?

The future theorist of the *semiotic* arrived in Paris from Bulgaria in 1965, holder of a French government scholarship. She had been schooled in French language and literature, as well as in mathematics and linguistics, and could well have developed into a pillar of the French academic establishment. This was not to be. Kristeva quickly became associated with the writer Philippe Sollers, and the avant-garde literary journal *Tel Quel*, both anathema to the establishment. Also associated with *Tel Quel* was Roland Barthes who, in 1966, invited Kristeva to give a paper at his seminar on the work of Mikhail Bakhtin, the Russian literary theorist who survived Stalin. Subsequently, a lengthy review article on Bakhtin appeared in *Critique* in 1967 (Kristeva 1967). Of particular concern in this article is the elucidation of the notions of 'dialogue' and 'carnival', notions which point to the text as a dynamic, polyphonic phenomenon, rather than the static vehicle of transparent prose characteristic of various forms of realism.

From a more political point of view, *Tel Quel* in the late 1960s endeavoured to develop a truly materialist theory of language. As the basis of the symbolic order, the materialism of language is a practice. For the *Tel Quel* group, it thus became possible to give the Marxist revolution a fundamentally cultural and artistic air, one that could not have been more calculated to displease the various communist parties, and particularly their leaders so carefully schooled in dogmatic Marxism. Subsequently, Kristeva showed that the key to grasping language as a practice depends on focusing on its poetic, or musical aspect, and not simply on its symbolic, representational, communicative aspect. If we add the problematic—inspired by Lacanian psychoanalytic theory—of the subject to this notion of 'poetic language', we have in a nutshell the key elements which have animated Kristeva's intellectual journey over the last quarter of a century.

At the height of the structuralist fever between 1965 and 1970, and in light of the emphasis on Saussure's theory of language as a system of differences—the theory that provided the key insight of structuralism—Kristeva turned to developing a theory of the logic of poetic language that could genuinely account for its dynamic, heterogeneous nature. The point was that existing modes of scientific knowledge based on the 'true–false' logic of 0–1 (where '0' is the empty set and '1' is equivalent to identity) could not account for the transgressive, ambivalent, and contradictory features of poetic language. Practically, this means that realist interpretations of art (interpretations exclusively concerned with language as communication) cannot account for the actual transgression of grammar, syntax, and narrative in, for instance, an 'unreadable' text like Joyce's *Finnegan's Wake*. Instead of coming to grips with Joyce's striking evocation of the sounds and rhythms of the prose, the critical establishment seemed—at the time of Kristeva's early theory of poetic language—to be impelled to restore the text's hidden, and more or less conventional, linguistic, narrative structure: the alleged source of the 'true' meaning of the novel.

However, the poetic element in artistic works—the sound of words, the colour of paint, the matter of sculpture, the forms of architecture—does not lend itself to this 'true–false' logic. Its significance and force rather lies in a transgressive materiality that shakes this logic. Whether an entire narrative structure in *Finnegan's Wake* can be recovered, and whether one particular reading rather than another accomplishes this task, is not directly pertinent to the poetic, material basis of the novel. Like Mallarmé, Joyce is seen by Kristeva to give form to poetic language, rather than simply deforming the symbolic dimension of language. The 'language' of this poetry keeps madness at bay.

In *Le Texte du roman* (1970), Kristeva investigates the way in which the modern novel as a truly heterogeneous text came into being. The concept of carnival, inspired by Bakhtin's writing on Rabelais and Dostoevsky (Bakhtin 1984a, 1984b), is here crucial to the attempt to formulate a theory of carnival as transgression. Carnival is no longer the simple mirror reversal of the existing order: the other, negative side of a symmetrical opposition. Carnival is precisely what cannot be predicted by the existing law. There is no language of carnival: it cannot be represented by existing symbolic means, but can be generative of new symbolic resources. Carnival is laughter—the ultimate transgression. Carnival is neither the Devil opposing God, nor the criminal element opposing the law, nor the revolutionary opposing the bourgeoisie—nor even the lowly people opposing, or taking the place of, high authority. In its joy and laughter, carnival transcends all of this. It conforms to the '0–2' logic of poetic language. This is because it constitutes the basis of an alternative system: it includes the possibility of a new law and its contrary within its own interstices.

In its theory of the evolution of novelistic discourse, *Le Texte du roman* elaborates terms like *inter-texuality* (the interpenetration of two different sign systems), *geno-text* (the material, poetic basis of the text), and *pheno-text* (the symbolic, narrative, or representational aspect), terms which have become very much associated with Kristeva's theory of writing. In the published version of her doctorate on the nineteenth-century avant-garde, *La Révolution du langage poétique* (1974), Kristeva points out that the poetic aspect of avant-garde writing both posits and transgresses the symbolic, discursive, and thus communicative aspect of language; it uses the latter to bring about a rupture—a *thetic* moment—constitutive of both subject and object, which would renew the existing configuration of the symbolic order.

Looked at from the perspective of the formation of the individual subject, drive activity (the basis of the poetic) binds the infant to its mother, while at the same time being the means of separating this originally united couple. At this pre-Oedipal phase of development—the phase prior to the acquisition of articulated language—the infant exists in a pre-symbolic world of holophrastic utterances, rhythmical gestures, vocal modulations, and laughter. These are the outcome of minimally controlled drive activity, the basis of what Kristeva calls the *semiotic* function of language, which she contrasts with the formally organised *symbolic* function. Just as scientific logic had been the only one available for understanding poetic language, so language had also been defined as exclusively symbolic: that is, as grammar, syntax, meaning, discursivity, representation and communication.

Kristeva's insight is that, firstly, while the semiotic may not have (symbolic) meaning, it nonetheless has *significance* (it is minimally organised and is not a purely arbitrary phenomenon), and, secondly, the

semiotic is always present in every instance of the symbolic. The uniqueness of avant-garde poetry like Mallarmé's (cf. Mallarmé 1945) turns out
to be centred on the way this poetry exploits the *semiotic* features of
language (its rhythm and music), but not as a way of eventually privileging the semiotic. The concept of *significance* is also closely linked with
the notion of *chora*—'a nonexpressive totality formed by the drives and
their stases . . . '. The *chora* is also described (following Plato) as a kind
of receptacle which corresponds to the unarticulated, rhythmed, maternal 'space' of flows and lines, rather than of articulations and positions.
Chora challenges many narrowly rationalistic views of language and art,
and has provided the theoretical weaponry for various 'feminist challenges' (cf. Pateman and Gross 1986).

To turn the subject into a purely symbolic, objective entity, that is,
into the homogeneous, self-present, punctual subject of everyday language, is to limit its potential for change. By contrast, the subject Kristeva
brings to light in *La Révolution du langage poétique* is a *subject in
process/on trial,* one that is continually renewing and dissolving itself in
and through its images and objects. This means there is no science of the
subject, because the prominence of semiotic drive activity turns the
process of subjectivity into a *practice,* one that dissolves the framework
of self-presence characteristic of scientific logic. Practice here is a form
of laughter. It is the presence of drive activity *in* the symbolic.

More pointedly, practice is what creates something new: 'Every practice which produces something new is a practice of laughter' (Kristeva
1984: 225). In her essay on Bataille, collected in *Polylogue* (1977),
Kristeva states clearly how, in this phase of her intellectual work, the
intersection between the semiotic and the symbolic, constitutive of subjectivity, was inseparable from a confrontation between drive *rejection*
taken in charge by avant-garde writing, and static historical and social
structures rooted in representation, a confrontation which could bring
about a transformation of these structures (1977: 133–4).

With the publication of *Powers of Horror* (Kristeva 1982), a new
direction emerges in Kristeva's work. Rather than focusing on language
per se, a new theory of subjectivity emerges, one that partially bypasses
the emphasis Lacan placed on the mirror stage (entry into language) and
the (virtual) object (*objet petit a*) in the formation of subjectivity. For
Lacan, the human being only becomes human in any meaningful sense
when he/she learns to use language as a system of signs, that is, as a
substitute for the (mother as the) absent object. Hence the importance
for Lacan of the object as the virtual object, 'petit *a*'. The full separation
of the individual from the mother is brought about precisely through the
intervention of the symbolic in the mother–child dyad.

For Kristeva, on the other hand, separation begins at a pre-objectal
level, where subjectivity begins to form on the basis of what is expelled
from the body, as well as through what is incorporated, accepted or

embraced. The pre-object that is in play, Kristeva calls the abject. It is what the individual finds painful, intolerable and repulsive: what makes one want to vomit.

At a social level, the abject is often the basis of purification rituals which assist a minimally elaborated symbolic structure deal with socially ambiguous phenomena. The corpse, or the boundaries of the body are, in this sense, instances of ambiguity which call for purification rites that might facilitate social integration. Morally speaking, the abject is evident in corruption and hypocrisy—the double dealing which puts into question any consistent moral stance. More pointedly, hypocrisy is a threat to the symbolic means necessary for distinguishing between 'right' and 'wrong', 'good' and 'bad', 'love' and 'hate', etc. Indeed, what is abject is 'beyond good and evil', often leaving the one who experiences it bereft of symbolic resources. A pile of shoes belonging to children killed by the Nazis is abject in this sense (Kristeva 1982: 4). It provokes nausea.

In her best-selling book, *Tales of Love* (1987b), Kristeva explains how love—both historically and contemporaneously—is, from a psychoanalytic point of view, essential to the formation of a capacity for idealisation, and hence symbolisation. In effect, each individual needs to develop an adequate capacity for narcissism. Ovid's Narcissus, made famous in the history of Western culture for apparently falling in love with his own image, is taken by Kristeva to be an example of how an adequate ego structure, based on narcissism, has failed to develop. Indeed, Narcissus' self-image fails as the means for opening him up to the other, as love requires, and rather becomes the point of a fixation that renders him impervious to the outside world. Because he has in fact only partially entered the symbolic, Narcissus exhibits a melancholic disposition, one that makes problematic the very possibility of love and social being.

Kristeva turns her attention to melancholia and depression in her book which addresses some aspects of postmodern experience, *Black Sun* (1989). According to Kristeva's psychoanalytic theory, melancholia and its less severe form, depression, occur because the thetic phase has not been fully realised. The melancholic, therefore, has not entered the symbolic and is, as a result, too much attached to the mother. Or at least he or she is unable to symbolise successfully the emotional trauma that the separation from the mother, and the intervention of the symbolic (father), entails for everybody. One historical instance where Kristeva sees art coming to the aid of a melancholic disposition is in Hans Holbein the Younger's painting of *The Corpse of Christ in the Tomb* (1521). Holbein is able to symbolise the death of Christ in a way that gives us an insight into how the melancholic disposition struggles to inject an emotional charge into forms of the symbolic. Unlike the one committed to an ideal, the melancholic often tends to use symbolic forms in an entirely detached, passionless way, so that, sometimes, language fails altogether, and a commitment to living evaporates.

The question today is: are we entering a phase of history in which it is becoming increasingly difficult to combat the melancholic disposition, because the symbolic means available for expressing our sadness have become inadequate? Is this part of the price to be paid for our postmodern experience where ideals have been rendered suspect because they are so often connected with dogma and totalitarian thought? Kristeva's answer seems to be 'yes', and artistic endeavour would seem to be an important antidote to this 'postmodern' depression. However, she does not appear to be willing to give any indication as to what social strategies might be appropriate for improving the status and importance of artistic endeavour in contemporary Western societies.

Towards the end of the 1980s the issue of the nature of modern society arose in light of the presence of diverse cultural groups within nations such as France and Australia. In *Etrangers à nous-mêmes* ('Foreigners to Ourselves') (1988), Kristeva outlines the origins of European cosmopolitanism and calls on people to recognise the fact that, as human beings, foreignness is always already within us, and that, as a result, it is not possible to understand one's relationship with (significantly different) others unless one understands one's relationship with oneself. In today's world, with the movement of people to all parts of the globe, the fostering of an ethic of cosmopolitanism is absolutely imperative if we are to avoid a slide into the worst excesses of racism and nationalist chauvinism. This is the thesis defended at length in Kristeva's contribution to the problem of racism, a problem that seems ever-present in this *fin de siècle*, which each one of us needs to consider carefully.

BIBLIOGRAPHY

Primary sources

Kristeva, J. (1967) 'Le mot, le dialogue et le roman' *Critique* 239: 438–65
——(1969) *Séméiotiké: Recherches pour une sémanalyse* Paris, Seuil
——(1970) *Le Texte du roman. Approche sémiologique d'une structure discursive transformationnelle* The Hague, Mouton
——(1974) *La Révolution du langage poétique. L'avant-garde à la fin du XIXe siècle, Lautréamont et Mallarmé* Paris, Seuil
——(1977) 'L'expérience et la pratique', in J. Kristeva *Polylogue* Paris, Seuil: 107–36
——(1982) *Powers of Horror.* Trans. by Leon S. Roudiez. New York, Columbia University Press
——(1984) *Revolution in Poetic Language.* Trans. by Margaret Waller. New York, Columbia University Press

——(1986) *About Chinese Women.* Trans. by Anita Barrows. London, Marion Boyers

——(1987a) *In the Beginning Was Love: Psychoanalysis and Faith.* Trans. by Arthur Goldhammer. New York, Columbia University Press

——(1987b) *Tales of Love.* Trans. by Leon S. Roudiez. New York, Columbia University Press

——(1988) *Etrangers à nous-mêmes* Paris, Fayard

——(1989) *Black Sun.* Trans. by Leon S. Roudiez. New York, Columbia University Press

Secondary sources

Bakhtin, M. (1984a) *Problems of Dostoevsky's Poetics.* Trans. by Carlyl Emerson. Manchester, Manchester University Press

——(1984b) *Rabelais and His World.* Trans. by Hélène Iswolsky. Bloomington, Indiana University Press

Grosz, E. (1989) *Sexual Subversions: Three French Feminists* Sydney, Allen & Unwin

Lechte, J. (1990a) 'Art, love and melancholy in the work of Julia Kristeva', in J. Fletcher and A. Benjamin *Abjection, Melancholia and Love* London, Routledge: 24–41

——(1990b) *Julia Kristeva* London, Routledge

——(1991) 'And is this all there is—postmodern melancholia?' *Thesis Eleven* 29

Nooy, J. de (1988) 'Double jeopardy: a reading of Kristeva's "Le texte clos"' *Southern Review* (Adelaide) 24 (2): 150–68

Mallarmé, S. (1945) 'Un coup de dés', in J. Mallarmé *Oeuvres Completes* Paris, Gallimard: 457–77

Pateman, C. and Grosz, E. (1986) (eds) *Feminist Challenges: Social and Political Theory* Sydney, Allen & Unwin

19

Jacques Lacan

Starting from the premise that the unconscious is structured like a language, the French psychoanalyst Jacques Lacan gave a new orientation to Freudian theory and practice that makes Lacanian psychoanalysis the most flourishing and dynamic form of psychoanalysis today. Through his seminars and writings he has had an inestimable influence upon the contributions of a generation of French 'structuralists' and 'post-structuralists' to philosophy, literary studies, social theory, and feminism.

The acknowledged stature of his work notwithstanding, Lacan remains a controversial figure within the field of psychoanalysis. Excommunicated from the International Psychoanalytic Association during his lifetime, his views are still regarded with suspicion or dismissed as wilfully obscure by the psychoanalytic orthodoxy.

After his training as a psychiatrist which culminated in an important thesis on paranoid psychosis, Lacan made his entry into psychoanalysis in 1936 with his theory of the *mirror stage*. With this theory as its centrepiece, his contributions up to the 1950s located psychoanalysis within what he would later call the register of the *imaginary*.

The theory of the mirror stage combines the psychological observation that between the ages of six months and eighteen months, the infant is fascinated by its image in a mirror with the biological fact of its physiological prematurity. The child greets its specular image with jubilation arising from the anticipation of a bodily unity that contrasts with the immaturity of its motor development. Captivated by the image and identifying with it, the child apprehends it both as its own image and as the image of another. Fundamental to the theory of the mirror stage is the view that the 'self' constitutes both itself and the *other*, its counterpart, through an *identification* with an image of itself as other; the child locates its own image in the other and, conversely, locates the other in the image of its own self.

While the theory of the mirror stage appeals to psychological and physiological evidence, its significance for Lacan is much greater, informing as it does his view that the *ego* is the outcome of a series of such identifications with the other over the course of development. Since the identity of the ego is constructed through its mirror image, the mirror stage entails that the inter-subjective relationship is essentially dual, characterised by imaginary identification and alienation, and marked by an ambivalent relationship of aggressive rivalry with and erotic attachment to the other.

The turning point in Lacan's work came in the early 1950s with the introduction of the distinction between the *symbolic* and the *imaginary*. Neither term is employed in its usual sense: 'imaginary' means based on an image; 'symbolic' means having to do with language. Lacan's focus shifted from the mirror stage, henceforth taken to typify the imaginary, onto the symbolic as the register within which the efficacy of psychoanalytic practice and the explanatory power of psychoanalytic theory are located.

Lacan initially divided the symbolic register into the two dimensions described by Saussure as *speech* and *language*. In characteristic fashion, Lacan combines the linguistic concept of speech with Hegel's master-slave dialectic to yield the claim that speech establishes a social bond or symbolic pact which overcomes the erotic-aggressive relationship of ego-to-ego characteristic of the imaginary. At a more specifically psychoanalytic level, the efficacy of psychoanalytic treatment is also to be understood as located at the level of speech. A neurotic symptom, to take an example, is regarded as an encoded message that has been excluded from the circuit of discourse and thus can only be communicated in disguised form. By means of the transference the analyst becomes the addressee of the symptom's hidden message and through interpretation inserts the communication back into discourse. Accordingly, symptoms and other *formations of the unconscious* (slips of the tongue or pen, bungled actions, memory lapses, jokes and dreams) are regarded as instances of failed communication. Operating solely by means of speech, analysis re-establishes the continuity of the subject's history through retroactively giving meaning to opaque elements of discourse.

Language, the second dimension of the symbolic, consists of a network of *signifiers* that can only be defined diacritically—i.e. signifiers possess no positive properties but are definable only through their differences. Signifiers are, strictly speaking, meaningless. Meaning is not a property of language but the product of speech; it is only produced at the level of the spoken chain of signifiers and unfolds according to a different temporality to that of the signifier; it is *prospectively anticipated* and *retroactively created*.

Inter-subjectivity, as the relationship based on the pact or bond between subjects that true speech establishes, is construed as the overcoming of the imaginary relationship between ego and other that Freud had described in his writings on narcissism and Lacan developed further in his theory of the mirror stage. However, Lacan's work then moved away from the inter-subjective dimension of speech onto the more purely formal level of language conceived as a pure network of signifiers located in the locus of the *Other*. Henceforth small other and big Other are contrasted and the imaginary relationship is regarded as subordinate to the symbolic relationship of the *subject* to big Other.

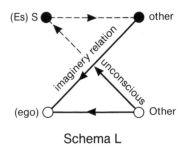

Schema L

No simple, single definition of the Other is possible: Lacan characterises it variously as the discourse of the unconscious; as the locus of good faith and the guarantor of truth; as the treasure of signifiers upon which all speech acts must draw. The common element in all Lacan's formulations is that the Other is a third place in discourse, radically external to both speaker and listener.

In urging a 'return to Freud' Lacan contended that the distinction between the symbolic, as the order of language, and the imaginary, as characterised by dual interpersonal relationships, was already implicit in Freud. Post-Freudian analysis had come to concentrate on the imaginary, and as a result psychoanalytic practice had failed to grasp the fundamental principles of psychoanalysis, which lay in the symbolic. This made it impossible to distinguish the essential in analytic practice from its contingent features, resulting in a conservatism that discouraged innovation and ritualised a technique misunderstood by its practitioners.

The introduction of the symbolic enabled Lacan to distinguish between the ego as constituted by a series of imaginary identifications and the subject regarded as the result of the effect of language upon the human being. Language subjects the living being to the signifier.

are clear evidence that language fragments the body according to its own divisions. The Freudian drive is not an instinctual force but possesses a logical grammar, analysed by Freud, from which no separate, biological component can be factored out.

As symbolic phenomena, both subject and Other contain a fundamental *lack*. On the side of the subject there is a 'lack' or 'want' of being (*manque-à-être*) which expresses itself as the *desire,* distinct from any biological need, for a lost object the subject has never possessed. The symbolic lack, which Lacan identifies with castration, is thus the counterpoise of, and the point of rent or rift in, the plenitude of the imaginary ego–other relationship (see *Schema L*) exemplified by the 'pre-oedipal' symbiosis of mother and infant. Desire is filtered through and structured by the signifier. Thus unconscious desire is not a psychological phenomenon, its object is variable, and it lies beyond the pleasure principle and the subject's interest in his or her own well-being. This is what is meant by Lacan's claim that desire and prohibition, or the (symbolic) law, are identical. However, this claim also implies that there can be no 'liberation' of desire, if by this is meant the possibility of giving free expression to desire upon the lifting of repression, nor any question of the adaptation or education, but only an ethics, of desire.

The second lack, the lack in the Other, is structural. The battery of signifiers that make up the Other is essentially incomplete, but it contains a key signifier which both represents and covers over this lack, $S(\emptyset)$. This lack, which was noted by Freud when he observed that the threat of castration only arises upon recognition of the mother's castration, is the key to Freud's theory of fetishism in which the fetish is a substitute for the woman's 'Missing' penis. For Lacan, the lack in the Other is the fundamental trauma that lies at the heart of human sexuality.

Lacan's claim that 'man's desire is the desire of the Other' has to be understood in two ways: firstly, as the claim that the subject desires to be desired by the Other, i.e. desires to be the object of the Other's desire, desires to fill the lack in the Other; and secondly, as the claim that the subject's desire is the Other's desire, that its origin lies in the locus of the Other.

The function of the father, called the *'Name of the Father'* to emphasise that its function is symbolic and that its significance is cultural, is to introduce the law and subject the human infant to its imperatives. At the same time it organises the sexual being of the subject. The phallus, Φ, a signifier distinct from the biological organ, the penis, is the primordial signifier of desire in the *Oedipus complex*. It is the sole means by which sexual difference is registered in the unconscious; there is no unconscious registration of masculinity or femininity as such, hence no 'sexual rapport', no relationship of natural complementarity, between the sexes. Gender, as distinct from sex, is a result of the way in which the subject is inscribed within the phallic function.

Freud introduced the concept of the death drive in response to his discovery that the subject 'loves his symptoms more than he loves himself'. Lacan's term *jouissance* characterises this hidden satisfaction that the subject derives even from what causes suffering. The Oedipus complex introduces the law that regulates and localises this *jouissance* through the introduction of the Name of the Father. Furthermore, while man is inscribed entirely within the phallic function and all his *jouissance* is subject to the law of the father, there is a supplementary, specifically feminine jouissance which remains outside the law.

For Lacan, there are three possible outcomes of the Oedipus complex, three ways in which the division of the subject can be introduced: the neurotic has assumed the law but *repressed* it; the psychotic has *foreclosed* the Name of the Father; while the pervert has *disavowed* castration. Normality is not an alternative outcome; for Lacan, in psychoanalysis 'normality' has no other meaning than a successful adaptation to the conditions of existence, and neither psychotic, neurotic nor perverse subjects are excluded from this. Lacan's structural approach enables a distinction to be drawn between a clinical picture and the structure of a subject—between, for example, clinical psychosis and a psychotic subject.

From the mid-1960s the category of the real became the focus of Lacan's work. Distinguished from reality, the real is excluded from the play of signifiers and has no specular dimension. While the real cannot be inscribed within the field of signifiers, it marks the place at which the symbolic breaks down. It is a point of failure of symbolisation that can never be apprehended in the symbolic itself, and can only be reconstructed on the basis of the structural distortion it produces in the symbolic order of the subject. Thus the real is not some positive entity that transcends the symbolic; it is an aporia internal to the symbolic itself. It is based on the concept of trauma that Freud initially considered the ultimate origin of all neurotic disorders.

However, Lacan opposes developmental approaches in psychoanalysis, maintaining that psychoanalytic theory does not describe the facts of actual development, but a structure which organises and manifests itself within an individual's history without being reducible to its developmental processes.

The most striking feature of the evolution in Lacan's thought is that he increasingly formalises and de-psychologises or depersonalises psychoanalytic theory. Whether this will be regarded as what is most valuable in him or as what can best be discarded still hangs in the balance. But what can be said with some certainty is that any rigorous and systematic exploration of the theory and practice of psychoanalysis can no longer avoid the work of Jacques Lacan.

BIBLIOGRAPHY

Primary sources

The focus of Lacan's teaching was his seminar (1951–80). The transcripts from 1953 on are being edited and published under the general title *Le Séminaire de Jacques Lacan* (Paris, Seuil, 1976–). To date three have appeared: see 1977b, 1988b and 1988c. *Ecrits* (Paris, Seuil, 1966) brought together the major written work from 1936 to 1965. Part of it has been published in English: see 1977a.

Lacan, J. (1977a) *Ecrits: A Selection* London, Tavistock

——(1977b) *The Four Fundamental Concepts of Psycho-Analysis* (Séminaire series XI, 1969) London, the Hogarth Press and the Institute of Psycho-Analysis

——(1977c) 'Desire and the interpretation of desire in *Hamlet*' *Yale French Studies 55, 56*

——(1982a) 'Guiding remarks for a congress on feminine sexuality', in J. Mitchell and J. Rose (eds) *Feminine Sexuality* London, Macmillan

——(1982b) 'Intervention on the transference' in J. Mitchell and J. Rose (eds) *Feminine Sexuality* London, Macmillan

——(1982c) 'The meaning of the phallus', in J. Mitchell and J. Rose (eds) *Feminine Sexuality* London, Macmillan

——(1982–83) 'Merleau-Ponty: in memorium' *Existential Psychology and Psychiatry* 18: 73–81

——(1988a) 'Logical time and the assertion of anticipated certainty: a new sophism' *Newsletter of the Freudian Field* 2 (2)

——(1988b) *The Seminar of Jacques Lacan. Book I: Freud's Papers on Technique, 1953–54*, Cambridge, Cambridge University Press

——(1988c) *The Seminar of Jacques Lacan. Book II: the Ego in Freud's Theory and in the Technique of Psychoanalysis, 1954–55* Cambridge, Cambridge University Press

——(1988d) 'The seminar on *The Purloined Letter*', in J.P. Muller and W.J. Richardson (eds) *The Purloined Poe* Washington, Johns Hopkins University Press: 28–54

——(1989a) 'Geneva lecture on the symptom' *Analysis* 1: 7–26

——(1989b) 'Kant with Sade' *October* 51: 55–75

——(1989c) 'Science and truth' *Newsletter of the Freudian Field* 3(1/2): 4–29

——(1990) *Television, and A Challenge to the Psychoanalytic Establishment* New York, W.W. Norton

Secondary sources

Benvenuto, B. and Kennedy, R. (1986) *The Works of Jacques Lacan: An Introduction* London, Free Associations

Grosz, E. (1990), *Jacques Lacan: A Feminist Introduction* Sydney, Allen & Unwin

Lee, J.S. (1990) *Jacques Lacan* Boston, G.K. Hall & Co

Muller, J.P. and Richardson, W.J. (1982) *Lacan and Language: A Reader's Guide to 'Ecrits'* New York, International Universities Press

Ragland-Sullivan, E. 1986 *Jacques Lacan and the Philosophy of Psychoanalysis* Chicago, University of Illinois Press

Schneiderman, S. (1980) (ed.) *Returning to Freud: Clinical Psychoanalysis in the School of Lacan* Yale, Yale University Press

Zizek, S. (1989) *The Sublime Object of Ideology* London, Verso

20

Claude Lévi-Strauss

Lévi-Strauss was born in Belgium in 1908, of a Jewish family. After studying philosophy in Paris, a subject which he did not enjoy, he became a schoolteacher for a short period of time, but seized the opportunity to go to Brazil in 1934 to teach sociology and to do fieldwork with South American Indian groups. Having returned to France in 1939, he escaped from war-torn Europe in 1941 to teach at the New School for Social Research in New York, where he fell under the influence of structural linguistics. After the war he became French cultural attaché in Washington, returning to France in 1950 to take up a teaching post in comparative religion in Paris. In 1958 he became Professor of Anthropology at the Collège de France, where he taught and researched for the rest of his long, distinguished career. In 1973 he was made a member of the French Academy.

While it might be conventional in discussions of social theory to sketch in the biographical background of an author so as to shed light on the particular problems the author has chosen to focus on, or to illuminate the particular approach adopted, Lévi-Strauss himself might regard such reference to an individual life as irrelevant, for structuralism embodies a very distinctive view as to what constitutes a scientific approach in the study of society. In his early book *Tristes Tropiques* (1955), Lévi-Strauss claims that he had three important mentors: Freud, Marx, and geology. What all three had in common was the view that the surface of phenomena can be very deceptive, and that reality must be discovered underneath the appearance of phenomena. Just as unconscious mental mechanisms can provide reasons for our actions of which we may not be aware; just as geological strata explain surface differences in vegetation; just as underlying techno-economic orders can account for patterns of values and ideologies, so for structuralism the scientifically privileged realm is that which lies hidden from normal human perception. For Lévi-Strauss existentialism, phenomenology and similar modes of describing our actions are not only superficial but self-indulgent, for on this level analysis will be mixed up with self-serving ideologies and flattering self-conceptions. A 'science' of mankind has to escape this level to sink to the truer, deeper logical levels that underlie the regularities that appear on the surface of social life.

This particular conception of scientific explanation accounts for why Lévi-Strauss has, somewhat strangely for an anthropologist, not written extensively about his own fieldwork material. Most practising anthropologists spend a considerable portion of their working lives publishing data arising from their fieldwork experiences. While Lévi-Strauss did fieldwork during the 1930s, his personal encounter with the 'savage' does not figure largely in his own massive output. As a recent collection of his essays was aptly entitled, structuralism is essentially *The View from Afar* (1983). The author is detached from the object of study, and the cultural descriptions do not dwell on concrete human lives, nor do they explore the world of human intentionality. Lévi-Strauss' central interest has been constant throughout his career; it has been to expose the underlying logical order which exists beneath all the richness and diversity of human culture. From his earliest writings on kinship systems, through the study of classification, to the analyses of mythology, his aim has been to expose this deeper level of order to establish universals of thought and behaviour.

Lévi-Strauss is not exploring human 'meaning', as that term is normally used. He is not discussing what native peoples 'mean by' their beliefs or customs, for their own conscious understandings are not scientifically privileged. He is exploring what we might term 'significance' rather than meaning, significance being the logical and communicative properties of systems of cultural signs. A set of kinship rules, a set of myths, a set of rules about eating, systems of tattoo designs, are all 'languages' and all have an underlying grammar which conveys cultural messages, independently of human consciousness. Culture and society, in the structural universe, are anonymous, objectified thought systems; they are systems of behaviour and thought that no individual human has authored or intended. Structuralism in anthropology thus shares with the structuralisms of other disciplines (such as literary analysis) and with other intellectual developments of the 1960s (the work of Foucault, for instance) a radical 'decentring' in the human sciences; significance, intelligibility, 'meaning' are properties of systems, not a matter of human will, subjectivity or intention. Lévi-Strauss' work does not privilege the level of the human subject at all.

Why was it that Lévi-Strauss seized upon the notion that language and linguistics were in some sense the key to understanding human social phenomena? Is language not very much bound up with how human beings make meaning? We need to recall here that the linguistics which Lévi-Strauss found so suggestive was the structural linguistics which scholars like Jakobson were introducing to the United States during the 1940s, and that this particular linguistic tradition did not privilege semantic concerns. For Lévi-Strauss, structuralism in the study of language made linguistics the most advanced of the social sciences. It did so precisely because such a scientific analysis of human language and speech, it was claimed, did not require the analyst to be bound up with speakers' intuitions; the linguist can access a level of reality and structure which escapes the speaker's consciousness. Thus linguistics could empirically discover universal features underlying the sound structure of human language.

Lévi-Strauss was extremely impressed by these rigorous, scientific achievements, and we can best understand his collection of early essays in *Structural Anthropology* (1958) as a search to find exactly how to utilise the idea that language was a key tool in decoding cultural reality. Did this mean that a society could be regarded as a language?; did it mean that there was some relationship between a culture and its language?; did it mean that detailed linguistic models could be employed in the analysis of cultural phenomena? Through the 1940s and into the 1950s, Lévi-Strauss struggled with this problem, abandoning several false trails as he went. Most importantly, he seized upon the general notion of semiology, conceived by Saussure early in the twentieth century, that beyond linguistics proper there was a much broader science of cultural signs. In a very real sense, Lévi-Strauss decided, as he admitted in *The Scope of Anthropology* (1960), that anthropology could be defined as the branch of semiotics which should analyse those systems of cultural signs—whether they be mythology, ritual, pottery, art, exchange systems, kinship rules, etc.—which linguists had not made their own.

Lévi-Strauss' initial field for this endeavour was that of kinship. In 1949 he released *The Elementary Systems of Kinship*, an attempt to find, underneath all the intricate details of marriage and descent rules in hundreds of societies, some simple logical rules by which we could understand them all. Ultimately, however, Lévi-Strauss found his explorations in the field of kinship to be unsatisfactory in that kinship systems were heavily influenced by historical, demographic and other material constraints. So he moved to the field of human classification where, he argued, the universals he was seeking would be more easily discovered in that, in this realm, the human mind simply converses with itself, so contamination by purely external factors would be absent.

In 1962 Lévi-Strauss published two works—*Totemism* and *The Savage Mind*—which firmly established his reputation as an anthropologist of worldwide importance. The appearance of those two books, with the redirection of attention they implied for anthropology, has had a lasting effect in the discipline. The two works are closely related. *Totemism* uses structural methods to demolish a classic anthropological problem about savage thought. *The Savage Mind* broadens the approach adopted there to the entire field of the classifying activities of human-kind.

The problem of totemism had exercised the minds of many anthro-pological theorists throughout the nineteenth century. Why did some savages claim that they were parrots? Why did clans often have animal names? Many explanations had been given—from intellectual confusion to utilitarian considerations—but Lévi-Strauss dismisses them all for falsely isolating a problem. 'Totemism', in his view, is only one instance of what he terms 'concrete logic': the use by the human mind of con-crete codes for constructing systems of significance. Societies are always internally differentiated, whether it be into clans or any other units, and the differences between animal species are a perfect image of heterogen-eity provided by nature. The realm of nature, in other words, provides a perfect code for making statements about social divisions. Animal spe-cies are chosen, in Lévi-Strauss' words, not because they are 'good to eat' but because they are 'good to think'.

In *The Savage Mind* Lévi-Strauss continues this line of inquiry in setting out a 'logic of the concrete'. A time-honoured problem in anthro-pology has been: what, if any, are the differences between civilised and savage thought? Lévi-Strauss does not accept that the so-called savage is swamped by emotion, incapable of logical thought, or is irrational. In his view mankind has always thought equally well, in fact the so-called savage has a thirst for intellectual order and an extensive knowledge of nature, sometimes more exhaustive than the knowledge embedded in scientific taxonomies of the natural order. But reality can be appre-hended on more than one level. While we in advanced industrial cultures use scientific, technical, specialised thought and employ specialist lan-guages and theoretical concepts, the 'savage mind' works on a concrete level, taking from nature and using, over and over again, the same intel-lectual bric à brac to create systems of significance. From nature, the mind can utilise concrete sensory codes, employing simple logical oppo-sitions between, for instance, hot/cold, raw/cooked, clothed/naked, male/female, left/right, wet/dry, black/white, and so on, to create logically coherent and extremely complex intellectual systems.

The mythology of pre-industrial society may appear to be very strange, even arbitrary in its operations, but this is an illusion, quickly dispelled when one analyses the concrete codes employed in their con-struction. These mental operations are unspecialised, rather like the operations of a 'jack of all trades' rather than an engineer. This type of thought is found in all societies, so Lévi-Strauss' expression 'savage mind' does not refer to the mind of the savage (i.e. primitive, primeval) but to the mental functioning of all of us in our untrained, unconscious operations.

The Savage Mind was succeeded by Lévi-Strauss' largest undertaking: four volumes of myth analysis in which, taking hundreds of myths, largely from the Americas, Lévi-Strauss aimed to prove that, however chaotic mythology may appear, it has a simple underlying logic; indeed, a simple logical transformation allows one to pass from one myth to another constructed by another code. Order and logic, in other words, are everywhere, even in realms where the mind appears most free. At least at the commencement of this search, Lévi-Strauss even hoped that his results could be expressed in a kind of mathematical logic—an aspired-for precision which he later abandoned. In response to the accusation that Lévi-Strauss himself may simply be imposing his own logic on the mind of the savage, he rejects even the point of the criticism. He is dealing with the unconscious operations of the human mind, and at that level the thought processes of the savage and his own are identical. Indeed, for Lévi-Strauss, in a very real sense it is not even a matter of his projecting his ideas onto another, or of the other becoming intelligible through his analysis, for, as an anonymous, objectified thought system, myths quite literally think themselves out via the medium of the human brain.

For Lévi-Strauss, concrete thought is as true and as valid as any other. One reason for this is that the logical order evident in the construction of these systems is a direct expression of the fundamental structures of the human mind which in turn are manifestations of the structure of the human brain. Why can the brain create structures that are true? It is because the human brain itself is a product of the evolutionary laws of the universe and thus the orders of nature are already part of the make-up of the brain. In the last analysis, for Lévi-Strauss, this is all that the elaborate systems of significance amount to.

The laws of thought themselves can be reduced to physico-chemical laws, and thus the regularities of human culture can all be re-expressed as invariants established by the natural sciences. As he put it at the end of *The Savage Mind* in his debate with Sartre, the goal of anthropology is not to constitute man, but to dissolve him; the establishment of cultural universals is only a step along the way. A genuine anthropological science will study human beings as if they were ants. There is no ultimate meaning behind the orders of significance which humanity has built. In the long run, as he puts it at the end of *The Naked Man* (1972), the laws of entropy will ensure that the earth will again fall silent, as it was before the appearance of life; all the civilisations that man has created through his period on the planet will disappear. This is the distant, detached, analytical, atheistic—if one will, 'anti-human'—facet of structuralism.

What are we to make of a conception of anthropology that puts so much emphasis on logic, intellect and on the unconscious? Where are human history, feeling, the richness of social context and the intricacy of events? Where is human intentionality and experience? Is 'meaning' really merely the outcome of logical combinations of elementary bits?

Has linguistics not moved on significantly since the 1940s? Are the structures located by structural methodology 'real' or merely created by the operation of structural analysis itself? Can we accept a theory which is so universal in its aims and yet so completely unreflexive? Are the phenomena brought into prominence by structuralism of more importance than those omitted?

In evaluating Lévi-Strauss' work it is vital to remember what goals he set himself. For many years he was unfairly criticised, particularly by Anglo-Saxon anthropologists, who could not comprehend the basic ways in which he had redefined the scope and nature of anthropology. But before one can criticise someone, one has to know what they are attempting to do so as to avoid judging them by irrelevant criteria. Lévi-Strauss was not continuing the traditions of British or American anthropology, but launching a different project. In the 1990s we can call our period of intellectual history poststructuralist, just as we might wish to call it post-industrial and postmodern. Lévi-Strauss has fewer followers now than during the 1970s, but that does not undo the fact that his bold vision has had an unquestionable influence on the development of anthropology. Much of what we do nowadays would be unintelligible without the contribution of Lévi-Strauss.

In Australia, partly because Lévi-Strauss himself frequently illustrated problems with Aboriginal data, local writers have had to engage with his writings on myth, totemism and classification. But such engagement was mainly at the ethnographic level. During the 1960s and 1970s, many anthropologists in the UK, Europe and the US defined much of their work in relationship to structuralism. In some universities, indeed, whole departments were significantly influenced. In Australia, that fundamental level of theoretical engagement never took place, perhaps partly because theory as such has not been a central strength of anthropology written in this country.

BIBLIOGRAPHY

Primary sources

Lévi-Strauss, C. (1949) The Elementary Structures of Kinship London, Social Science Paperbacks, 1970
——(1955) Tristes Tropiques Harmondsworth, Penguin Books, 1976
——(1958) Structural Anthropology New York, Basic Books, 1963
——(1960) The Scope of Anthropology London, Cape Editions, 1967
——(1962a) The Savage Mind London, Weidenfeld & Nicholson, 1972
——(1962b) Totemism Harmondsworth, Penguin Books, 1973
——(1964) The Raw and the Cooked Chicago, University of Chicago Press, 1983
——(1966) From Honey to Ashes London, Cape, 1973

——(1968) *The Origin of Table Manners* New York, Harper and Row, 1978

——(1972) *The Naked Man* London, Cape, 1981

——(1973) *Structural Anthropology* Vol 2 New York, Basic Books, 1976

——(1978) *Myth and Meaning* New York, Schocken Books, 1979

——(1982) *The Way of Masks* London, Cape, 1982

——(1983) *The View from Afar* New York, Basic Books Inc, 1985

——(1984) *Anthropology and Myth, Lectures 1951–82* Oxford, Blackwell, 1987

——(1985) *The Jealous Potter* Chicago, University of Chicago Press, 1988

Secondary sources

Ardener, E. (1971) (ed.) *Social Anthropology and Language* London, Tavistock Publications

Austin-Broos, D. (1987) (ed.) *Creating Culture. Profiles in the Study of Culture* Sydney, Allen & Unwin

Badcock, C. R. (1975) *Lévi-Strauss: Structuralism and Sociological Theory* London, Hutchinson

Charbonnier, G. (1970) *Conversations with Claude Lévi-Strauss* London, Jonathan Cape

Clarke, S. (1981) *The Foundations of Structuralism: A Critique of Lévi-Strauss and the Structuralist Movement* Brighton, Harvester Press

Crick, M. (1976) *Explorations in Language and Meaning. Towards a Semantic Anthropology* London, Malaby Press

Glucksmann, M. (1974) *Structuralist Analysis in Contemporary Social Thought* London, Routledge & Kegan Paul

Hayes, E. N. and Hayes, T. (1970) (eds) *Claude Lévi-Strauss. The Anthropologist as Hero* Cambridge, Mass., MIT Press

Jenkins, A. (1979) *The Social Theory of Claude Lévi-Strauss* New York, St Martin's Press

Leach, E. (1974) *Lévi-Strauss* London, Fontana/Collins

——(1968) (ed.) *The Structural Study of Myth and Totemism* London, Tavistock Publications

Macksey, R. and Donato, E. (1972) (eds) *The Structuralist Controversy. The Languages of Criticism and the Sciences of Man* Baltimore, Johns Hopkins Press

Pace, D. (1983) *Claude Lévi-Strauss. The Bearer of Ashes* Boston, Routledge & Kegan Paul

Paz, O. (1971) *Claude Lévi-Strauss. An Introduction* London, Cape

Rossi, I. (1974) (ed.) *The Unconscious in Culture. The Structuralism of Claude Lévi-Strauss in Perspective* New York, E. P. Dutton & Co

Shalvey, T. (1979) *Claude Lévi-Strauss. Social Psychotherapy and the Collective Unconscious* Sussex, The Harvester Press

Skinner, Q. (1985) (ed.) *The Return of Grand Theory in the Human Sciences* London, Cambridge University Press

Sturrock, J. (1979) (ed.) *Structuralism and Since. From Lévi-Strauss to Derrida* London, Oxford University Press

PETER BEILHARZ

21

Karl Marx

One Marx, or many? Both, or all of the above. The work of Marx can be interpreted in various different ways, including the early romantic critique of the 'Paris Manuscripts', Marx the philosopher, the historical anthropology of *The German Ideology*, the critical history of the *Eighteenth Brumaire* or *The Civil War in France*, Marx the historian, the private brainstorming of *Grundrisse*, the later critical economy of *Capital*, Marx the economist, and so on. And there is a panoply of interpretations, and the subsequent 57 varieties of Marxism—Bolshevism, social democracy, Trotskyism, Maoism, critical theory, Western Marxism, council communism, and so forth—all of which pick up one theme or other in Marx's writing—too much to make sense of.

One way to argue the unity of Marx's thought, rather than its fragmentation and subsequent proliferation into various Marxes, is to read his project as possessing a single over-arching theme: the critique of political economy. Marx's theoretical work began as romantic critique, subsequently to become ensnared within political economy itself. It was only after Marx's death in 1883 that his work was to become widely influential, but in the truncated forms of propaganda developed by the Soviets in the east and in the models of society encouraged by professional sociologists in the West. Like Weber's thought, Marx's theory lost much of its critical impact in the hands of stratification theorists. But the trajectory of Marx's own theory was also one which became progressively less critical and more fully locked into the logic of industrialism.

THE PARIS MANUSCRIPTS

The question of the relationship between the young and the 'mature' Marx was a major motif in the Marx renaissance that spread from the 1960s on. It was not just a spectacle organised by publishers and academics. The fundamental question involved was whether Marx's theory was continuous or whether there was some kind of qualitative shift in his work. Whatever the continuity, the path of Marx's own work is one from *praxis* to structure, from action to system.

Marx set out in his *Paris Manuscripts*, published in German in 1932 and in English only in the 1960s, to put political economy to the test. Classical political economists such as Smith and Ricardo had recognised the central economic contribution which labour made to the production of wealth or value, but they would not give labour its proper place in politics or in society. Partly they did this by fudging the nature of the *process* of the production of wealth, as though property preceded labour, whereas property was actually the result of creative labour or *praxis*, the sensuous human activity through which humanity constituted itself. Labour thus expended its lifeblood in creating capital which (to use a later image) turned on labour like a vampire (Marx 1867: 245; 1844: 322–34). This critique of political economy took Marx to the philosophical critique of the division of labour. His early work echoes the German romantics, such as Schiller; the orientation is to cast backward, and to contrast a postulated image of humanity as a whole before industrialism, a species which does not know alienation, to its dismembered, dethroned condition under capitalism. Alienation, the division of humans and their individual subdivision: these only arrive with capitalist civilisation.

The undercurrent in this argument is the necessity of human or proletarian redemption, which Marx progressively redefines as he enters the labyrinth of economy itself. By redemption Marx imagines the simultaneous supersession of private property (capital) and the recovery of human integrity. The issue here is that while Marx chooses to identify human suffering as a central social and theoretical problem, he also ascribes a central status to labour as the suffering and redemptive agent. The bearer of socialism, Marx tells, is the proletariat, the 'last class'—he portrays it as a mythical actor, inserting a teleology in history but also imputing the historic task of socialism to a particular class, as though a general cause could be pursued by a particular agent (Marx 1844: 333–48). The image of socialism in Marx's early work is thus that of a society of craft-labourers. By *The German Ideology* Marx's image of the socialist future is closer to the Renaissance (Marx and Engels 1845: 47).

In *The German Ideology* Marx and Engels also began to address the question of ideology, criticising—ironically, given the privileging of the proletariat in their theory—the pretensions of the bourgeoisie that their own interests were the popular and general interests. In 1848 Marx and Engels published their most famous work, *The Communist Manifesto*, a brilliant polemic sketching one key dimension of Marx's project: the profoundly *ambivalent* assessment of capitalist civilisation, which made everything possible, as it were, and simultaneously denied humanity its

SOCIAL THEORY

potential for self-realisation. It was a brilliant achievement, anticipating Tönnies, Simmel, Seabrook and Berman, and drawing on inspiration such as Carlyle ('the cash nexus') and on Goethe's image of the sorcerer's apprentice. The bourgeoisie conjured up an economic spell of manic growth which it could not control; Marx simply sidestepped the question of whether this was a problem for which the proletariat was the solution.

The *Manifesto* also returned to the theme of history, discussed in *The German Ideology*. Here came the axiom that all history was the history of class struggle. For the young Marx, class struggle was the pivot; for the later Marx, it was class structure, labour and capital as formal categories. Here Marx planted the two-class model which sociologists and historians were later to seize upon and which also became concepts central to *Capital*. History was not merely the history of struggling classes—modern history was the titanic struggle between the two fundamental classes: bourgeoisie and proletariat.

THE GRUNDRISSE

Marx's shift from action to structure was politically determined by the defeat of the 1848 revolutions. If the world did not change, the obvious question was why not. How did it reproduce itself? (Korsch 1938: 114). This was to become the essential logic of *Capital*, a systems logic, an explanation of capitalist production, how it functioned and how it would allegedly dysfunction, collapse and inaugurate socialism. Marx's major transitional work here was the *Grundrisse*, the Notebooks for *Capital*. There are three major themes worth indicating here. First, in the '1857 Introduction' Marx discussed questions of epistemology and methodology (Marx 1857: 100–8). Marx's views were not novel, but his canvassing of the issues enabled the English readers of the *Grundrisse*, sometimes under the influence of Althusser, to begin to pose questions about claims to knowledge and premises of the construction of knowledge. Certainly the logic of Marx's approach was that knowledge is constructed and not 'discovered', and though Marx sometimes claimed the status of science for his work, this suggested that human science was a qualitatively different kind of endeavour to natural science. Thus Marx implicitly aligned his project back to Vico's proposition that humans know best that which is unique to them: human history itself.

This brings us to the second theme. Marx also discusses here the question of the transition from feudalism, in a passage much discussed in the *Science and Society* debate of the 1950s (Marx 1857: 471–98; Hilton 1976). The point here is less the content of Marx's views than the fact that his project was still governed by a sense of what apparently had happened in history; by *Capital*, history was marginalised, being introduced only into chapter 10. By *Capital*, then, Marx returned to his earlier sense that History was necessity, a necessary process leading from feudalism to capitalism to socialism rather than a contingent process in which masses of men and women *chose* socialism. This problem of automatism or teleology also underlines the third pertinent theme of the *Grundrisse*. In a passage picked up later by Marcuse (1964: 42), Marx shifted to the proposition that the technological revolution and not the class struggle might inaugurate socialism. The internal developmental logic of capitalism was such that automation would pull the rug out from under class relations (Marx 1857: 704–6). The agent of history again became mythologised: the actors were not the sensuous, suffering human beings who populated the pages of Marx's early work, but the forces of history, or now, of economy, and even technology.

The *Grundrisse* has left us some of the most fascinating evidence of Marx's intellectual process, that twenty-year long labour which eventually culminated in the final publication of *Capital* Volume One in 1867. In 1859, however, Marx published another signpost to *Capital*, his 1859 *Contribution to the Critique of Political Economy*. Partly because of the codification of Marxism by his followers into the twentieth century, the book was less frequently read than the preface was. It was in the 1859 *Preface* that Marx, in passing, offered a thumbnail sketch of his project: to find the secret of bourgeois society in political economy. This was necessary, Marx claimed, because economy was the fundamental determinant, upon which there arose a legal and political superstructure and definite forms of social consciousness. In broad outline, humanity progressed from Asiatic, ancient and feudal to bourgeois modes of production, as productive forces came into conflict with existing class relations (Marx 1859: 20–1). This relatively innocent sketch of an intellectual agenda subsequently became catechism for generations of socialists and communists: base-determined superstructure; explain economy and all else is explained; socialism is inevitable, and so on. Marx, for his own part, may not have subscribed to all these cliches, but he did provide elaborate reasons for viewing capitalism as the central phenomenon of modernity, simultaneously the agent of its own self-promotion and its own downfall.

CAPITAL

The culmination of Marx's science and of his mythology is *Capital*. Chapter 1, 'Commodities', is the most theoretically significant part of the work and also the most difficult. Marx provides a devastating critique of capitalist and utilitarian ethics. He sets the cue on the opening page of the 1859 *Contribution*, where he refers to Aristotle's *Politics*: a shoe is made for wearing, not for exchange—things have their own reasons for being, they are not commensurable. Yet commodification makes everything commensurable—two books are 'worth' one coat, four meals—everything, lamentably, has its price. Bourgeois society, in short, reduces human value to economic value, and it levels out the differences which ought to be characteristic of everyday life. Our labours disappear into things, which then come to dominate us, appear to precede us and, fetish-like, we fall into praise of this artificial world. Thus Marx begins the carefully constructed narrative of *Capital*, leading us from the surface or end of the process into the Dante's inferno of production.

The substance of the book concerns a critical analysis of capitalist production; it is, in a sense, a pioneering sociology of the modern factory. It is not a *history* of capitalism, although history is discussed—the history of labour legislation, primitive accumulation: the bloody emergence of capitalism via the enclosure acts—and it reappears in the penultimate chapter, where socialist revolution steps unexpectedly on the stage: negations are negated, the expropriators expropriated, etc. Here, at least, there is one element of continuity with the *Paris Manuscripts*: the inevitability of socialism as redemption is again asserted, and the struggle is still primarily that between the two fundamental classes and the concepts they represent—labour and capital. What, then, happens to the class struggle, which Marx earlier viewed as the central fact of history? One response would be that *Capital* is not a work of history, but of theory; but the obvious response would be, what happens to history in Marx's theory? Where have the actors gone? What has happened to the other classes? (Rundell 1987; Beilharz 1985). Such is the objection raised, in different ways, by Castoriadis and Touraine; and there are numerous other criticisms such as Pateman's refusal of Marx's category labour-power as disembodied. For if Marx, in a sense, leaves the class struggle out, he also leaves the sex struggle out (except that he makes one important point: capitalism as a system itself is indifferent to gender: it will happily exploit anyone and everyone).

Capital remains, in all, one of the most extraordinary of works in social theory. Its architecture is splendid, and its narrative compelling and replete with insight. Its difficulty, by contemporary standards, lies in its attempt to produce the proper general theory of capitalism. Consequently, everyday life and the world system, the endless peculiarities and complexities of particular experience, are left out. The obvious response to such criticism is that it is a general work, but this is to beg the question whether it is better to shift from the general to the particular or the other way round. Certainly the idea of discussing capital today outside the world system is less than persuasive. The more general issue remains, however, whether this is an economic theory or a social theory; whether a theory of capitalist production can claim to comprehend all that is social and cultural; whether, in plainer terms, life can be reduced to labour. Marx himself was no enthusiast for the centrality of economy—he directed the first chapter of *Capital* against it. Yet he also came to accept industrialism as fate, and to reconstruct his image of socialism in the grey colours of the city rather than the shades of the countryside. At the same time, his longing was always for the past, as well as the future (Prawer 1978). In terms of social theory, he is arguably still best read as a critic of capitalist culture rather than as a system builder for, like Weber, Nietzsche and Freud, he was nothing if not critical.

Marx's reception has been complicated, in Australia as elsewhere, both by his political and scholarly followers. Marxism has a long tradition of influence through the labour movement. With the expansion and radicalisation of the tertiary education system into the 1960s, Marcuse (and Gramsci) became popular, along with the writings of the young Marx. Marxism became influential in sociology via the work of Connell and Irving (1980), via Habermas in Theophanous (1980) and Frankel (1983) and Pusey (1991), via Althusser in cultural studies and political economy, as well as through the influence of Europeans and North Americans such as Braverman (1974), Mandel (1975) and Carchedi (1977). Enthusiasm for Marx's early works was also fuelled by the Australian sojourn of Agnes Heller. We are left with a situation in which, thanks to postmodernism, Marx is not even read to be 'forgotten' let alone remembered. This is unfortunate, because the end of Marx's own grand narrative also represents a potential beginning for many smaller, more local stories which remain to be told, heard, argued about and acted upon.

BIBLIOGRAPHY

Primary sources

Marx, K. (1844) 'Paris Manuscripts', in L. Colletti (ed.) *Marx—Early Writings* Harmondsworth, Penguin, 1975
——(1857–58) *Grundrisse* Harmondsworth, Penguin, 1973
——(1859) *A Contribution to the Critique of Political Economy* Moscow, Progress, 1970
——(1867) *Capital* Volume One, Moscow, Progress n.d.
——and Engels, F. (1845) *The German Ideology*, in Marx-Engels *Collected Works* London, Lawrence and Wishart, 1976, Volume 5
———(1848) *The Communist Manifesto* (any edition)

Secondary sources

Beilharz, P. (1985) 'Theorizing the Middle Class' *Arena* 72
Berki, R. N. (1983) *Insight and Vision. The Problem of Communism in Marx's Thought* London, Dent

173

Berman, M. (1982) *All That Is Solid Melts Into Air* New York, Simon and Schuster

Braverman, H. (1974) *Labor and Monopoly Capital* New York, Monthly Review

Carchedi, D. (1977) *On the Economic Identification of Social Classes* London, Routledge

Connell, R. and Irving, T. (1980) *Class Structure in Australian History* Melbourne, Longman Cheshire

Frankel, B. (1983) *Beyond the State?* London, Macmillan

Hilton, R. (1976) *Transition from Feudalism to Capitalism* London, New Left Books

Kolakowski, L. (1978) *Main Currents of Marxism* 3 volumes, Oxford, Oxford University Press

Korsch, K. (1938) *Karl Marx* New York, Russell and Russell

Lowith, K. (1982) *Max Weber and Karl Marx* London, Allen & Unwin

Mandel, E. (1975) *Late Capitalism* London, New Left Books

Marcuse, H. (1964) *One Dimensional Man* London, Sphere

Prawer, S. (1978) *Karl Marx and World Literature* Oxford, Oxford University Press

Pusey, M. (1991) *Economic Rationalism in Canberra* Cambridge University Press

Rundell, J. (1987) *Origins of Modernity. The Origins of Modern Social Theory from Kant to Hegel to Marx* Cambridge, Polity

Theophanous, A. (1980) *Australian Democracy in Crisis* Melbourne, Oxford University Press

PAUL RAYMOND HARRISON

22

Friedrich Nietzsche

The work of Friedrich Nietzsche (1844–1900) has returned to the centre of philosophical and sociological attention over the past two decades. Nietzsche always retained a philosophical presence due to the influence of Heidegger's preoccupation with Nietzsche's place in the history of Western metaphysics. Furthermore, Nietzsche always maintained a sociological presence through the reception of several of his ideas by Max Weber. However, Nietzsche's subterranean influence on both philosophy and sociology probably served more to block the path back to a more direct appropriation of Nietzsche's thought.

There were, of course, political reasons for being content with the repression of Nietzsche's thought, especially in the postwar context of a return to liberal democracy and a faith in the rationality of history. This postwar optimism is now gone and Nietzsche's return arrives at the beginning of several ends. The sense of an end has emerged over the past two decades: in social theory there is talk of an end to modernity; in politics of an end to history; in the arts of an end to modernism; and in philosophy of an end to philosophy or, at least, a particular kind of philosophy. In this context there is a return to a Nietzsche as a thinker of *endings*.

POWER AND DISSIMULATION

The two most important receptions of Nietzsche's work in recent times have both occurred in the context of what is conventionally called French poststructuralist thought; that is, in the context of another ending, that of structuralism. In the work of Foucault it has been the Nietzschean concept of genealogy which has received attention. A genealogy traces the contingent emergence of discourses out of relations of force and power which govern their production. In Foucault's thought, Nietzsche is received essentially as a thinker of *power*. In the work of

Derrida it has been the Nietzschean deconstruction of the idea of truth and the history of metaphysics that has received attention. Here again it is the contingent nature of metaphysical ideas which is emphasised, but in the thought of Derrida the implication of this idea leads to the reception of Nietzsche as a thinker of *dissimulation*.

These two receptions of Nietzsche's thought correspond to a distinction that can be drawn in Nietzsche's thought between its culture-critical dimension, which has very strong implications for social theory, and its metaphysical dimension, which is of more relevance to the situation of post-metaphysical thought. In the thought of Nietzsche these two dimensions are united in the concept of power. Power appears in Nietzsche's culture-critical works as that which lies behind the emergence of those 'ideal interests' which are the generative matrices of *cultural complexes*, whereas in his more metaphysical works power as *will-to-power* appears as the principle of all cultural creativity as such. In other words, the notion of power functions to unmask culture either as a product of the non-cultural or as a charismatically governed, aesthetico-poetic force which lies behind all existence.

POWER AND CULTURE

Nietzsche's earliest writings are mainly concerned with classical Greek culture. What concerns him most is the simultaneous emergence of both philosophy and tragedy. In *Philosophy in the Tragic Age of the Greeks* (1873b) Nietzsche presents Greek philosophy as coming to an end with Socrates. The cosmos-philosophy of the pre-Socratics had reached its high point in the thought of Anaxagoras, according to Nietzsche, with the discovery that becoming is an aesthetic phenomenon. In the *Birth of Tragedy and the Case of Wagner* (1872) Nietzsche presents to us the Dionysian 'substratum' underlying the Apollonian form of Greek tragedy. For Nietzsche, therefore, tragedy is not so much the product of culture, but a product of those 'art impulses of nature' which lie beneath culture. This idea leads to his celebrated dictum that it is only as an *aesthetic phenomenon* that existence is justified.

Greek tragedy meets its end in the same way as Greek philosophy— through Socrates. Socrates as the representative of theoretical knowledge destroys the creativity of those two cultural forms by destroying their connection to the natural through reflection. As Nietzsche puts it in the *Twilight of the Idols and the Anti-Christ* (1888), Socrates represents the plebeian against the strong, unreflective culture of the aristocracy that once ruled the polis. What we see here, therefore, is both an attempt to ground culture in forces which are non-cultural (that is, a naturalisation of cultural creativity); and an attempt to ground culture in its most unreflective forms such as custom (that is, a de-intellectualisation of cultural creativity). These two themes are a constant in Nietzsche's thought, even though they undergo many variations.

With regard to monotheistic cultural complexes such as Judaism and Christianity, Nietzsche's criticism is even more devastating. Unlike polytheism with its 'plurality of norms', as Nietzsche puts it in the *Gay Science* (1882, 1887), monotheism is 'monotono-theism'; that is, it represents a vast diminution of social and cultural creativity. In *On the Genealogy of Morals and Ecce Homo* (1887) Nietzsche continues his attempt at a non-theological, natural history of morals in relation to the emergence of the distinctions between good and bad and good and evil. The affirmative morality of the noble operates with the distinction between good and bad, while the morality of resentment of the slave operates with the distinction between good and evil.

The characterisation of certain instincts as evil, as opposed to merely natural, results in the turning of the instincts against themselves and in the emergence of 'bad conscience'. Instead of the open affirmation of the instinctual, there occurs the turning of the instincts against themselves in Christianity. Nietzsche then traces the emergence of the 'ascetic ideals' of poverty, humility and chastity from early Christianity to modern science. Science is, for Nietzsche, the latest form of the ascetic ideal and as such is essentially reactive. In the face of the scientific fact, Nietzsche postulates the plurality of *interpretation*; and in the face of science's will to truth, the value-creating power of art. Christianity as a cultural complex is, therefore, one which results in a reduction of cultural creativity through the emasculation of those instinctual forces and powers which are culture-creating. Nietzsche's identification of these reactive forces with the power interests of the lower classes leads on to his critique of the political form of modern society: democracy.

Throughout his writings Nietzsche was concerned with the culture of modernity. As a result of his power-theoretical standpoint, however, Nietzsche's treatment of modern culture is reductionist. Modern culture is judged to have become inimical to life and to the instincts from the Renaissance on, with the partial exception of the seventeenth century, due to the influence of such forces as the Enlightenment, romanticism, democracy, utilitarianism, science and socialism. These forces represent a domestication of power in an increasingly universalistic culture. The result is a culture that loses its belief in its ability to create and to value, the culture of *fin-de-siècle* European nihilism. In his early text 'On the Use and Abuse of History for Life' in *Untimely Meditations* (1874) Nietzsche argues against the scientisation of history in modernity because it robs history of any relation to life. He makes a plea for forgetting (the *unhistorical*) and for art and religion (the *suprahistorical*).

Nietzsche's most penetrating dissection of modern nihilism occurs in his notebooks which were partially published in book form after his death in the *Will to Power* (1901). For Nietzsche, nihilism is the condition where 'the highest values devaluate themselves'. In relation to Western culture this means, first of all, as Nietzsche announces in *Thus Spake Zarathustra. A Book for Everyone and No One* (1883–86), the death of God. Nihilism is, in short, our 'postmodern condition' as it is the end of all meta-narratives. Yet, what is to be done given this condition? In one note from 1888 Nietzsche observes the ambivalence of the phenomenon of nihilism by carefully distinguishing between passive and active nihilism. Passive nihilism reacts to this situation by eschewing all prospect of positing goals and creating anew, whereas active nihilism reacts to it by an act of self-assertion or overcoming. It is on this theoretical foundation that Nietzsche fashioned his doctrine of the overman (*Uebermensch*). Modern culture's domestication of power through the religio-cultural complex is to be broken.

POWER AND TRUTH

Nietzsche's thought is also a genealogy of the *will to knowledge*. More specifically, it is a critique of the will to knowledge embedded in the greco-occidental tradition which has resulted in the development not only of modern philosophy, but of modern science. In his early essay 'On Truth and Lies in a Nonmoral Sense' Nietzsche deconstructs the logic of identity which informs our modern notions of the concept, truth and the subject (1873a). Nietzsche criticises the modern idea of the concept for its suppression of the non-identical; the notion of truth for its denial of the metaphorical origins of truth; and the notion of the subject as self-consciousness for forgetting the artistic and creative nature of the subject.

In the later works where the power-theoretical framework comes to the fore, it is not so much the multiple and dissimulatory nature of truth which is emphasised, but that 'the criterion of truth lies in the enhancement of the feeling of power'. However, this biological foundation to power and this power-theoretical undermining of truth does not totally exclude the earlier perspective. Instead, it reappears in the notion of *interpretation*. In the *Genealogy of Morals* Nietzsche opposes the absolute, metaphysical value placed on the will to truth with a notion of interpretation that allows for dissimulation. In *Beyond Good and Evil: Prelude to a Philosophy of the Future* (1886) he argues that physics is simply just an interpretation of the world, rather than an explanation for it. In short, as Feyerabend would put it, 'anything goes'.

In the *Twilight of the Idols* Nietzsche presents us with the genealogy of the onto-theological concept of truth. According to Nietzsche our concept of reason is embedded in the spontaneous metaphysics of Indo-European languages, hence his celebrated dictum that 'we are not getting rid of God because we still believe in grammar'. Instead of remaining content with the apparent world as the only world, we have invented a higher world as the cause and truth of this world. Hence, greco-occidental thought reaches its height with the pre-Socratics and begins it downfall with Plato.

It is significant that Nietzsche praises nineteenth-century positivism for beginning the breakdown of this idea, for in many ways Nietzsche's power-theoretical reductionism is a version of nineteenth-century positivism. However, as mentioned earlier, the notion of power escapes from its positivist background in Nietzsche's thought and becomes, as will-to-power, a charismatically governed (the doctrine of the overman), bio-aesthetic force. In sum, the notions of life and power provide Nietzsche with a biological basis for creativity which replaces the earlier natural philosophical basis.

NIHILISM AND THE POSTMODERN CONDITION

In the thought of Nietzsche the grand narrative whose end inaugurates the postmodern conditions is Christianity. From the beginning of the sixteenth century, modernity and Christianity had proved difficult but not incompatible partners. It is only in late nineteenth- and early twentieth-century thought that the split becomes irrevocable. The death of God brings with it the end of the cosmological correlate of the idea of God; namely, divine providence. In its place Nietzsche posits the overman and its cosmological correlate; namely, a world with no end, a world of *eternal recurrence*.

The task of thought in this situation is not to succumb to a passive nihilism which is the result of thinking that now that the moral interpretation of the world has come to an end, all interpretation must come to an end. The task of thought is to develop an active nihilism which is both ironical and creative, which both posits new values and multiplies new interpretations. Nietzsche is a thinker of endings, and this should be understood first and foremost in terms of the ending of the Christian world-interpretation with all its social, psychical and philosophical correlates. It must also be added that Nietzsche, through his notions of interpretation and eternal recurrence, is a thinker of a world horizon without endings.

BIBLIOGRAPHY

Nietzsche, F. (1872) *The Birth of Tragedy and The Case of Wagner* New York, Vintage Books, 1967
——(1873a) 'On truth and lies in a nonmoral sense', in *Philosophy and Truth: Selections from Nietzsche's Notebooks of the Early 1870s* Atlantic Highlands, Humanities Press, 1979
——(1873b) *Philosophy in the Tragic Age of the Greeks* Chicago, Henry Regnery, 1962

——(1874) *Untimely Meditations* Cambridge, Cambridge University Press, 1983

——(1882, 1887) *The Gay Science* New York, Vintage Books, 1974

——(1883–86) *Thus Spake Zarathustra. A Book for Everyone and No One* Harmondsworth, Penguin, 1961

——(1886) *Beyond Good and Evil: Prelude to a Philosophy of the Future* Harmondsworth, Penguin, 1973

——(1887) *On the Genealogy of Morals and Ecce Homo* New York, Vintage Books, 1969

——(1888) *Twilight of the Idols and the Anti-Christ* Harmondsworth, Penguin, 1968

——(1901) *The Will to Power* New York, Vintage Books, 1968

23

Talcott Parsons

Talcott Parsons was born in Colorado in 1902, the son of a Congrega-tionalist minister and teacher, interested in 'the social gospel'. He was an outstanding student in both his senior school in New York and Amherst College, Massachusetts, where the foundations were laid for his later interests in biology, philosophy, economics and sociology (Wearne 1989). After a year at the London School of Economics he went to Heidelberg, where Max Weber was still a major influence, and a principal figure from then on in Parsons' life work. He joined Harvard University in 1927, and stayed until his retirement in 1973. *The Structure of Social Action* (1937) established him as a leading sociological theorist, and his work in the 1940s brought him wide recognition. His bibliography finally included over 270 items (Parsons 1978). His great influence probably peaked in the 1950s, but he continued to develop 'the theory of action' until his death on a lecturing visit to Munich in 1979. His work was enjoying a major revival in Germany at that time.

THE THEORY OF ACTION

In social science Parsons is unsurpassed in the sustained elaboration of a theoretical scheme—'the theory of action.' Although many work in this field (see Inkeles and Barber 1973; Loubser et al. 1976) it remains largely identified with him. His first great work, *The Structure of Social Action*, aimed to demonstrate that four outstanding theorists of the turn of the century were not in disparate 'schools', but converging on one funda-mental scheme. Three of them were economists but all had faced up to the non-rational aspects of economic activity. The great English econ-omist, Marshall, had insisted that the most important outcome of econ-omic behaviour was character formation, and not consumer satisfaction. Pareto, the leading Italian economist–sociologist, gave a crucial place to non-logical, as opposed to illogical factors in social life. Durkheim had

SOCIAL THEORY

challenged Spencer's conception of individual contracts as the basis of
society by pointing to the institution of contract which inserted the
'non-contractual elements' into all particular contracts, through law and
custom. Parsons was so taken with Weber's thesis—that the Puritan
social ethic accelerated Europe's transition from traditional society to
modern capitalism (Weber 1904–5)—that he translated it into English in
1930, and remained closely interested in it.

Aspects of the ancient opposition between materialism and idealism
came to a head in their works, in various forms of positivism and
idealism which Parsons codified and reconciled in his 'voluntaristic
theory of action' (1937: 77–82). 'Action' was behaviour with a subjective
aspect of 'effort' intended to bring situational conditions, or 'matters of
fact', nearer to a normatively defined, or 'ideal' state of affairs.

In the positivistic tradition the 'Hobbesian problem of order' had
arisen through Hobbes' misprizing of normative regulation. As individuals naturally competed to satisfy their passions, which their reason
merely served, force and fraud became the most efficient means to their
ends, and the only solution to the resulting 'war of all against all' was to
eliminate individual freedom by a coercive authority conceived as an
external, factual source of order.

Similarly, in the idealist tradition, the guiding 'spirit' of nation, folk,
age, law or religion had effectively determined social life, and deprived
'the subjective point of view of the actor' of all theoretical significance.
But the relation of action to both facts and values was best expressed by
'orientation to', not 'determined by' as the actor had invariably to decide
between alternative possible acts.

THE SOCIAL SYSTEM

In 1949–50 Parsons convened a group of nine who produced *Toward a
General Theory of Action* (Parsons and Shils 1951). Its major monograph,
'Values, Motives and Systems of Action', presented the general action
system as comprising three independent but interpenetrating systems,
the social, the personality and the cultural systems, giving a chapter to
each. At the same time, Parsons published his own version of the social
system chapter, twelve times longer, as *The Social System* (1951). While
this was 'a theory of systems', he pointed out that between 1937 and
1951 'no fundamental change has been made' in the action frame of
reference (1951: 8 n.4).

The first half of this work built up the institutional structure of an
ideal-type social system, 'deductively' from the basic concepts of action
theory. The second half analysed the principal social processes involved
in the states of equilibrium and change: socialisation, deviance, social
control, the nature of systems of ideas and beliefs, and of expressive
symbolism, and social change. This apparatus was applied in chapter X,

'Social Structure and Dynamic Process: The Case of Modern Medical Practice', which is perhaps his most widely known analysis.

The key concept of this stage of Parsons' theorising was 'value-orientation'. Regularities of choice between basic ways of relating to people formed 'patterns of value-orientation' which were a major part of the cultural system. The patterns came out of a matrix of five dichotomous choices called 'the pattern variables'. These patterns of choices became part of the personality system through internalisation, and part of the social system through institutionalisation. Parsons emphasised that 'This integration of common value-patterns with the internalized need-disposition structure of the constituent personalities is the core phenomenon of the dynamics of social systems' (1951: 42).

STRUCTURAL FUNCTIONALISM

At this time Parsons believed that the most appropriate methodology was that of 'structural functionalism', although this was only 'a second best type of theory' (1951: 20). An adequate theory of dynamic process was not available, he argued, but it was possible to analyse regularities in relationships which could be treated as 'structure'. The notion of 'function' served to keep constantly in view what any part of the structure contributed to the system being analysed, that is, what function it served in the system. He regretted being labelled 'a structural functionalist', as he wished to keep function, as an explanatory term, separate from the descriptive pair, structure and process (Parsons 1975: 100–17). While the three terms were essential, the dominance of 'function' became apparent with the next stage of his theorising.

THE FOUR-FUNCTION PARADIGM

Every action system faced four functional problems in seeking to persist. Parsons developed this idea with Robert F. Bales who was working on 'interaction process analysis' with small problem-solving groups. Group tasks entailed adapting to the given environment and submitting to the discipline of instrumental activity. As these efforts generated tensions in the group, action shifted from an instrumental–adaptive to an expressive–integrative dimension (Bales 1950). Parsons used his pattern-variables to analyse the Bales cycle as a series of four problems, classified by their function for the group: Adaptation to the given environment; Goal-gratification (or Goal-attainment, including matters of group policy, later); Integration of the group as a social system; and pattern-maintenance, as concern for the Latent value-pattern or deep structure of the group (Parsons, Bales and Shils 1953: chs 3, 5). Known from then on by its initial letters, AGIL, the four-function paradigm became the foundation of all subsequent Parsonian theory.

With Bales, Parsons then used the paradigm to revise, in effect, the personality system chapter of the 1951 Parsons–Shils monograph (Parsons and Shils 1951: part 2, ch.2), emphasising now the 'input–output' relations between systems and sub-systems, conceived in terms of the four AGIL functions (Parsons and Bales 1955).

ECONOMY AND SOCIETY

Parsons developed the paradigm further, with Neil J. Smelser, to demonstrate that economic activity should not be treated as uniquely rational behaviour in a theoretically random environment, as if only economics could be a social science (*Economy and Society* 1956). Economic activity was social activity, and part of society as a social system. A society faced the four functional problems. The economy was the Adaptive sub-system, organising society's gaining of a living in its environment; the polity specialised in Goal-attainment, through 'governments' both public and private; the Integrative sub-system was later named more descriptively the societal community; and the Latent-Pattern-Maintenance sub-system, called later the fiduciary system, was responsible for the stabilisation of the value-patterns which constituted the character of the society (1956: 16–29).

In a developed society, the relations between the economy and the other three sub-systems were mediated by money. Money had no use-value, but only a conventional meaning of exchange-value. In effect, 'money talked'. The recognition of money as a language, or as the 'symbolic generalised medium of interchange' of the economy, prompted the search for the media anchored in the other three sub-systems.

THEORIES OF SOCIETY

Theories of Society (Parsons, Shils, Naegle and Pitts 1961) stands near the middle of Parsons' long theoretical development. He had rejected nineteenth-century evolutionism, avoided biological reductionism and treated classical physics as a scientific model, but he now proposed an evolutionary social theory linked to modern biology (pp 32, 40 n.12, 89–91). Excerpts from the works of some hundred authors, principally nineteenth- and twentieth-century, were organised in terms of their contributions to the revised components of the general action system.

The four-function paradigm had led to a fourth system, as a sub-system of the general action system, and the four were organised into a 'cybernetic hierarchy', with superior-subordinate relations modified by 'feed-back' up the levels. The hierarchical order was down through LIGA, with the cultural system's value-patterns (L) controlling the social system's norms (I), controlling the personality system's motives (G), which controlled the new system, the behavioural organisms's (later, system's) relations with the physical environment (A).

THE GENERALISED SYMBOLIC MEDIA OF INTERCHANGE

The search for the three further generalised media of the social system was completed by using money, the economy's (A) 'language', as a model. These were: political power, anchored in the polity (G); influence in the societal community (I); and value-commitments in the Latent-Pattern Maintenance (later, fiduciary system, L) (Parsons 1963a, 1963b, 1968). With this he had worked out the functional differentiation and the main structure and processes of the social system.

THE EVOLUTION OF SOCIETY

In 1937 Parsons rejected positivistic 'linear evolutionism', with either its inevitable progress through science, or its biologically driven natural selection (1937: 122–4). The theory of action called for an active, not a passive adaptation. It entailed the active transformation of the environment, against resistance, in order to realise human values. Human effort affected the complex balance of factors inhibiting and facilitating evolutionary change, and the increasing rationalisation of social systems was an uneven, not a mechanical process.

When the key evolutionary concept of adaption entered the four-function paradigm it was contrasted with goal-attainment (G). The latter entailed specific goal states, while adaptation (A) fulfilled 'a *generalised* interest in establishing and improving control over the situation in various respects' (Parsons and Smelser 1956: 18). Parsons' version of evolutionary adaptation was to be both active and generalised.

A specific concern with comparative and evolutionary perspectives reappeared with Parsons' historical review of social science in *Theories of Society* (Parsons et al. 1961: 89–91, 240–1, 985–8), and was developed over the next decade (1961, 1966, 1971). Social evolution proceeded through the master process of differentiation and integration. Structural differentiations arose with the potential for enhancing the social system's 'adaptive capacity.' They survived to the extent that they were integrated, through institutionalisation, in a process analogous to natural selection, and resulted in the 'adaptive upgrading' of the system (1966: 21–6; 1975: 112–14). The latest, post-Weber, adaptive upgrading of the West had come with the educational revolution, equal in significance to the industrial and democratic revolutions (1971: 97–8).

THE AMERICAN UNIVERSITY AND THE PROFESSIONS

With *The American University* (Parsons and Platt 1973), his work reached its sociological, as distinct from 'general action', culmination.

SOCIAL THEORY

He presented an ideal type of the university as the powerhouse of 'cognitive culture'. Academic professionalism based on graduate training and research was 'the core of the modern academic system' (ch.3 and p. 110). Higher education, including research, had become, in his view, 'the most critical feature of modern society' (p. vi).

He had long believed that the professional was the type-case of fiduciary role: '. . . trained in and integrated with, a distinctive part of our cultural tradition, having a fiduciary responsibility for its maintenance, development and implementation' (1952: 381). This line of thought came to fruition in *The American University* with the focus on society's Latent-Pattern-Maintenance sub-system (L) as the fiduciary system (Parsons and Platt 1973: 19, 20, 426, 428). As a vital part of that system, the university was effectively society's agent for the maintenance, development and implementation of the Western rational tradition.

THE HUMAN CONDITION

There were two final collections of papers. The first, *Social Systems and the Evolution of Action Theory* (1977), included Parsons' intellectual autobiography and other retrospective papers. The last, *Action Theory and the Human Condition* (1978), provided new developments at the general theory level. At this level, the four systems, cultural, social, personality and behavioural, had long had 'beneath' them the physical-organic environment, and ultimate reality 'above' them (Parsons 1966: 28). In his last years Parsons pursued these two 'outside' environments of the action system.

While so far the general action level had been the highest, a higher one, called the human condition system, was now introduced, in which the general action system was only one of its four sub-systems. The previous 'upper' environment of ultimate reality became the telic system (purposive, from 'teleological') as the L sub-system of the human condition. The (general) action system occupied the position of the I sub-system; the human organic system formed the G sub-system; and the 'lower' physical-organic environment became the physico-chemical system, with the Adaptive function, A.

The human condition, as the ultimate system in Parsonian theory, was '. . . a version of whatever universe may in some sense be knowable' (1978: 382). This echo of Spencer's dichotomy of the knowable and the unknowable casts Parsons' work in the scientific tradition of increasing the knowable. In these last major essays he brought this tradition to bear on Kant and his concept of the unknowable, the *Ding an sich*.

Parsons' whole theoretical effort can be seen as an attempt to rescue the 'non-empirical'—the rejected residual category of positivist thought—from its inferior status in a scientific culture. Even in 'idealistic' Germany Weber had to introduce 'The *Spirit* of Capitalism' as '. . .

the somewhat pretentious phrase' in Parsons' 1930 translation (Weber 1904–5: 47). It is Parsons' achievement that, in integrating the two great Western traditions of positivism and idealism, he provided social science with a most impressive alternative to their mutual rejection.

BIBLIOGRAPHY

Primary Sources

Parsons, T. (1937) *The Structure of Social Action* 2 vols. New York, Free Press, 1968

——(1939) 'The Professions and Social Structure' Reprinted in 1954

——(1951) *The Social System* New York, Free Press

——(1952) 'A sociologist looks at the legal profession' Reprinted in 1954

——(1954) *Essays in Sociological Theory* rev. ed., New York, Free Press

——(1960) *Structure and Process in Modern Societies* New York, Free Press

——(1961) 'Evolutionary Universals in Society' Reprinted in 1967

——(1963a) 'On the Concept of Influence' Reprinted in 1969

——(1963b) On the Concept of Political Power' Reprinted in 1969

——(1966) *Societies: Evolutionary and Comparative Perspectives* Englewood Cliffs, NJ, Prentice-Hall

——(1967) *Sociological Theory and Modern Society* New York, Free Press

——(1968) 'On the Concept of Value-Commitments' Reprinted in 1969

——(1969) *Politics and Social Structure* New York, Free Press

——(1971) *The System of Modern Societies* Englewood Cliffs, NJ, Prentice-Hall

——(1975) 'The Present Status of Structural-Functional Theory in Sociology' Reprinted in 1977

——(1977) *Social Systems and the Evolution of Action Theory* New York, Free Press

——(1978) *Action Theory and the Human Condition* New York, Free Press

——and Bales, R.F. (1955) *Family: Socialisation and Interaction Process* New York, Free Press

————and Shils, E.A. (1953) *Working Papers in the Theory of Action* New York, Free Press

——and Platt, G.M. (1973) *The American University* Cambridge, Mass., Harvard University Press

——and Shils, E.A. (1951) (eds) *Toward a General Theory of Action* Cambridge, Mass., Harvard University Press

————Naegle, K.D. and Pitts, J.R. (1961) (eds) *Theories of Society: Foundations of Modern Sociological Theory* New York, Free Press

—and Smelser, N.J. (1956) *Economy and Society*, London, Routledge & Kegan Paul; New York, Free Press

—and Platt, G.M. (1973) *The American University* Cambridge, Mass., Harvard University Press

Secondary sources

Alexander, J.C. (1983) *Theoretical Logic in Sociology* Vol 4: *The Modern Reconstruction of Classical Thought: Talcott Parsons* Los Angeles, University of California Press

Bales, R.F. (1950) *Interaction Process Analysis: A Method for the Study of Small Groups* Cambridge, Mass., Addison-Wesley

Black, M. (1961) *The Social Theories of Talcott Parsons: A Critical Examination* Englewood Cliffs, NJ, Prentice-Hall

Grathoff, R. (1978) (ed.) *The Theory of Social Action: The Correspondence of Alfred Schutz and Talcott Parsons* Bloomington, Indiana University Press

Habermas, J. (1981) *The Theory of Communicative Action Vol 2: Lifeworld and System: A Critique of Functionalist Reason.* Trans. by Thomas McCarthy. Boston, Beacon Press, 1987.

Inkeles, A. and Barber, B. (1973) (eds) *Stability and Social Change* Boston, Little, Brown

Lockwood, D. (1956) 'Some remarks on "The Social System" ' *British Journal of Sociology* 7(2): 134–46

Loubser, J.J., Baum, C.R., Effrat, A. and Lidz, V.M. (1976) (eds) *Explorations in General Theory in Social Science: Essays in Honor of Talcott Parsons* New York, Free Press

Martindale, D. (1960) *The Nature and Types of Sociological Theory* Boston, Houghton Mifflin

Mills, C.W (1959) *The Sociological Imagination* New York, Oxford University Press

Mŭnch, R. (1987) *Theory of Action: Towards a New Synthesis Going Beyond Parsons* London, Routledge & Kegan Paul

Spencer, H. (1862) *First Principles* London, Williams and Norgate, 1908

Wearne, B.C. (1989) *The Theory and Scholarship of Talcott Parsons to 1951: A Critical Commentary* Cambridge, Cambridge University Press

Weber, M. (1904–5) *The Protestant Ethic and the Spirit of Capitalism.* Trans. by Talcott Parsons. London, Allen & Unwin, 1930

24

Carole Pateman

Carole Pateman is a British political theorist who entered academe as a mature-age student through Ruskin Hall, Oxford University. Her first book, *Participation and Democratic Theory* (1970), established her reputation as a serious political theorist and critic of liberal democratic theory. This book was written and published in Britain. Pateman's first tenured academic post was in the Department of Government, University of Sydney, and she spent over a decade in Sydney where she established an active relationship with feminist theory and the Australian women's movement. In 1990, Pateman took up a full professorship in political science at the Los Angeles campus of the University of California. Also in 1990, she was the executive's nominee for president of the International Political Science Association. This honour confirmed within the political science profession both her stature and the significance of her book, *The Sexual Contract*, published in 1988.

Pateman's work is that of a democratic theorist oriented within Anglo-American literature and theorising. Her work represents a sustained critique of the dominant ideology of liberal contractualism. Notwithstanding the dominant representation of democracy in terms of liberal contractualism, Pateman has argued that this is an undemocratic conception of the political community.

Pateman's critique of liberal contractualism takes the form of three interconnected arguments (although she herself does not systematise these interconnections and the general critique of which they are part). The first argument is a critique of the liberal equation of freedom with the social contract and the kind of political obligation established through the social contract. The second argument is a critique of how liberal constructions of democracy authorise elitist and authoritarian modes of governance which pre-empt the participatory involvement of citizens within both politics and employment. The third argument is a critique of the way in which the modern social contract entails a distinctively modern form of patriarchy whereby women are subjected to the mastery of men as freely contracting property owners.

One of the central themes of Pateman's work concerns how modern contractualism does not express or guarantee the freedom of the contracting parties, but entails their exchange of obedience for protection. While this is a specific critique of the marriage and employment contracts (see 1988, chs 3 and 5) in relation to the respective statuses of wives and workers, it is a general point about the nature of the social contract. In *The Problem of Political Obligation* (1979), Pateman shows that the central line of liberal reasoning as to why individual private proprietors 'in the state of nature' agree to enter a social contract whereby they establish a public authority or government over themselves concerns prudential or utilitarian grounds for this agreement. Her point is that it is not the principle of free agreement—consent—which grounds the type of government established through the fictional mechanism of the social contract. Instead it is the instrumental principle of obtaining from such government protection for the private property rights of the individuals concerned.

In effect, this is an exchange of freedom for subjection to a statist form of the political community. Since the contract becomes a device for establishing this exchange of obedience for protection, Pateman insists that it has nothing to do with the freely assumed obligation of promising. Promising involves the consensual assumption of social ties and responsibilities where their basis depends on reciprocal relations of trust. Here Pateman indicates something of her own democratic utopian vision, one which mixes together the republican democratic tradition's emphasis on participation with anarcho-syndicalist emphases on non-statist, voluntarily maintained associations based on trust. Hers is a vision of multiple horizontal political relationships counterposed to the hierarchical relations of the liberal state: 'The members of the community are citizens in many political associations, which are bound together through horizontal and multifaceted ties of self-assumed political obligation' (1979: 174).

This is an argument which depends on an immanent critique of liberal contractualism, i.e. one which shows that the very terms of the liberal argument require individuals to surrender their 'substantive political freedom and equality' for the protection of the liberal state (1979: 169–70). It permits a gloss on Pateman's first major work, *Participation and Democratic Theory*, where she shows the dominant ideological interpretation of liberal democracy to be one which substitutes the principle of competition of elites for control of the state for that of citizen participation in voluntarily maintained political communities. In this work Pateman counterposed the participatory approach to democracy of Rousseau and J.S. Mill to the elite theory of democracy championed by Schumpeter among other twentieth-century theorists of capitalist democracy in the face of the development of what sociologists called 'mass society'. She understood herself at this point to be rescuing a tradition of democratic theory which has been buried or discredited by the elite democratic theorists. Accordingly she emphasised the normative features of the participatory tradition, especially its emphasis on a process of education into creative and responsible citizenship through the access of individuals to participatory modes of decision-making. Like the new left politics of its time, this work stressed the importance of extending participatory principles to the workplace. In more general terms, it questioned how democratic a liberal democratic state could be if all the institutions of everyday life—including the family—were structured in terms of authoritarian principles of governance.

With her 1979 critique of liberal accounts of political obligation, Pateman shows that liberal contractualism does not occlude the distinctive characteristics of the employment contract under capitalism: it establishes them, the logical import of which is to suggest that liberal democracy precludes workers' participation or industrial democracy. Like Marx, Pateman accepts that the worker is formally free in the sense of being accorded status as proprietor of his or her capacity to labour. She also accepts the Marxian point that the worker does not have a choice as to whether to enter an employment contract: he or she has to obtain the wherewithal to live (a wage), and this means that he or she is positioned to exchange obedience to the employer for protection (1988: ch. 5). However, Pateman's development of the Marxian critique of the contractual relation of private property relies on a feminist emphasis on the necessarily embodied quality of the worker's capacity to labour. The worker cannot detach the service he or she provides from his/her embodied self. This means that it is not, as the Marxist formulation would have it, the worker's *capacity* to labour that is sold to the capitalist employer. That suggests the separability of this capacity from the worker. Instead 'the worker and his labour . . . are the subject of contract' (1988: 151).

This regime makes sense only in terms of the employer's contractual right as *master* of his employees: 'The employment contract creates the capitalist as master; he has the political right to determine how the labour of the worker will be used, and—consequently—can engage in exploitation' (1988: 149). This explains the open-ended character of the employment contract, that the employer can extend the hours of labour and intensify its speed with the only check on the prerogative of the master being the combined resistance of workers organised as trade unions. This is why, in Pateman's view, there is no substantive distinction to be made between the employment contract and wage slavery.

Pateman's emphasis on the *political* nature of the employer's regime is an important and original one. It represents a revision of the Marxian critique of the capitalist employment contract by directing us away from an exclusively economic explanation of the employer–worker relationship. For Pateman, it is not because the employer economically exploits the worker that the former subordinates the latter. Instead, it is because the employer becomes the master of the worker that the former can exploit the latter (1988: 149). The reason why capitalist employers will not fully automate the work process is because a political relationship of mastery cannot be established over machines.

Pateman (1988; 1989: ch. 4) establishes an analogy between the employment contract and the marriage contract. Through supposedly freely consenting to marry a man, women also exchange obedience for protection where the services they provide are via the medium of their embodied selfhood. The husband's mastery is limited only by his private benevolence. His is a complete contractual freedom of mastery over his wife: hers is a contractual unfreedom. Nowhere is this more underlined, Pateman insists, than in those jurisdictions which maintain a husband's right to conjugal sex independent of his wife's consent.

However, the wife's status is not the same as that of the male worker. While he at least can attain domestic mastery over his wife, women are consistently positioned as subject to the political mastery of men. This means that their relationship to 'freedom of contract' is qualitatively distinct from that of male workers. Women enter contractual relations not as citizens or workers in the abstract but as female citizens and workers. Theirs is a citizenship and an employee status which work to subject them to men (1989: ch. 8). Thus, women's access to the social citizenship of the welfare state is primarily as dependents of men, and the vast majority of women employees are located within poorly paid, lowly valued feminised occupations where positions of authority and management prerogative belong to men.

That women do not enter the social contract on equal terms with men but, indeed, enter the social contract as subordinate to men's collective and several mastery, is Pateman's third argument. It represents a feminist critique of liberal contractualism, and, as suggested above, a feminist gloss on socialist critique of liberal contractualism. This is the thesis of *The Sexual Contract* (1988).

This thesis assumes especial strength in Pateman's treatment of the prostitution and surrogacy contracts. With the resurgence of liberal contractualism in the 1980s it is not uncommon to find a contractual defence of the free choice of women who sell their embodied selves into prostitution and surrogate motherhood. This construction of freedom depends again on making it appear that the woman is selling a service that is separable from her selfhood. If she was selling her selfhood then the paradox of maintaining the freedom of the individual to subject themselves to the unrestrained mastery of another would become evident. Pateman emphasises that such is the nature of sexual interaction and carrying a foetus within one's womb that these 'services' fundamentally entail the embodied selfhood of the women concerned. As Pateman (1988: 198, emphasis in the original) points out, since 'there is no natural necessity to engage in sexual *relations* to assuage sexual pangs,' prostitution reflects men's need to express their sexuality as a matter of their mastery over women. Inherent in modern, contractual masculinity is the law of male sex right over women (1988: 199).

The relationship of surrogate motherhood, once examined, evinces the same assertion of masculine sex right over women who become surrogate mothers. The private property in this relationship concerns the way in which the male's semen establishes his proprietary right in the foetus/child:

> A surrogacy contract differs from a prostitution contract in that a man does not make direct sexual use of a woman's body; rather, his use is indirect via artificial insemination. The man's seed, to use Locke's language, is mixed with the woman's uterus, and if she performs her service faithfully, he can claim the property thereby produced as his own (1988: 214).

If women enter the modern contractual political order as subjected to the mastery of men, this would suggest, Pateman reasons, that what she terms the sexual contract or modern patriarchal right precedes the social contract.

The social contract is a fraternal contract whereby men agree to constitute each other as equal proprietors of sex right. Elsewhere I have criticised this tendency of Pateman to make the sexual contract the foundational base and 'secret' of the social contract (1990; Gatens 1990). How could it be more foundational than the mastery Locke's possessive individual establishes over 'the Grass my Horse has bit; the Turfs my Servant has cut'? (*Two Treatises on Government*, 2nd treatise: ch. 5, par. 28; Macpherson 1962). How indeed could it be more foundational than the way in which the biblical origins myth of God commanding Adam 'to multiply and people the Earth and to subdue it' is invoked by Locke (1st treatise: ch. 3, par. 14) to require these possessive individuals to conquer non-European territories and to enslave their peoples? All these relations of modern contractual/private property are mutually constitutive. Together they indicate the class, gender and race dimensions of the modern liberal contractual relationship of mastery.

There is a point at which Pateman appears to recognise this: 'The men who (are said to) make the original contract are *white* men, and their fraternal pact has three aspects; the social contract, the sexual contract and the slave contract that legitimises the rule of white over black' (1988: 221). Pateman has not to date expatiated on the relationship between these three aspects, nor has she accorded the racial/imperial aspects of the modern regime of private property anything like the salience she has given to the modern patriarchal and economic class relationships.

It is to be hoped that Pateman, as others, will begin to explore the systemic features of her critique of modern contractualism. This will be to recover and extend a critique of modern private property and in such a way that the Marxian tradition of such critique is read and interpreted anew with the contemporary emphases on the gender, race and colonial aspects of modern private property. In this context, Pateman's insistence that the political relationship of mastery is central to the intelligibility of modern private property is likely to prove very creative and fruitful. Of course, it is both ironic and inevitable that the renewal *and* extension of the Marxian critique of private property is attended by an extraordinary renaissance of liberal claims on behalf of contractualism and property right.

The reading I have offered of Pateman's work is, of course, selective. Not all of her concerns have been accorded the visibility or emphasis they arguably deserve. Indeed, I have accorded the still incomplete work of an author a not entirely arbitrary coherence of a kind that the author herself has not claimed. Pateman, at this stage of her work, has completed her feminist critique of liberal contractualism. It is not clear where she will go next. One possibility is to follow through the systemic direction I have indicated to be latent within her work.

Pateman, like all feminist political and legal studies theorists in the 1980s, has confronted the issue of 'difference' in respect of the formally universal terms of modern political culture. As Jones puts it:

> The dilemma confronting modern political theory from the eighteenth century on was how to recognize the political relevance of sexual differences, and how to include these differences within definitions of political action and civic virtue without constructing sexually segregated norms of citizenship. In short, the task was to construct a theory of political equality and citizenship that granted the individual personhood of women without denying that women had differing needs and interests from men (1990: 792–3).

Pateman argues that the fraternal bond of the social contract which ensures a sameness of masculine individuals *qua* masters of women precludes a political vision which reconciles freedom with differences between individuals, especially that of sex difference. If not for this reason alone, it is for this reason in particular that she claims 'a new story about freedom is urgently needed' (1988: 233). This suggests that a further possibility for where Pateman goes next is to work on this normative task. Her recent rejoinder to her critics within a review symposium on *The Sexual Contract* suggests her own discernment of this task:

> At present, neither I, nor other feminists as far as I know, have an alternative conception of freedom to hand. Many old arguments and structures are now crumbling at rapid rates, although contract seems to be preserving its attractions, and, whatever insights might be gleaned from conventional sources, feminists cannot simply look to the standard texts or theories for alternatives. The pleasure and reward of feminist political theory is exactly that new territory is being staked out so that, for the first time, a genuinely democratic theory may be formulated (1990: 82).

BIBLIOGRAPHY

Primary sources

Pateman, C. (1970) *Participation and Democratic Theory* Cambridge, Cambridge University Press
——(1979) *The Problem of Political Obligation: a Critical Analysis of Liberal Theory* Chichester, John Wiley
——(1988) *The Sexual Contract* Cambridge, Polity Press
——(1989) *The Disorder of Women: Democracy, Feminism and Political Theory* Cambridge, Polity Press
——(1990) 'Reply to reviews on *The Sexual Contract*' *Political Theory Newsletter* 2: 78–83

Secondary sources

Gatens, M. (1990) 'The return of the repressed', part of a review symposium on *The Sexual Contract, Political Theory Newsletter* 2: 69–73
Jones, K. (1990) 'Citizenship in a woman-friendly polity' *Signs* 15: 781–813
Locke, J. (1963) *Two Treatises of Government* Laslett edition, Cambridge, Cambridge University Press
Macpherson, C.B. (1962) *The Political Theory of Possessive Individualism: Hobbes to Locke* London, Oxford University Press
Pringle, H. (1990) 'Belmont and Venice: Carole Pateman, *The Sexual Contract*' *Political Theory Newsletter* 2: 73–8
Yeatman, A. (1990) 'Carole Pateman's *The Sexual Contract*' *Thesis Eleven* 26: 151–60

TREVOR HOGAN

25

Jeremy Seabrook

Jeremy Seabrook stands within the tradition of English ethical socialism. His central concern is the failure of the modern project, defined as a 'race for riches'. The domination of nature and the accumulation of wealth through the exploitation of human labour has led to the replacement of material scarcity by social scarcity and to the domination of money instead of nature.

For Seabrook, the cult of productivism (whether capitalist or communist) has not only failed to conquer the scourge of poverty in the South—a scourge now returning to haunt the advanced societies of the North—but also to recognise ecological limits. The deepest scourge of all for Seabrook, however, is the impoverishment of the human soul, the dismembering of human identity, and the enslaving of human capacities and creativity to money fetishism. If this is a moral and religious critique, it is also a democratic and socialist one, for the battle over the human soul is not for its orderly protection by a cultural elite (contra the literary tradition of Arnold, Eliot and Leavis) but a battle for and by the common person for the creation of a common culture which nurtures cooperation and creativity rather than competition and acquisitive materialism.

Seabrook's project is a search for a substantive rationality which will 'prise apart those processes which simultaneously gut human beings and eviscerate the planet itself' (1988c: 3). This search involves the task of 'unveiling' the true nature of our desires and physical needs and translating them into a collective project, a 'politics of social hope'. For Seabrook, such a politics needs to name personal hurts, wants and dreams and link them to a world of physical needs and social forms without subsuming one life sphere to the other.

In form and vision, Seabrook represents a revival of Carlyle and Marx as much as he represents English ethical socialism. His vision is organicist, emblematic and global. His chosen form is fragmentary, analogical and typological.

If Seabrook does not end with Carlyle and Marx, he certainly starts where they began. Marx's initial social and political concern was the dual problem of poverty and citizenship. The vast majority of the population in Germany in the early part of the nineteenth century was landless, masterless, and unemployed—peasants, servants or apprentices—and consequently had no fixed place in the feudal order. These unincorporated poor were by definition outside civil society and beyond the reach and responsibility of the state. The poor, for the young Marx, were not only without property but were denied social and political rights as well.

In the *Paris Manuscripts* (1844), Marx shifts from being the advocate of the outcast poor who have been stripped of their social and political rights, to the anthropologist of the estranged *homo faber*. This shift in focus represented a significant narrowing of his conception of the poor—from citizens to workers and from their exclusion as fellow humans qua humans to their oppression as workers. Carlyle, however, while preaching a 'Gospel of Work' ('Produce! Produce!') and condemning unemployment of all kinds, was more concerned to overcome the horrors of poverty (of which ignorance and hunger were perceived to be its worst vices). He sought a 'disimprisoning' of the social order from both the stultifying strictures of privilege (as symbolised by the feudal order) and the exploitation of the poor by the wealthy (as symbolised by the 'Gospel of Mammonism; embodied in laissez faire capitalism).

Carlyle's purpose was first to offer a critique of dominant bourgeois doctrines of laissez faire, egoism, rationalism, and utilitarianism, and of the residual and decadent aristocratic doctrine of 'do-nothingism' and then to imagine the possibilities of a radically new social order. He achieved this via three experiments of form: philosophical-biographical fragments (*Sartor Resartus* 1832–34), historical epic (*The French Revolution* 1837) and social criticism (*Chartism* 1839; *Past and Present* 1843).

Seabrook shares at least three of Carlyle's and Marx's common themes and concerns. With Carlyle, he works outwards from a biographical and phenomenological position, tracing the 'structures of feeling' of his own life and that of his own time, place, class and society. With the young Marx, he emphasises how the doctrines of economic reason radically subvert the fuller flourishing of the individual human person and impoverish the vast majority of humanity by excluding them from participation in civil society. With Carlyle, too, he shows how capitalism ('the Gospel of Mammonism') not only pauperises the poor but impoverishes the rich as well. Third, together with Carlyle and

Marx, he searches for a new social order and for emergent social forces which have the capacity to establish such a vision and order.

'STRUCTURES OF FEELING': AUTOBIOGRAPHY AND THE ENGLISH MANUFACTURING WORKING CLASS

Seabrook intertwines novelistic and social documentary conventions with polemical commentary, participant-observer ethnography and autobiography. He collects and recounts stories in a non-linear fashion, offering them as emblematic fragments, as 'signs of the times'.

Seabrook uses his own story as an emblem of the cultural and structural transformations of the English manufacturing working class since World War II (1967; 1976; 1979; 1985b; 1988b). Born in Northampton in 1939, he has moved between two social worlds in each dimension of his life, be it class, place, or sexuality. His journey has been from the working class to the professional middle class and in part a redemptive return to his roots through social work, commitment to the labour movement and teaching with the Workers' Educational Association; from a regional manufacturing town of the north to the metropolitan centre, London; and a gradual journey of discovery and self-acceptance made manifest in public declaration of his homosexuality.

Seabrook argues that, during its cultural ascendancy from the 1890s to the 1940s, the English manufacturing working class had oral familial traditions which recalled pre-industrial memories of arcadia, an everyday practice of community solidarity, and a political movement which offered an alternative vision and competing myth to that of capitalism. This embodiment of the working class is now but a ghostly reflection of its once great strength. A repressive, because oppressed, culture which was unable to celebrate difference, autonomy or creativity, its true nature was exposed at the very historical juncture its socioeconomic function was made redundant in an emergent epoch of consumer capitalism. As the older generation of the manufacturing working class discovered their obsolescence as productive workers, they were left bereft, bemused, and nostalgic. One hundred and fifty years of resilient self-reliance and thriftiness was suddenly presented to them as nothing but a bad joke (1978; 1982a). For the young, the liberation offered from material want proved to be a new and joyless subjection, a trade of one form of oppression and exploitation with another: of body and material deprivation to a 'market economy of the emotions' (1985a: 107).

POVERTY AND WEALTH: THE GLOBAL PROCESSES OF SYMBIOSIS AND DISSIMULATION

The costs of poverty are not just unfortunate externalities of the race for riches—costs which can be counted and then offset—but are bound up in the very nature of the race and its destiny. The search for riches, the maintenance of social scarcity, and the worship of money as the solution to all human problems impoverishes the rich as fast as it pauperises the poor (1985a). For the poor, the process of pauperisation is a process of social fragmentation and political disenfranchisement. It veils the social causes of private woes and it contributes to the loss of social purposive activity. Not least, it leads to economic impoverishment, that which is most commonly recognised as the condition of poverty.

The impoverishment of the rich is a process of spiritual desolation and social fragmentation. It is the creation of a new set of externalities for the rich: not only are there rising costs associated with surveillance, aid and administration of the 'problems of the poor' and because of the desecration of landscapes, but they also now face rising costs associated with minimising exposure to 'environmental risks' such as toxic wastes and hazards, air and noise pollution.

Both rich and poor are bound up in a symbiotic dependency on money and an 'immitigable sense of insufficiency'. Because poverty evades definition, proclaimed as 'relative deprivation' it serves as a goad to all to struggle for more—'its perpetuation is ensured; and therefore a justification is created for an eternity of striving beyond satiation for everybody else' (1978: 212). Although the rich are able to buy exemption from material insufficiency this very act sets in motion a constant struggle against a socially constructed sense of insufficiency. The drive for the acquisition of more consumer goods emerges from a residual fear of falling and an existential feeling of dissatisfaction that consumption leaves. This in turn engenders a feeling that the vacuum can be filled only by still further acts of acquisition.

Seabrook views Britain's decline as an industrial power to be the harbinger of a larger transnational reorganisation of capitalism. He calls this process 'dissimulation', whereby the spheres of production and consumption are separated geographically as well as conceptually; the house of politics is locked into eighteenth-century aspirations while the economic order is globalised, and a new international division of labour is developed (1988c).

For the advanced nations of the North, a sectoral employment revolution is occurring on a scale to match that of the industrial revolution of the late eighteenth century and first half of the nineteenth century in Britain. Whereas industrial capitalism required labour power, market/consumer capitalism requires a proportionally small sector of highly skilled, high-consuming information workers/technocrats. The rest—the disabled, the infirm, the casualised, deskilled workers, the elderly, the young, and women employed in 'use-value' work are the 'new poor'. If the phenomenon is not new, the context is; in the rich North the 'lumpen-proletariat' now outnumber 'the proletariat'.

The second identifiable group of 'new poor' Seabrook calls the new 'serving class' (1988a): those deskilled, casualised, non-unionised workers lured from the yoke of heavy manual labour, whether of manufacturing (men) or processing and domestic labours (women), into a new working world of waiters, nannies, croupiers, domestic helpers, chauffeurs, door-people, escort agents, security guards, word processors, and shop attendants, etc. These are analogous to Marx's incorporated poor of the old feudal order. They are the new servants of the rich and the new 'artificial peasantry' (1985b: 18). As servants, they are anonymous, silent, politically unorganised and fragmented, and replaceable.

Whether the analogy is with the commoners, servants or the peasants, both the welfare-dependent and the new serving class under consumer capitalism occupy one and the same position in relation to the rich: 'a protean vassalage that can be counted upon to accommodate itself to whatever will make money for others' (1985a: 24). This scheme is then writ large onto the world system as such (1985a; 1988c).

THE POLITICS OF HOPE

By retrieving Carlyle's depiction of capitalism as a protean myth, Seabrook grants capitalism the status of a mythic story by which we live. The fundamental task of the social critic, therefore, is to unmask the central logic and myths of capitalism so that its spiritual roots may be unveiled, named and overcome. Like Carlyle and Marx before him, Seabrook is fascinated by the dynamism and energy of the modern world but distrusts the ubiquitous display of semblances, surfaces, images and forms, and instead seeks to reveal its immutable essence.

The search for vehicles of social hope, emergent communities of resistance, is not merely a matter of drawing up shopping lists and offering reform packages. Rather it necessitates the telling of stories which remember the riches of radical traditions of resistance while imagining possibilities for a new social order. A search for an alternative social order is one which recognises itself as a 'culture of resistance'—a moment, a movement and a politics from within the dominant social order. Unless these communities of resistance strike at the spiritual roots of capitalism as world system and as everyday 'habits of the heart', they cannot hope to transform and overcome its processes of domination, exploitation, and inbuilt obsolescence.

The politics of hope, for Seabrook, then, is a moral necessity which makes possible cultural resistance to the logic of capitalism as world economic and cultural system on the one hand, and constructs alternative social imaginaries and practices that sustain self-reliant, materially sufficient communities on the other. The social identity of the individual and the possibility of social solidarity require a storytelling and a politics that unite the structure of feeling with our feelings regarding the abstract processes, rationalities and structures that shape our material world. Such is the logic of Seabrook's project.

BIBLIOGRAPHY

Primary sources

Seabrook, J. (1967) *The Unprivileged*, London, Longmans, Green and Co
——(1971) *City Close-up* London, Allen Lane
——(1974) *Loneliness* Text by J. Seabrook. Picture sequence by Bryn Campbell. London, Temple Smith in association with New Society
——(1976) *A Lasting Relationship; Homosexuals and Society* London, Allen Lane
——(1978) *What Went Wrong? Working People and the Ideals of the Labour Movement* London, Victor Gollancz
——(1979) *Mother and Son: An Autobiography* London, Victor Gollancz
——(1980) *The Way We Are*, Mitchan, Surrey, Age Concern England
——(1982a) *Unemployment* London, Quartet
——(1982b) *Working-Class Childhood* London, Victor Gollancz
——(1984) *The Idea of Neighbourhood: What Local Politics Should be About* London, Pluto Press
——(1985a) *Landscapes of Poverty* Oxford, Basil Blackwell
——(1985b) (with Trevor Blackwell) *A World Still To Win: The Reconstruction of the Post-War Working Class* London, *Faber and Faber*
——(1987) *Life and Labour in a Bombay Slum* London, Pluto Press
——(1988a) *The Leisure Society* Oxford, Basil Blackwell
——(1988b) (with Trevor Blackwell) *The Politics of Hope: Britain at the End of the Twentieth Century* London, Faber and Faber
——(1988c) *The Race for Riches: The Human Cost of Wealth* Basingstoke, Green Print, Marshall Pickering
——(1990a) (with Winin Pereira) *Asking the Earth: Farms, Forestry and Survival in India* London, Earthscan
——(1990b) *The Myth of the Market: Promises and Illusions* Bideford, Green Books

26

MICHAEL TAVEIRA

Georg Simmel

Simmel was born in the centre of Berlin in 1858 and lived through its expansion into a great metropolis. He studied history, psychology and philosophy at the University of Berlin. In 1881 he obtained his doctorate for an essay on Kant's theory of matter, and in 1885 he became a *Privatdozent*, a position remunerated only by students' fees. He taught a wide variety of courses, proving immensely gifted and popular as a lecturer. He also wrote and published widely, securing an international reputation as a scholar.

Although he was born to ex-Jewish, Christian parents, and never professed the Jewish faith, anti-Semitism combined with jealousy and accusations of dilettantism to keep him out of mainstream academic life. He was granted the title of *Ausserordentlicher Professor*, a purely honorary rank, in 1900. He finally left to become a full Professor of Philosophy at the University of Strasbourg in 1914. He died there of liver cancer in 1918. His legacy was his students (he taught Georg Lukács and Ernst Bloch, amongst others), his friends (including Max Weber), his participation in and influence on Berlin's cultural life, and his publications (25 books and hundreds of articles and other writings). His work is currently enjoying a belated revival and reassessment.

Three overlapping periods may be established in his intellectual development. At first he was influenced by 'pragmatism, social Darwinism, Spencerian evolutionism and the principle of social differentiation' (Landmann in Frisby 1984: 23). During this phase he wrote *On Social Differentiation* (1890), *The Problems of the Philosophy of History* (1892), and *Introduction to Moral Philosophy* (2 vols 1892–93). Then followed the period of his greatest interest in sociology, during which he published *The Philosophy of Money* (1907: second enlarged edition following the first edition of 1900) and *Sociology* (1908). The third period saw him turning to philosophy, literature and art and to the working out of his *Lebensphilosophie*. The influences here were principally Bergson but also Goethe, Hegel, Schopenhauer and Nietzsche. He published *Philosophical Culture* (1911), *Fundamental Problems of Sociology* (1917), *The Conflict in Modern Culture* (1918) and *Interpretation of Life* (1918).

These three phases underlie, without coinciding with, three roles that Simmel has played in the history of English-language sociology. Until recently he has been principally regarded as the founder, with Ferdinand Tönnies, of a distinct German sociology. His claim was that there was no discipline dealing with the common forms which civilised social life takes everywhere, as distinct from those disciplines focusing on such content as the economic or the historical. For example, the effect of the number of members on any sort of group was an isolable problem; or the pecularities of the two-member group, the dyad; or the ubiquitous role of 'the stranger'. As it treated of social forms, as distinct from content, this was called formal sociology; and as he likened it to geometry (1950: 21; 1959a: 317, 320–21) and it attracted diagrams of relationships, it appeared to imply a mathematical perspective. For the pioneers of a scientific sociology in America, Simmel was a useful ally. Albion Small, the influential editor of *The American Journal of Sociology*, published translations of Simmel's articles between 1896 and 1910. His junior colleagues at Chicago, Park and Burgess, gave more space to Simmel than to anyone else in their 1921 *Introduction to the Science of Sociology*, the 'Green bible' of interwar American sociology. This was the Simmel revived after the war, when his *Sociology* was translated, and he became a source of hypotheses in research on small groups and social conflict.

The emphasis on the distinction between form and content is the most distinctive feature of Simmel's work. 'Forms are the synthesizing principles which select elements from the raw stuff of experience and shape them into determinate unities'. On the other hand, 'Contents are those aspects of existence which are determined in themselves', being without structure and beyond apprehension in their immediacy (Levine 1971: xv). 'Society' itself is one of these forms, and specifically one of the forms of 'sociation' (*Vergesellschaftung*); for 'it is *sociation* which synthesizes all human interests, contents, and processes into concrete units' (Simmel 1964: 4). Sociology studies these forms in a unique way by asking 'what happens to men and by what rules they behave ... insofar as they form groups and are determined by their group existence because of their interaction' (p. 11). Simmel's 'geometrical' claim was that 'However diverse the interests are that give rise to these sociations, the *forms* in which the interests are realized may be identical', hence the varieties to be found within such forms as 'superiority and subordination, competition, division of labour ... a religious community, a band of conspirators ... an economic association ... art school ... family' (p. 22).

A second role for Simmel emerged with the American views of his turn away from sociology after his *Sociology*, and the implication that he was not really a sociologist. Even his sympathetic expositor, Spykman, offered only to deal 'with a restricted field of Simmel's work' (Spykman 1966: xv), and his lack of system helped prompt the charge that he was 'not only a sociologist, but . . . especially in his last years [after 1910] . . . pre-eminently a philosopher'. And damagingly: 'His need for metaphysics at last overcame his original leanings toward empiricism' (Wiese and Becker 1932: 705). But the most influential criticism was probably that of Sorokin: '. . . Simmel's sociological method lacks scientific method . . . experimental approach, quantitative investigation, or any systematic factual study of the discussed phenomena . . . What there is represents only the speculative generalization of a talented man . . . Without Simmel's talent the same stuff would appear poor' (Sorokin 1964: 502, n.26). He was reduced to the role of 'a talented man'.

A similar conclusion about Simmel was arrived at by at least some of his German contemporaries, and this was a factor in his prolonged exclusion from a full professorship. One major difference from the American views quoted above was that his involvement in sociology was itself made grounds for rejecting him; one negative referee remarked that 'sociology has yet to earn its position as a scholarly discipline', while at the same time dismissing his 'world view and philosophy of life' as prompted by 'a thirst for notoriety' (Schaefer 1908: 640–1).

It was Simmel's 'world view and philosophy of life', however, which formed the basis for his third role. The letter of the negative referee, Schaefer, was published in a commemorative issue of *The American Journal of Sociology* on Durkheim and Simmel in 1958, the centenary of their birth. In this issue, Kurt Wolff, translator of Simmel's *Sociology*, wrote; 'We hardly know him yet. We are just discovering, thanks to new translations, that there is more to him than the invention of formal sociology' (Wolff 1958: 593). In 1959 Wolff edited a commemorative volume, *Georg Simmel 1858–1918; A Collection of essays, with Translations and a Bibliography* (see Simmel 1959a) which was republished in 1965 with a significantly more informative title, *Essays on Sociology, Philosophy and Aesthetics* (see Simmel 1965). Wolff initiated, in English, the study of Simmel in the round, but while translations and studies have continued of Simmel's sociology (Levine 1971), and philosophy (Weingartner 1962), and more recently, philosophy of history (Oakes in Simmel 1892 and 1980). Simmel's third and most comprehensive role is that of 'cultural philosopher', specialising in 'modernity'. This ambiguous description may serve to cover the current tendency to put any aspect of Simmel's diverse works in the perspective of the whole. This would seem to be consonant with Simmel's own outlook: 'When we look at an isolated segment of existence, we find in it fragmentary realizations, simultaneous intimations of opposing fundamental concepts. It is one and it is many, it is action and passion, it is being and

becoming, it is somehow absolute and at the same time somehow relative ... only when we step back do we obtain an image that is dominated by a *single* point of view' (Simmel 1910: 309, in 1959a, 1965: 309).

What, then, is culture? Simmel describes it as 'coming into being by a
meeting of the two elements, neither of which contain culture by itself:
the subjective soul and the objective spiritual product' (Simmel 1918:
30). Such 'products' as art, morality, technology, religion and science are
forms which are part of culture insofar as they are vehicles for the
development of human personality (Scaff 1990: 288). But cultural
phenomena develop an immanent logic of their own and the human
being 'becomes the mere carrier of the force by which this logic dominates their development and leads them on' (Simmel 1918: 43). This is
the tragedy of culture; human beings become dominated by their own
products. Simmel takes the disproportion between life and the multiple
worlds it has created to its logical conclusion in his discussion of the
monetary economy, the big city, the division of labour, and modern
science with its own peculiar division of labour.

As a sociologist of modernity, Simmel's emphasis is on the everyday
experience and interpretation of the contingent and the new 'in terms of
the *reactions of our inner life,* and indeed *as an inner world*' (essay on
Rodin, 1911, cited Frisby 1990b; 59, Nedelmann 1990: 235, Simmel's
emphasis). He focuses on the individual, the metropolis and the mature
money economy.

The modern individual in the metropolis is exposed to various new
stimuli and to new forms of social interaction. Yet there is also an inner
loneliness as he or she is confronted with 'the deepest problems of
modern life' and tries to 'maintain the independence and individuality of
his existence against the sovereign powers of society' (Simmel 1971: 324)
Faced with close physical proximity to an enormous number of people
and the professional and social networks of urban culture, nervous and
restless individuals strive to build up an 'inner boundary and reserve'
between themselves and their social environment (Simmel 1907: 477).

This 'inner boundary and reserve' might be reflected in eccentricity or
agoraphobia but usually takes the form of either cynicism or a total
indifference that is located in a blasé attitude to life (Simmel 1971: 329).
Cynicism and the blasé attitude are seen as 'almost endemic to the
heights of a money culture' (Simmel 1907: 255). Money, the 'most
terrible leveler' (Simmel 1971: 330) reduces everything to the common
denominator of exchange value, and it is 'money transactions [which]
erect a barrier between persons' (Simmel 1907: 477). Cynicism most
generally occurs where large amounts of money change hands frequently, and leads to a mocking and frivolous attitude to the higher
values of life. 'The concept of a market price for values ... is the perfect
objectification of what cynicism presents in the form of a subjective
reflex'. On the other hand, the blasé person 'has completely lost the

feeling for value differences. He experiences all things as being of an equally dull and grey hue, as not worth getting excited about' (p. 256). This cultivation of subjective states in order to deal with objective culture ultimately devalues both the objective world and the individual person (1971: 330).

Simmel pursues the theme of 'the atrophy of individual culture through the hypertrophy of objective culture' (p. 338) in his analysis of money. Money as a form of exchange links individuals together and symbolises what holds society together (1907: 175). 'There is no more striking symbol of the completely dynamic character of the world than that of money ... money is nothing but the vehicle for a movement in which everything else that is not in motion is completely extinguished. It is, as it were, on *actus purus*' (p. 510–11).

Money links us all together as consumers and in financial transactions. It makes us cooperate with each other but the cooperation is that of strangers in the marketplace. We become objects ourselves and treat others as objects. Ultimately, the individual human being is devalued. Simmel's point is that the alienated forms of existence become the objective forms within which we exist (Frisby 1990b: 66). Frisby comments that 'A decade later Simmel was to speak of this increasing separation of subjective and objective culture not merely in terms of a 'crisis of culture', or even as a 'tragedy of culture', but also as the 'pathology of culture' (1984: 110). As for Simmel, we in Australia hardly know him yet.

BIBLIOGRAPHY

Works in English

Primary sources

Simmel, G. (1892) *The Problems of the Philosophy of History: An Epistemological Essay* Trans., ed. and introd. by G. Oakes. New York, Free Press, 1977

——(1907) *The Philosophy of Money* (2nd enlarged edition). Ed. and introd. by D. Frisby. Trans. by T. Bottomore and D. Frisby. London, Routledge

——(1910) 'On the nature of philosophy' (trans. by Rudolph H. Weingartner), in K.H. Wolff (ed.) *Essays on Sociology, Philosophy and Aesthetics* New York, Harper and Row, 1965: 282–309

——(1918) *The Conflict in Modern Culture and Other Essays* Trans. and introd. by K. P. Etzkorn. New York, Teachers College Press, 1968

——(1950) *The Sociology of Georg Simmel*. Trans. and introd. by Kurt H. Wolff. Glencoe, Ill., Free Press

——(1955) *Conflict and the Web of Group Affiliations* Trans. by Kurt H.

Wolff and R. Bendix. Foreword by Everett C. Hughes. Glencoe, Ill., Free Press

——(1959a) *Georg Simmel 1858–1918; A Collection of Essays, with Translations and a Bibliography* Ed. by K.H. Wolff. Columbus, Ohio, The Ohio State University Press (see 1965)

——(1959b) *Sociology of Religion* Trans. by C. Rosenthal. Introd. by F. Gross. New York, Philosophical Library

——Simmel, G. (1964) *The Sociology of Georg Simmel* Trans., ed. and introd. by K.H. Wolff. Glencoe, The Free Press

——(1965) *Essays on Sociology, Philosophy and Aesthetics* Ed. by K.H. Wolff. New York, Harper and Row (reprint of 1959a)

——(1971) *On Individuality and Social Forms*: Selected Writings Ed. and introd. by D.N. Levine. Chicago, University of Chicago Press

——(1976) *Georg Simmel: Sociologist and European* Trans. by D. E. Jenkinson et al. Introd. by P. A. Lawrence. Sunbury, Middx., Nelson

——(1980) *Essays on Interpretation in Social Science* Trans., ed. and introd. by G. Oakes. Totowa, NJ, Rowman & Littlefield

——(1984) *Georg Simmel: On Women, Sexuality and Love* Trans. and introd. by G. Oakes. New Haven/Boston, Yale University Press

——(1986) *Schopenhauer and Nietzsche* Trans. by H. Loiskandl, D. Weinstein and M. Weinstein. Amherst, University of Massachusetts Press

Secondary sources

Borgatta, E.F. and Meyer, H.J. (1956) (eds) *Sociological Theory: Present-Day Sociology from the Past* New York, Alfred A. Knopf

Coser, L.A. (1956) *The Functions of Social Conflict* London, Routledge & Kegan Paul

——(1977) *Masters of Sociological Thought: Ideas in Historical and Social Context* (2nd edition) New York, Harcourt Brace Jovanovich

Frisby, D. (1984) *Georg Simmel* Chichester, Sussex, Horwood

——(1985) 'Georg Simmel: first sociologist of modernity' *Theory, Culture and Society* 2(3): 49–67

——(1990a) 'Georg Simmel's concept of society', in M. Kaern et al. (eds) *Georg Simmel and Contemporary Sociology* Dordrecht, Kluwer Academic Publishers

——(1990b) 'Georg Simmel and the study of modernity', in M. Kaern et al. (eds) *Georg Simmel and Contemporary Sociology* Dordrecht, Kluwer Academic Publishers

Levine, D.N. (1971) 'Introduction', in G. Simmel *On Individuality and Social Forms*. Ed. and introd. by D.N. Levine. Chicago, University of Chicago Press

Nedelmann, B. (1990) 'On the concept of "Erleben" in Georg Simmel's Sociology', in M. Kaern et al. (eds) *Georg Simmel and Contemporary*

Sociology Dordrecht, Kluwer Academic Publishers

Oakes, G. (1984) 'The problem of women in Simmel's theory of culture' in *G. Simmel: On Women, Sexuality and Love*. Trans. and introd. by G. Oakes. New Haven and London, Yale University Press

Park, R.E. and Burgess, E.W. (1969) *Introduction to the Science of Sociology* 3rd rev. edition, Chicago, University of Chicago Press

Scaff, L.A. (1990) 'Georg Simmel's theory of culture', in M. Kaern et al. (eds) *Georg Simmel and Contemporary Sociology* Dordrecht, Kluwer Academic Publishers

Schaefer, D. (1908) 'A contemporary academic view of Georg Simmel', Appendix to L.A. Coser 'Georg Simmel's style of work: a contribution to the sociology of the sociologist' *American Journal of Sociology* LXIII (6): 635–41

Sorokin, P.A. (1964) *Contemporary Sociological Theories* New York, Evanston and London, Harper and Row

Spykman, N.J. (1966) *The Social Theory of Georg Simmel* New York, Atherton Press

Turner, B.S. (1986) 'Simmel, rationalisation and the sociology of money' *The Sociological Review* 34 (1): 93–114

Weingartner, R.H. (1962) *Experience and Culture: The Philosophy of Georg Simmel* Middletown, Connecticut, Wesleyan University Press

Wiese, L.V. and Becker, H. (1932) *Systematic Sociology: On the Basis of the Beziehungeslehre and Gebildelehre* New York, Wiley

27

Alain Touraine

It is difficult to separate Touraine's intellectual project from his personal biography. Born into a prominent Parisian medical family in 1925, Touraine followed the path of France's interwar intellectual elite to the Ecole Normale. There he broke with the classics-dominated curriculum and went to work as an unskilled worker in the coalmines of northern France. Here Touraine encountered the core of the French labour movement, as well as the sociology of Georges Friedmann. During the post-war labour conflicts in 1947 and 1948, Touraine decided on sociology as his intellectual direction. He returned to study, in 1950 joining the small and marginal sociology section of the CNRS (the French national research organisation), then under Friedmann's direction. Touraine's first work was in industrial sociology, based on extensive research on patterns of work organisation and worker action at the Renault factories. From this early period Touraine's work shows a pattern of periods of extensive fieldwork followed by periods of theoretical work.

During the Cold War, the Communist Party had a great influence amongst French intellectuals, opposing sociology as a 'bourgeois science'. The discipline remained marginal within the conservative universities as well. In 1952 Touraine left to study in the US with a sense of the crisis of French intellectual life dominated by Cold War ideologies (1977b). He studied under Parsons, Merton and Lazarsfeld in the US, an experience which left him a resolute opponent of the then triumphant functionalism. In this period he began what would become ongoing research on social change and social movements in Latin America, first researching the Chilean labour movement in 1956.

In 1967 Touraine went to Nanterre, a new social sciences university on the outskirts of Paris, as Professor of Sociology. Nanterre was one of the centres of the May student movement that shook France in 1968. Touraine played a key role in attempting to mediate between the university and student revolutionaries (many of whom were his students). In the period that followed, many of the hopes that had been associated with Nanterre soured, and in 1969 Touraine left to return to the Ecole des Hautes Etudes en Sciences Sociales where he teaches today. The May movement had a decisive impact on Touraine's work. He saw the movement made up of two forms of action: on the one hand, action dominated by the crisis of the old society; but on the other, action pointing to new forms of power and new social conflicts. The year after the May movement he published *The Post-Industrial Society* (1974), and in 1973 his major theoretical text, *The Self-Production of Society* (1977b).

Touraine developed the hypothesis that new social conflicts were forming which opposed new forms of technocratic power. The decade 1975 to 1985 involved an ambitious program of research with new social movements, based on a new research method, the *sociological intervention*. The results of the decade of research into the development of new social movements have led to another period dominated by theoretical questions, centred on rethinking modernity (see Touraine 1989).

At the centre of Touraine's work is the argument that society needs to be understood as the product of social actors or social movements. But Touraine does not see any group that simply marches on the street as a social movement. Touraine recognises that there are many forms of collective action, but argues that a social movement is a collective action involved in a social conflict around the social organisation of a society's central cultural orientations that he calls *historicity*. Social movements are the centre of the conflictual self-production of society.

Modern societies for Touraine are defined in terms of their self-transforming capacities. On this basis he argues that we need a concept of 'types' of society, representing the level at which a society transforms itself. Touraine's early work centres on developing a theory of industrial society, arguing that the labour movement and the industrialising class are involved in a conflict around the forms of social organisation of the historicity they share. He argues that each societal type will produce a particular form of knowledge, moral categories, and establish a particular relationship with nature. In industrial society the privileged locus for the production and social conflict around this form of historicity is the labour process.

For Touraine the self-transforming capacity of a society will not be monopolised by one particular social group. Rather it will constitute the stakes in a social conflict. In industrial society both the industrialising class and the labour movement share a common faith in progress, science and the work ethic. Yet they are involved in a conflict around the social organisation of their shared cultural orientations, above all in terms of power relationships in the workplace.

Touraine's earlier research indicated the extent to which social actors have a dual identity: on the one hand, attempting to monopolise social change, on the other, taking up a defensive identity. For the labour movement this defensive identity took the form of types of action rejecting industrialisation, such as the destruction of machines or nostalgias for pre-industrial community. The offensive identity took the form of contesting, not rejecting, industrialisation: this involves struggles for workers' control. Dominant social actors will have a similar dual identity: the conservative defence of privilege, contrasted with the modernising role of the industrialist. Historicity is most at stake when the modernising aspects of both industrialists and labour movement are central to social life. It is possible, however, that social conflict is primarily shaped by defensive anti-modernising identities. Touraine argues that each societal type is characterised by a central social conflict, pointing to a central social relationship. In industrial society that conflict is around the social organisation of work, the central social movement being the labour movement which most directly shares and contests the social project of the industrialising class.

May 1968 pointed to the decline of the capacity of the labour movement and the industrialising class to both generate and contest central cultural patterns. In the period of theoretical elaboration and the decade of field research that were to follow, Touraine attempted to test this hypothesis, seeking to identify the social movement that would play the central role in post-industrial society as the labour movement had in industrial society.

NEW SOCIAL MOVEMENTS

In the mid-1970s Touraine embarked on a decade of field research with new social movements, at the same time developing the sociological intervention as a research method. If social movements had been seen as forms of collective action shaped by the experience or social status of the individuals involved, the appropriate form of research would be the individual survey. If they were understood in functionalist terms as the product of modernisation or of capitalist crisis, the object of research would shift to the system that produced these social movements. Touraine argued instead that social movements are involved in a social conflict around the production and appropriation of historicity: the object of research was therefore a *social relationship*. A social movement could only be understood in terms of its struggle with another social actor. It is this social relationship that is researched in the sociological intervention.

Touraine argues that a social movement will be constituted by three poles: an identity (both an experience of domination and a capacity of action), an opponent, and the stakes that constitute the shared but contested object of the conflict between the movement and its opponent. The intervention method involves constituting a number of groups made up of actors in a social conflict. These groups meet with allies in their conflict, and then with representatives of social opponents, in a process that seeks to crystallise the identity of the actor, who their social opponent is, and what issue is at stake in the conflict. The researchers play a role of facilitator in this process, formulating hypotheses interpreting the conflict, but the development of the intervention depends on the actor moving to the position of analysing the conflict they are engaged in.

Touraine established CADIS, a new centre for the development and analysis of interventions, and over the decade 1975 to 1985, six major interventions were undertaken. These were with the French student mobilisations of 1975–76 (Touraine et al. 1978), the anti-nuclear movement in 1978 (Touraine et al. 1983a), the Occitan regional movement in 1979 (Touraine et al. 1981), Solidarnösc in Poland in 1981 (Touraine et al. 1983b), the French labour movement in 1983 (Touraine at al. 1987), and the women's movement in 1984–85.

In the first two of these interventions the researchers were looking to see if the social conflict that the student movement and anti-nuclear struggle were involved in could be understood in terms of the social production of knowledge. This drew on Touraine's theorisation of the post-industrial society, where knowledge and its production constituted the central social field of post-industrial society, in much the same way as the factory constituted the central social field of industrial society. The interventions on the labour movement in France and with Solidarnösc pointed to different issues. Solidarnösc represented a convergence point for three types of movement: democratic, worker and nationalist. The intervention with the French labour movement pointed to the decline in its role as a social actor, and to its movement into the political system. A key question coming from this intervention was the relationship that labour, as a political actor, would develop with emerging new social conflicts. The two other interventions underlined the question of the identity of the actor: the nationalist Occitan movement and the women's movement.

It is difficult to summarise the outcomes of these interventions, all of which, except the intervention with the women's movement, were completed and led to the publication of books. They were conceived as attempts at identifying an emerging movement contesting post-industrial social power. They led to the conclusion that where such a movement is present, it is in a far more diffracted form than first envisaged, and emphasised the need for a return to theoretical work.

The first interventions had aimed at analysing social conflict around the production of knowledge, as the central social field of post-industrial society. Over the decade Touraine reconceptualised this theme, arguing that the central form of social self-transformation lies in the capacity of symbolic production of a society (1985, 1988). Forms of social power are characterised by the attempt to mobilise all levels of personality and culture (1988). The analysis of the contested social production of this symbolic or communicative capacity for Touraine requires a rupture with evolutionary classical sociology, which was essentially concerned with the problem of reconciling order and progress, the solution being found in the idea of society as an evolutionary subject. For Touraine, the analysis of modernity must be separated from the analysis of modernisation, whereas these are fused into one process within evolutionary theories.

Contemporary social theory, Touraine argues, is in a period of decomposition. Its reconstruction involves opposing representations of social life as a pure system of change or market (analyses associated with the work of Michel Crozier), as well as those which conceive of society uniquely in terms of order and exclusion (analyses associated with the popularised receptions of Althusser or the early Foucault).

The centrality of symbolic production and communicative capacity means for Touraine that the decisive step in the recomposition of social theory lies in the replacement of the theme of labour with that of communication. For Touraine this represents the return of the subject, a subject no longer defined in terms of identification with the universal but defined in terms of difference and communication with the other, themes that were raised particularly by the women's movement (1985: 20). While the early interventions were looking to a rapid recomposition of a post-industrial social field, later work is based on the hypothesis of a much more fragile emergence of new forms of conflictuality, a process similar to the slow formation of the labour movement.

This has led to a widening out of the scope of the sociological intervention, and to an emphasis on the role of social movement analysis as central to the recomposition of social theory as a whole. François Dubet (1987) led a CADIS intervention with marginalised youth in French cities. The action patterns identified were dominated by themes of rage, disorganisation and exclusion. Nonetheless these did not form the stable responses to social exclusion represented by subcultures or gangs, but pointed towards emerging forms of social conflict from 'below', constituted as cultural forms of action. This led Dubet to develop the suggestive hypothesis of the emergence of new 'dangerous classes'. This points to an emerging social movement in the same way as the dangerous classes of the last century pointed towards a workers' movement that had not yet developed. The earlier thinking behind the intervention had looked for signs of an emerging social movement in terms of positive action capacities. This later research recognised the greater complexity involved in the formation of a social field.

The centrality of social movements to social policy analysis has also been developed. Anne Marie Guillemard (1985, 1986), who also worked with Touraine, has looked at the cultural and social organisation of ageing as a product of the shared culture of the labour movement and the industrialists, the industrial social conflict leading to the creation of 'retirement' as a cultural model for the management of old age. The decline of the ability of the social actors of industrial society to generate ways of life points to a crisis in the model of ageing represented by retirement. This may open out the possibility of new conflicts around the meaning of ageing, or it may lead to its decomposition and an absence of meaning.

RETHINKING MODERNITY, RECONSTITUTING THE POLITICAL

Touraine does not romanticise 'new social movements'. He is acutely aware of the decline in conceptions of social life associated with the passage from industrial society, particularly in a context where the economic internationalisation of societies is leading to social dualisation. This period of passage from industrial society involves a crisis of the model of social change associated with the Left, which had successfully combined demands for social reform and economic development in a model of progress. This model of social progress and evolution that was created in the process of development of industrial capitalism is in crisis, leading to a crisis for the Left and for its conception of social change, unable to oppose the representation of society as a market.

The decline of the social actors of industrial society does not necessarily usher in new social movements contesting new forms of post-industrial power. It can lead to a situation characterised, above all, by what appears as the absence of social conflicts and debates, with the triumph of categories such as the 'nation' over social categories (Touraine 1990b). Touraine is increasingly concerned with the possibility of a situation shaped by the weakness of new social movements, a dynamic where the representation of society as a market is opposed only by populist forms of defensive nationalist reaction. Such forms of action are evident in the development of new forms of defensive racism or the development of action patterns that are the defence of communities in crisis: skinheads in Britain, the development of 'urban tribalism', the return of forms of action dominated by social exclusion. While Touraine's program in the 1970s and 1980s looked to the emergence of new social movements, the 1990s look more fragile, to be grasped in terms of the urgency of developing a language to express new forms of social conflictuality and creativity, and in terms of the possible costs of the failure to do so.

BIBLIOGRAPHY

Primary sources

Touraine, A. et al. (1965) *Workers' Attitudes to Technical Change* Paris, OCDE
——(1974) *The Post-Industrial Society* London, Wildwood House
——(1977a) *The Self-Production of Society* Chicago, University of Chicago Press
——(1977b) *Un désir d'Histoire* Paris, Stock
——et al. (1978) *Lutte étudiante* Paris, Seuil
——(1981) *The Voice and the Eye: An Analysis of Social Movements* New York, Cambridge University Press, 1983
——et al. (1981) *Le pays Contre L'Etat: Luttes Occitaines* Paris, Seuil
——et al. (1983a) *Anti-Nuclear Protest* New York, Cambridge
——et al. (1983b) *Solidarity: The Analysis of a Social Movement* New York, Cambridge University Press
——(1985) 'Les transformations de l'analyse sociologique' *Cahiers Internationaux de Sociologie* LXXVIII
——et al. (1987) *The Workers' Movement* New York, Cambridge University Press
——(1987) *Return of the Actor: Social Theory in Postindustrial Society* Minneapolis, University of Minnesota Press
——(1988) 'Modernity and cultural specificities' *International Social Science Journal* 118
——(1989) 'Is sociology still the study of society?' *Thesis Eleven* 23
——(1990a) 'Peut-on encore être de gauche' *Le Monde* 23 January (translation forthcoming in *Thesis Eleven*)
——(1990b) 'L'hymne à la nation' *Le Monde*, 18 September

Secondary sources

Dubet, F. (1987a) 'Conduites marginales des jeunes et classes sociales' *Revue Française de Sociologie* XXVIII
——(1987b) *La galère: jeunes en survie* Paris, Fayard
——(1990) 'Les territories des bandes' *Libération* 29 March
Guillemard, A. (1985) (ed.) *Old Age and the Welfare State* Beverley Hills, Sage
——(1986) *Le déclin du social* Paris, Presses Universitaires de France
Leccardi, C. (1988) 'Quando il futuro è dark: rappresentaazioni del tempo e stili di identità dei giovani in Italia' *Il Mulino* 317

28

Immanuel Wallerstein

'World-system analysis' is not a theory about the social world, or about part of it. It is a protest against the ways in which scientific inquiry was structured for all of us in the middle of the nineteenth century
(Wallerstein 1987: 309).
The dominant organizing myth of the historiography of the nineteenth and twentieth centuries portrayed a premodern (precapitalist) past . . . It is precisely to [its] historiographical failures that world-systems analysis addressed itself in proposing an alternative organizing myth
(Wallerstein 1983: 301–2).

World system theory can be viewed as a theoretical schema, or organising myth, for understanding the patterns of European development and Third World underdevelopment as interrelated phenomena. The 'gains' of the one generated the impoverishment of the other. The principal theses of world system theory as a 'historical social science' (Wallerstein 1976b; Alexander 1981) suggest that a European world economy was established during the course of the long sixteenth century (c. 1450–1650) by the uneven structuring of trade and development patterns between a West European 'core' and an East European and Latin American 'periphery'. This pattern of uneven development and unequal exchange persists to the present even though core, semiperipheral and peripheral regions may have changing memberships.

Wallerstein's substantive writings (1974a; 1980; 1989) utilise large-scale historical comparisons to fill out and expand the broad picture of world system expansion, fluctuation and change. The scope of analysis is akin to the historical sociology of Barrington Moore (1966) or more recently Theda Skocpol (1979). His comparisons, however, lead to quite different conclusions than theirs (Skocpol 1977). But the most striking aspect of Wallerstein's work as a social theorist is the constant concern with epistemological and methodological issues evident in all his occasional writings. This concern sets his writings apart from the work of other world system theorists who have elaborated the theory as a set of hypotheses amenable to quantitative cross-national and time-series testing (Chase-Dunn 1989). To read Wallerstein as a social theorist, therefore, we need to consider the dual concerns of his own writing and the more empirically-oriented applications of the theory by its other proponents (Taylor 1986).

HISTORICAL MYTH-MAKING: DEFINING THE WORK OF HISTORICAL SOCIAL SCIENCE

Wallerstein presents world system theory as a synthesis of a longer tradition of counter-theorising which questions the theoretical fundamentals of Western social science. World system theory offers and demands a different conception of historical truth; a different heuristic. It can only be, Wallerstein asserts, the elaboration of a series of historical propositions about the origins of the contemporary world economy, its possible form of development and its possible transformation into some other form of global organisation. Moreover, as a series of hypotheses, its claims to truth rest not on criteria of empirical validity as usually conceived but on their heuristic value; i.e. whether they make sense to the people and organisations who are seeking to act in world-historical contexts and need to understand the dynamics of change and reaction in these contexts.

For Wallerstein, world system analysis must be uncompromisingly interdisciplinary. It neither expects the key disciplines of history and the various social sciences to have a neatly shared division of labour (Wallerstein 1987: 314) nor will it allow social sciences to work with concepts of societies or polities as timeless forms of organisation conceived independently of their world-historical contexts. The historical patterns of technological and social development have a major impact on any society or polity as do the larger and historically specific patterns of interstate and inter-societal (or international) relations. The capitalist world economy is only one such configuration, although it is obviously the most important in the contemporary era.

It is the application of these iconoclastic perspectives to the definition and discussion of capitalism that has generated much dispute between Wallerstein and his Marxist critics (Aronowitz 1981; Brenner 1977; Worsley 1980). Because world system theory sees the capitalist world economy as a historically specific system of uneven development and accumulation, Wallerstein's definition of capitalism relates to this *systemic* dynamic. The very starting point of his definition is grounded in historical mythology and hence contrasts markedly with the more formal and abstract Marxist definition of capitalism as a set of class relations generated by a commodity exchange network. In contrast to the Marxist (and Smithian) view, Wallerstein comes to see forms of monopoly as the key element in the uneven accumulation of capital in the capitalist world economy. If the *system* is capitalist in that it allows the accumulation of capital, this element of monopoly control is the critical one which defines its historical specificity. The control of technological and industrial innovations which Marx and Smith saw as the essence of capitalist endeavour are, for Wallerstein, just one more important example of this systemic structuring of monopoly advantage (1987: 319–20). World system theory therefore turns conventional theory on its head. Whereas conventional theory sees monopoly as a degeneration of pure capitalism, Wallerstein sees technological innovation, the epitome of industrial capitalism in the conventional view, as a special form of monopoly.

The capitalist world economy is, therefore, the system of exchange and accumulation taking place within the framework structured by the political system of the interstate competition, rivalry and balance. The interstate system generates a framework of trading regimes which structure and channel the international (and national) exchange of commodities, capital, labour power and information. The institution of different forms of labour control in different zones of the world economy is, for Wallerstein, a major mechanism of surplus extraction. States and corporations both seek to position themselves to capture this surplus by controlling the crucial links in the commodity chains that traverse the space from initial production to final consumption.

The elaboration of world system theory as an alternative organising myth undermines any easy acceptance of the conventional, generally optimistic 'facts' of Western history. Its redefinition of capitalism and its critique of progress undermine the eschatology—the belief in material progress and scientific enlightenment—implied in both liberal and Marxist views of history and change (Wallerstein 1983b). With this rethinking of the substantive content of received historical social science, it is little wonder that world system analysis has led Wallerstein to constantly question the epistemological and methodological assumptions of Western social science traditions.

THE STRUCTURING OF THE CAPITALIST WORLD ECONOMY: THE PROBLEM OF THE SEMIPERIPHERY

Even with the traditions of counter-theorising that Wallerstein sees as the precursors of world system theory, this theory is unique in that it proposes a three-part structuring of the world economy. To the division of core and periphery it adds a third category, the semiperiphery. The idea of the semiperiphery is an important one as it recognises many cases and situations which do not fit easily into the simple categories of core and periphery (Garst 1985). Australia is such a case. Approaching world system theory through such problems, however, exemplifies the underlying tension within Wallerstein's paradigm between the demands of his heuristic theorising and the analysis of particular empirical cases.

In Wallerstein's occasional writings the semiperiphery has assumed an imprecise and ambiguous meaning and is variously used to specify a state's position within the economic hierarchy of the capitalist world system, the geopolitical hierarchy of the nation-state system, or some combination of both (Arrighi and Drangel 1986: 14). Within the heuristic overview of world system development it has primarily served to explain the stabilisation of the capitalist world system (Wallerstein 1974b, 1976b). In the broad overview, Wallerstein does not provide specific insights into the relationship between economic participation in the capitalist world economy and geopolitical position and power. Wallerstein's discussion of the European semiperiphery (1980: 179–241), the situation of postwar semiperipheral countries (1976a) and settler decolonisation (1989: 193–256) explores these relationships in particular instances. However, in these discussions, the way that the semiperiphery contributes to the stability of the capitalist world system is not clearly theorised.

For other world system theorists, the semiperiphery has been utilised as a category of empirical analysis 'in isolating a zone of political analysis' (1985: 36), particularly in Southern Europe. Here, it has been argued, states have exhibited broadly similar patterns of economic dualism and interventionist state policies (Arrighi 1985: 11–13). Again, however, the relationship between economic participation in the world economy and geopolitical position is not systematically addressed. The analysis tends to subordinate questions of geopolitical power to a conception of semiperipheral politics which 'emphasizes the voluntary action of states to improve the relative position of their countries by accepting competition but by pursuing a policy of catching-up' (Aymard 1985: 40).

The most careful elaboration of the economic conception of the semiperiphery is that of Arrighi and Drangel. They define it as 'a position in relation to the world division of labour' and argue that the concept should never be used 'to refer to a position within the interstate system' (1986: 15). They conceptualise the world economy as a network of commodity chains 'that cut across state boundaries' and argue that core and peripheral activities (not regions) are unevenly distributed both within and between nation-states (p. 11). Commodity chains link these core and peripheral activities. The core activities 'command a large share of the surplus produced within a commodity chain while peripheral activities are those that command little or no such surplus' (pp. 11–12). Arrighi and Drangel argue that there is no empirical means of directly measuring the mix of activities in any country or region but use GNP per capita as an indirect measure. They demonstrate that there is a distinctly trimodal patterning of the international economy which, they argue, correlates with a relatively stable division between core, periphery and semiperiphery for the 50-year time period they cover (pp. 31–71).

Arrighi and Drangel's analysis also confirms that there is no simple correlation between core, semiperipheral and peripheral economic position and geopolitical position. For instance, the USSR, although a major power within the nation-state system, is classified in their formulation as an organic member of the semiperipheral zone (p. 69). Similarly, the oil-rich states of Libya and Saudi Arabia, although not major geopolitical powers, are seen as presently occupying a transitory position in the core. On the other hand, the economic analysis gives no systemic clues as to the relationship between economic position in the world economy, geopolitical position and the emergence of semiperipheral politics. This problem of the semiperiphery illustrates the difficulties of matching the heuristic and empirical strands of world system theorising.

AUSTRALIA AS A SEMIPERIPHERAL COUNTRY?

Arrighi and Drangel locate Australia as an organic member of the core (p. 61). Wallerstein, by contrast, locates Australia in the semiperiphery (1976a: 466). This ambiguity of Australia's position illustrates the deeper ambiguity between the heuristic and problem-oriented aspects of world system theory. Analysis of the semiperiphery as a 'zone of political activity' extends world system analysis in the direction of a more state-centred approach. Skocpol (1977), Booth (1985) and Mouzelis (1988: 23) argue for such an extension to overcome the impasses of world system theory. This extends the parameters of Wallerstein's historical sociology by seeing the modern, territorially demarcated nation-state not just in terms of its role in securing the conditions of capital accumulation but also in terms of its central role in constituting political and economic regimes and orders (Skocpol 1985: 9; Mann 1980, 1984). On the broader heuristic level, however, such a theoretical extension reopens questions about the dynamic of world system change; is it a system process of dynamic contradictions and balances or is it a contingent process of regime construction and shifting hegemonies? Furthermore, if world system analysis is extended by using a more state-centred approach, there is a danger that the more rationalistic assumptions which this embodies may undermine the methodological and epistemological positions which Wallerstein has established for world system theory.

Australia can be categorised as a core country in terms of its GNP per capita and standard of living. In global geopolitics it is a relatively successful middle-order power. Its mode of participation in the world economy has some of the economic dualism of a peripheral region, given the position of its producers in the international commodity chains and its reliance on foreign capital. If, however, one views semiperipheral politics as the active involvement of the state in strategies of nation-building, the Australian situation seems to fit. Despite the current fashion for deregulation amongst policy-makers, Australia has had a long history of involvement of the state in the management of economic affairs and the maintenance of Australia's status as a sub-imperial power (Gow 1990). The difficulty of fitting world system analysis to Australia's situation clearly illustrates the dilemmas of the theory.

CONCLUSION: AUSTRALIA AND THE THREE FACETS OF WORLD SYSTEM THEORY

Wallerstein's heuristic elaboration of world system theory offers a corrective to many assumptions of Western superiority embedded in both liberal and Marxist perspectives. The problems raised by treating the semiperiphery and Australia as a 'zone of political analysis' do not fit easily with the 'Third Worldist' direction of his heuristic. A more state-centred approach has other dangers. The articulation of this problem and its resolution within world system theory are of particular interest to Australian social theorists.

The other arena of world system analysis is the mapping of world economic structures along the lines pioneered by Arrighi and Drangel (1986). This economic analysis is still in its early stages. World system analysis also needs more parallel work which maps global geopolitical regimes to internal political movements (Gow 1990). Although remaining within the stricter parameters of world system analysis stipulated by Wallerstein's methodological concerns, these approaches need further development before they will adequately address the empirical problems of world system theorists, such as those associated with the situation of semiperipheral countries.

BIBLIOGRAPHY

Primary sources

Wallerstein, I. (1974a) *The Modern World System I: Capitalist Agriculture and the Origins of the European World Economy in the Sixteenth Century* New York, Academic Press
——(1974b) 'The rise and future demise of the world capitalist system: concepts for a comparative analysis' *Comparative Studies in Society and History* 16(4)
——(1976a) 'Semiperipheral countries and the contemporary world crisis' *Theory and Society* 3(4)
——(1976b) 'A world-system perspective on the social sciences' *British Journal of Sociology* 27(3)
——(1980) *The Modern World System II: Mercantilism and the Consolidation of the European World Economy, 1600–1750* New York, Academic Press

——(1983a) 'An agenda for world-systems analysis', in W.R. Thompson (ed.) *Contending Approaches to World System Analysis* Beverley Hills, Sage

——(1983b) *Historical Capitalism* London, Verso

——(1985) 'The relevance of the concept of the semiperiphery to Southern Europe', in G. Arrighi (ed.) *Semiperipheral Development: The Politics of the Semiperiphery in the Twentieth Century* Beverley Hills, Sage

——(1987) 'World systems analysis', in A. Giddens and J. Turner (eds) *Social Theory Today* Oxford, Polity Press

——(1989) *The Modern World System III: The Second Era of Expansion of the Capitalist World Economy* San Diego, Academic Press

Secondary sources

Alexander, M. (1981) 'Historical social science: class structure in the modern world system' *Australian and New Zealand Journal of Sociology* 17(1)

Aronowitz, S. (1981) 'A metatheoretical critique of Immanuel Wallerstein's *The Modern World System*' *Theory and Society* 10(4)

Arrighi, G (1985) 'Introduction', in G. Arrighi (ed.) *Semiperipheral Development: The Politics of Southern Europe in the Twentieth Century* Beverley Hills, Sage

——and Drangel, J. (1986) 'The stratification of the world economy: an exploration of the semiperipheral zone' *Review* X(1)

Aymard, M. (1985) 'Nation-states and interregional disparities of development', in G. Arrighi (ed.) *Semiperipheral Development: The Politics of Southern Europe in the Twentieth Century* Beverley Hills, Sage

Booth, D. (1985) 'Marxism and development sociology: interpreting the impasse' *World Development* 13(7)

Brenner, R. (1977) 'The origins of capitalist development: a critique of neo-Smithian Marxism' *New Left Review* 104

Chase-Dunn, C. (1989) *Global Formation: Structures of the World-economy* Oxford, Basil Blackwell

Garst, D. (1985) 'Wallerstein and his critics' *Theory and Society* 14

Gow, J.F. (1990) The construction of hegemony: a world-historical study of Australian politics and external relations, PhD thesis, Division of Humanities, Griffith University

Mann, M. (1980) 'State and society, 1130–1815: an analysis of English state finances', in M. Zetlin (ed.) *Political Power and Social Theory* New York, JAI Press

——(1984) 'The autonomous power of the state: its origins, mechanisms and results' *Archives Européenes de Sociologie* XXV

Moore, B. (1966) *Social Origins of Dictatorship and Democracy: Lord and Peasant in the Making of the Modern World* Boston, Beacon Press

Mouzelis, N.P. (1988) 'Sociology of development: reflections on the present crisis' *Sociology* 22(1)

Skocpol, T. (1977) 'Wallerstein's world capitalist system perspective: a theoretical and historical critique' *American Journal of Sociology* 82

——(1979 *States and Social Revolutions* Cambridge, Cambridge University Press

——(1985) 'Bringing the state back in: strategies of analysis in current research', in P. Evans, D. Rueschemeyer and T. Skocpol (eds), *Bringing the State Back In* Cambridge, Cambridge University Press

Taylor, P. (1986) 'The poverty of international comparisons: some methodological lessons from world-system analysis' *Studies in Comparative International Development* XXII (1)

Worsley, P. (1980) 'One world or three? A critique of the world system theory of Immanuel Wallerstein' *The Socialist Register*

PETER BEILHARZ

29

Max Weber

Of all the classical social theorists, it is probably fair to say that none have suffered such distortion as Marx and Weber (though this transformation is also a broader trend, including Freud and Durkheim). Marx and Weber have been turned into apologists for the very phenomena which they set out to criticise, Marx set up as an apologist for Soviet 'primitive communism', Weber as an enthusiastic advocate of bureaucracy, the 'value-free' science, and the onward march of rationalisation. An accompanying problem in the reception of Weber has been the widespread tendency to set Marx and Weber against each other, as adversaries, with Weber as 'the bourgeois Marx' (cf. Bittman 1986; Beilharz 1983). We need to scrape off some of these accretions on Weber before we can begin to indicate something of the nature of his thought, because it is really only quite recently that Weber scholarship has begun this exercise of reading Weber with new (or, in a historical sense, old) eyes.

Before we proceed to Weber's sociology, a word is appropriate about his politics. Marx's communism is universally declared or declaimed, as though it were uncommon for social theorists to engage in politics. Nothing could be further from the truth. Indeed, Weber, and Durkheim, and more recent theorists such as Castoriadis and Habermas, are all, by definition, political animals. Weber was political from the first to the last. The young Weber was an active researcher into social policy and labour conditions; the later Weber conducted research into the psychophysics of industrial work, but was also a participant in the Versailles peace negotiations and a contributor to the Weimar Constitution (Tribe 1989; Mommsen 1989; Weber 1988).

In all this, his sympathies were arguably closer to the German Social Democratic Party than has been acknowledged, at least to its reformist current (Mommsen and Osterhammel 1987). It is no accident that two of his young friends, Lukács and Michels, were revolutionaries, for Weber also had his romantic impulse. Writing closer to the turn of the century, though, he believed the hope of redemption to be decisively lost, a redundant Victorian dream. As recent scholarship in English has finally recognised, the vital figure in Weber's shadow (along with Goethe) is Nietzsche. If Weber's world is one without great hopes, it is also, like Nietzsche's, one without the traditional great illusions. Where Marx's lifespan was 1818–1883, Weber's was 1864–1920. Weber's moment, rather like our own today, was one of circumspection, introspection, and modest hopes. Right-and left-wing myths of progress were both too fearful for Weber, but he was not the defeatist he is often portrayed as.

THE 'PROTESTANT ETHIC' AND WEBER'S SOCIOLOGY

To turn to Weber's published work is immediately to be overwhelmed— sociology of religion, medieval and ancient law and history, sociology of music ('The History of the Piano'), action, the city, methodology, charisma . . . The binding thread is Weber's concern with culture, or how we live, and its rationalisation. Weber's leading and most controversial work here is *The Protestant Ethic and the Spirit of Capitalism* (1904–5). Contrasted to massive and arid texts such as *Economy and Society* (in English, 1968), it is Weber at his reflective and conversational best. Weber's essay is often cast as a narrowly religious inquiry, or as a metanarrative about ideology and the primacy of ideas in social life. Neither proposition manages to capture Weber's purpose, which is to discuss problems of rationality and the rationalisation of culture. Where Marx draws out commodification as the central trend of modernity, Weber draws attention to the tendency to universal calculation, itself underpinned by the rationalisation, disenchantment or demagification of everyday life (Weber 1904–5: 18).

In common with Marx and Durkheim, Weber takes a stand against utilitarianism or the cult of utility, that which would replace all matters of quality with calculus about quantity (Seidman 1983). Weber regards rationalisation as an inexorable, yet ambivalent process (Löwith 1982). As he argues later, citizens of modernity need bureaucracy, justice, legality and administration, yet they all, in turn, also feed upon us. Weber does not, however, construct his theory in terms of the bureaucratic system. In form and content his method is essayistic. It is neither exhaustive—heaping up empirical evidence—nor systematic in the manner of Marx's *Capital*. Weber's approach to knowledge is conversational, in the manner of hermeneutics; he uses exemplary instances, the historic figures of Franklin and Baxter, in order to illustrate the claim that with capitalism there emerges a new way of living: or more precisely, that capitalism emerges together with a new, rationalised and calculative way of life.

Calvinism encourages asceticism, the gathering of wealth to God's greater glory, and not for worldly luxury; this accumulation of capital makes possible the transition from feudalism to capitalism. Now the logic of the worldly pursuit of gain for God turns back on itself; if religion helps to bring about the advent of capitalism, capitalism itself promptly sets about destroying religion. Weber quotes Goethe: asceticism seeks ever the good, but creates evil (Weber 1904–5: 172). Thus Weber appeals to the theme present throughout his work, the Hegelian cunning of reason or irony of history, what in everyday life we less elegantly call unintended consequence. The implication is clear—what we call rationality becomes irrational. Capitalist rationality produces a self-sufficient, self-sustaining cosmos, to the extent that its citizens forget the plurality of rationalities (p. 78). Bound, like Sisyphus, to the stones of our specialisation, we become entrapped within the steel-hard housing of our own unwitting manufacture (p. 181). Disenchantment confronts us. Like Marx, Weber summons Goethe to judge the human condition: we are 'Specialists without spirit, hedonists without heart; this nullity imagines that it has attained a level of civilization never before achieved' (p. 182). Little wonder that Weber is often read as a pessimist, or paired together with Nietzsche as a nihilist.

But there is more to the story. If this is Weber's common visage in social theory, then there is another Weber in mainstream sociology, the one who wrote about (and allegedly was enthusiastic about) bureaucracy and model-building. Most undergraduates are fortunate to meet the reflective or philosophical Weber at all. What they typically find served up as Weber in sociology is the proposition that status and political power offer a counterbalance and qualification to the power of class, and the model concerning the ideal-typical attributes of bureaucracy (Weber 1948: chs. 7 and 8). The significance of status and political power are indeed considerable for Weber, for they indicate a plurality of forms of domination and spheres of action not routinely recognisable to Marx.

For Marx, the problem of modernity is capitalism; for Weber, capitalism is a fundamental part of the problem, but only part of it. Weber makes the elementary observation that classes do not, cannot act—groups do, including groups and representatives which identify with classes. Weber retains a pragmatic sense of action compared, say, to Lukács or the young Marx, for whom the proletariat was a collective actor. The forms of action, authority and legitimation Weber then identifies as traditional, charismatic and rational-legal, roughly sequential viewed schematically, but always in mixed historical fusion. Bureaucracy becomes predominant in all spheres of public life because of the increasing formalisation of public relations; this begins the Weberian process later explained by Habermas as the colonisation and juridicalisation of the life-world.

The increasing centralisation of bureaucracy proceeds hand-in-hand with the increasing centralisation of wealth (Weber 1948: 221). Ironically, just as capitalism erodes religion, so does organisation undermine the mass democracy which it emerges in league with (Weber 1948: 224; Michels 1915). As with the *Protestant Ethic*, however, Weber's claim is not simply that bureaucracy exists in some narrow institutional or organisational sense; rather it is that our culture, our practices and beliefs become bureaucratic. It is not ideas which bring about this process, but material and ideal *interests*, as actors conceive them (Weber 1948: 280). If the popular image of Weber's sociology and its buzz words—status, bureaucracy, charisma—are then reinserted into this context, a more striking image of Weber's purpose can be allowed to emerge. His is a sceptical social theory, governed by concerns of complexity, action, individual motivation, forms of association, and social consequence.

POLITICS AND SCHOLARSHIP

The nature of Weber's project becomes further apparent when it is located in the context of his three famous lectures, on politics and knowledge as vocations and on socialism. The lectures reward careful reading. Parts of them address a world long gone; parts pierce the heart of the present. Even without knowing the timbre of his voice or the inflection of his native German prose, the lectures tell us a great deal both about Weber and about ourselves. Weber viewed the social world as necessarily consisting of distinct spheres and ethics. The problem with bureaucracy, for example, was to keep it where it belonged; similarly with other practices.

In the context of the growing political demagoguery of the emerging Weimar Republic—the collapse of the Empire left insurrection widespread, fascism incipient—Weber was anxious that politics and scholarship be kept separate, not because they were unconnected, but because each had its own distinct purpose. Politics proper concerned matters of state. Politics needed to be kept separate from bureaucracy or administration; each practice was significant, for all societies, real or imagined, were compelled to secure their own order (Weber 1948: 91–2). Administration calls on coolness; politics, for Weber, is primarily the scene of struggle and passion. Yet ironically, like much else in social life, political action is also given to turning back on itself. This is a general predicament for Weber, part of a broad societal process in which *means* come to dominate *ends* (Weber 1948: 120).

Politics and scholarship alike demand persistence, which is difficult in both spheres because each is given to corruption. Scholarship is, if anything, more arbitrary. Insight can be the product of accident or coincidence just as much as of deskwork, but deskwork remains the formal precondition of knowledge (1948, p. 136). Anticipating Foucault's concerns about power and knowledge, Weber also sketches the idea of the specific as opposed to the renaissance intellectual (p. 137) and, like Lévi-Strauss, he proposes that we moderns do not know ourselves any better than the 'primitives' (p. 139).

In all this Weber's is an astonishingly contemporary presence—his scholarship is committed yet contingent, and he relies upon the case study rather than the master work, microsociological insights emerging from macrosociological thinking. Above all, Weber's social theory is consistently historical, located within a sense of the epoch as one where science and religion have been sundered. Science can no longer generate meaning. But this does not leave us without hope, or without meaning. It throws upon us the responsibility to create our own meaning out of our own chests, for within the disenchantment of modernity there remain gods or orienting values to choose between (p. 155). So Weber exhorts us, via Goethe, to take up our vocations (p. 156). God is not dead, rather polytheism reigns; the shift, historically, is that research can no longer inform us of our values, which we must rather each grasp or forge. We make our own gods, but ours is not a godless-valueless world; God is no longer given by tradition, but chosen.

Scientisation is thus a dominant trend, but this does not mean that knowledge is no longer possible. Weber is concerned with the limits to knowledge, but he is no epistemological nihilist. Views of culture are always perspectival (Weber 1949: 81). And while perspectives are obviously socially formed, they are also individual. Weber put great stress on the individual, and on individual responsibility. In the collision of world views or gods, it was individuals who needed to take their stand and to argue. Weber would doubtless have agreed with Goethe's maxim that we aspire to the truth still, even though we know it to be elusive. Now clearly these kinds of sympathies in Weber make possible certain potential openings to existentialism and to phenomenology.

The question then returns: whether we do live in a metaphorical iron cage or prison and, if so, whether we can flee it to a sphere of value where we must create our own meaning (Scaff 1987). The least that need be said here is that the iron cage metaphor is overblown. It is essentially a mistranslation which too easily aligns Weber with the nihilism of Nietzsche and the anthropological pessimism of Foucault's prison-society image. Here it is important to remember that, like Foucault the prison activist, Weber was indeed a reformer. He understood that there was a strong relationship between social theory and social policy. The intransigence of the world did not tempt him to turn his back on politics or on scholarship as kindred vocations.

Was Weber, then, a socialist? The answer to this question is no, but it raises another, more interesting question about the relation between liberalism and socialism. Weber was in some ways a cultured bourgeois like Keynes, but this did not prevent either from being a reformer. The logic of his social theory, however, was that the prospect of a qualitative break between capitalism and socialism was simply inconceivable. The day after the revolution—here he would agree with Gramsci and Durkheim—it would still be necessary to have bread in the shops and to get the children to school. In this regard Weber's distaste may be said to be for certain socialists more than for socialism, which he viewed as an historic form of economic organisation (Weber 1978: 251).

In his lecture on socialism Weber discusses the *Communist Manifesto* as a document of scientific achievement in the first order (Weber 1978: 256). What he objects to is its assertion that socialism could mean the end of domination. Weber sympathetically discusses the possibility of cooperation, but views state and capital as the central institutions of economic life, and fears the tyranny of the state more than that of capital. And in this, too, his social theory is perspectival, for he can immediately accept that from the position of the working class the view is different, even if the problems faced across society are similar. Social-ism for Weber is one of the warring gods, but it is not the one he will choose. Given the irreconcilability of the modern gods, it is impossible for Weber to accept that there could ever be any kind of end to history or to struggle, to difference or to conflict. Modernity tests our mettle, each one of us: it demands to see how much we can stand, and this goes on every day of our lives.

Weber's influence in Australia has been strong but late, retarded, arguably, by the institutional emergence of sociology as a discipline only into the 1960s. Weber's influence on pioneers such as Davies (1964) and Encel (1970) is clear. Later followers include Wild (1978). On the whole, however, the philosophical Weber is a recent arrival in Australia, as in other English-speaking academic cultures. Weber has been re-read cul-turally or philosophically by teachers such as Zawar Hanfi and Harry Redner and by those enthusiastic for Habermas (Arnason nd; Brand 1990) or Lukács (Grumley 1988), and has an increasing if indirect pres-ence in the present enthusiasm for the historical sociology which he largely pioneered, but which has yet to settle accounts with this debt (see, for example, Kennedy 1989).

BIBLIOGRAPHY

Primary sources

Weber, M. (1904–5/1958) *The Protestant Ethic and the Spirit of Capi-talism* New York, Scribners
——(1948) *From Max Weber* Ed. by H.H. Gerth and C.W. Mills. London, Routledge
——(1949) *The Methodology of the Social Sciences* New York, Free Press
——(1968) *Economy and Society* 2 vols, New York, Bedminster

——(1978) *Selections in Translation*. Ed. by W.G. Runciman. Cambridge, Cambridge University Press

Secondary sources

Albrow, M. (1990) *Max Weber's Construction of Social Theory* London, Macmillan

Arnason, J.P. (nd) *Rationalisation and Modernity. Towards a Culturalist Reading of Max Weber* Bundoora, Vic., La Trobe Sociology Paper 9

Beilharz, P. (1983) 'Marx and Weber—beyond the great divide?' *Politics* November

Bittman, M. (1986) 'A bourgeois Marx? Max Weber's theory of capitalist society' *Thesis Eleven* 15

Bologh, R. (1990) *Love or Greatness—Max Weber and Masculine Thinking* London, Unwin Hyman

Brand, A. (1990) *The Force of Reason* Sydney, Allen & Unwin

Brubaker, R. (1984) *The Limits of Rationality* London, Allen & Unwin

Davies, A.F. (1964) *Australian Democracy* Melbourne, Cheshire

Eden, R. (1983) *Political Leadership and Nihilism: A Study of Weber and Nietzsche* Tampa, University of Florida

Encel, S. (1970) *Equality and Authority* Melbourne, Cheshire

Grumley, J. (1988) 'Weber's fragmentation of totality' *Thesis Eleven* 21

Hennis, W. (1987) *Max Weber: Essays in Reconstruction* London, Allen & Unwin

Kennedy, R. (1989) *Australian Welfare—Historical Sociology* Sydney, Macmillan

Löwith, K. (1982) *Max Weber and Karl Marx* London, Allen & Unwin

Michels, R. (1915) *Political Parties* London, Jarrolds

Mommsen, W. (1989) *The Political and Social Theory of Max Weber* Cambridge, Polity

——and J. Osterhammel (1987) *Max Weber and His Contemporaries* London, Unwin Hyman

Parkin, F. (1982) *Max Weber* London, Ellis-Horwood

Scaff, L. (1987) 'Fleeing the iron cage' *American Political Science Review* September

Seidman, S. (1983) *Liberalism and the Origins of European Social Theory* Oxford, Blackwell

Tenbruck, F. (1980) 'The problem of thematic writing in the works of Max Weber' *British Journal of Sociology* September

Tribe, K. (1989) *Reading Weber* London, Routledge

Weber, Marianne (1988) *Max Weber. A Biography* New Brunswick, Transaction

Whimster, S. and S. Lash (1987) *Max Weber: Rationality and Modernity* London, Allen & Unwin

Wild, R. (1978) *Social Stratification in Australia* Sydney, Allen & Unwin

Raymond Williams

Raymond Williams, who died in January 1988 at the age of 66, and who had been until his retirement Professor of Drama at Cambridge University, is perhaps the single most important 'left-wing' figure in postwar British intellectual life. His various contributions, as a literary critic, as a central source of theoretical inspiration for the proto-discipline of cultural studies, as a key figure in the New Left intelligentsia, even as a realist novelist, have all been variously acknowledged. Less common is a recognition of his role as social theorist. And yet Williams himself came to characterise his *cultural materialism* as, among other things, a kind of sociology: hence, the inclusion of his *Culture* (1981) in the Fontana New Sociology series. Trained in the discipline of English literature, he was a former student of Leavis, the literary critic whose work provided English studies with its dominant paradigm for much of the postwar period.

Formed by the biographical experience of Welsh working-class life, Williams was also a lifelong socialist: very briefly a member of the British Communist Party, a Labour Party supporter during the 1950s and 1960s, an enthusiast for various New Left causes (especially that of the Campaign for Nuclear Disarmament) and, in his last years, a fairly close associate of the left-inclined Welsh nationalist party, Plaid Cymru. Such political involvements led to an enduring interest in Marxian and quasi-Marxian versions of social and cultural theory. In one sense, the key to an understanding of Williams's intellectual evolution consists in an appreciation of how he variously negotiated his own doubly ambivalent relationship to Leavisism on the one hand, and to Marxism on the other.

From Leavisism, Williams inherited a commitment to organicist and holistic conceptions of culture and methods of analysis; a strong sense of the importance of the particular, whether in art or in 'life'; and an insistence on the absolute centrality of culture. He rejected its cultural elitism, however, especially as displayed in the mass civilisation versus minority culture topos. From Marxism, Williams inherited a radically socialistic critique of ruling class political, economic and cultural power. But he rejected both the economic determinism of orthodox communist Marxism, which had sought to characterise culture as a merely epiphenomenal 'superstructure', and the later structural determinism of Althusserian and quasi-Althusserian theories of ideology, which belied the reality both of experience and of agency.

It is possible to identify three main 'phases' in Williams' thought, each explicable in terms of its own differentially negotiated settlement between Leavisism and Marxism, and each characterisable, in perhaps overly political terms, in relation to a relatively distinct, consecutive moment in the history of the British New Left. In the first such phase, that of the moment of '1956' and the foundation of the New Left, Williams addressed himself directly to the definition of a third position, simultaneously dependent upon but in contradictory relation to Leavisite criticism and orthodox communism. Williams was to play a central role in the development of a peculiarly 'culturalist' post-communist Marxism, a kind of indigenously British 'Western Marxism'. The key texts from this period are *Culture and Society* (1958) and *The Long Revolution* (1961).

Williams insisted that 'culture is ordinary' and, more famously, that 'a culture is not only a body of intellectual and imaginative work; it is also and essentially a whole way of life' (Williams 1958: 311). In principle this is little different from T.S. Eliot or from Leavis. But in the practical application of the principle, Williams so expands its range as to include within 'culture' the 'collective democratic institution', by which he means, primarily, the trade union, the cooperative, and the working-class political party (p. 313). Thus Eliot's and Leavis' notions of a single *common culture* become supplemented, and importantly qualified, by that of a plurality of *class cultures*. Yet, despite such qualification, the normative ideal of a common culture remains important to Williams.

A common culture may not yet properly exist, but it is nonetheless desirable and, moreover, it provides for Williams, as it had for Eliot and for Leavis, the essential theoretical ground from which to mount an organicist critique of utilitarian individualism. But a common culture could never be properly such, Williams argues, if established on the basis of that kind of vicarious participation which Eliot and Leavis had sanctioned. 'The distinction of a culture in common,' he writes, 'is that ... selection is freely and commonly made and remade. The tending is a common process, based on a common decision' (p. 322). Characteristically leftist, Williams thus relocates the common culture from that idealised historical past it had occupied for Eliot and Leavis, to the not too distant, still to be made, democratically socialist future.

If the common culture is not yet fully common, then the literary and cultural tradition should be seen not so much as the unfolding of a group mind, as it had been for Eliot, but as the outcome, in part at least, of a set of interested selections made in the present. Selection, Williams observes, 'will be governed by many kinds of special interest, including class interests ... The traditional culture of a society will always tend to correspond to its *contemporary* system of interests and values' (Williams 1961: 68). Where English literature had revered a 'Great Tradition', Williams would thus detect a *selective tradition*. But even as he insisted on the importance of class cultures, Williams was careful also to note the extent to which distinctions of class are complicated, especially in the field of intellectual and imaginative work, by 'the common elements resting on a common language' (Williams 1958: 311).

Any direct reduction of art to class, such as is canvassed in certain 'leftist' versions of Marxism, for example in Maoism, remained entirely unacceptable. Hence, Williams' development of the concept of *structure of feeling* for the analysis of literary and cultural texts. 'In one sense', he writes, 'this structure of feeling is the culture of a period: it is the particular living result of all the elements in the general organization' (Williams 1961: 64). He continues: 'in this respect ... the arts of a period ... are of major importance ... here ... the actual living sense, the deep community that makes the communication possible, is naturally drawn upon' (pp. 64–5). So, for example, the English novel from Dickens to Lawrence becomes, for Williams, one medium among many by which people seek to master and absorb new experience, through the articulation of a structure of feeling the key problem of which is that of the 'knowable community' (Williams 1974a).

Such deep community must, of course, transcend class, and yet remain irredeemably marked by class. In Williams' early writings, this remains a circle which refuses to be squared. But in the second phase of his work, that of the moment of '1968' and the emergence of a new New Left, it finally became possible for Williams to explain, to his own satisfaction at least, how it could be that structures of feeling are common to different classes, and yet nonetheless represent the interests of some particular class.

In this second phase, Williams' engagement with a series of continental European Western Marxisms, each only recently translated into English (Lukács, Goldmann, Althusser, Gramsci), and with various forms of Third Worldist political 'ultraleftism', parallels, but nonetheless neither reduplicates nor inspires, that of the younger generation of radical intellectuals associated with the *New Left Review*. Initially, this engagement had meant little more than a recognition that not all Marxisms were necessarily economically determinist; and a discovery of theoretical preoccupations similar to his own in the work of writers such as the Franco-Rumanian cultural sociologist Lucien Goldmann (Williams 1971a). Later, however, it came to entail a much more positive redefinition of Williams' own theoretical stance. *The Country and the City*

(1973) heralds a markedly 'leftward' shift in Williams, by which a developing critique of various mythological accounts of rural life (including Marx's own dismissal of 'rural idiocy') eventually culminates in a defence of Third World insurrectionism (Williams 1973: 304). The cultural politics implied therein are neither communist nor labour in inspiration, but rather more obviously akin to Maoism.

This renewed interest in and enthusiasm for unorthodox Marxisms is formally announced in Williams's *Marxism and Literature* (1977). Here Williams argued against the orthodox communist base–superstructure model for cultural analysis, on the grounds that culture is both real and material: 'From castles and palaces and churches to prisons and workhouses and schools; from weapons of war to a controlled press ... These are never superstructural activities. They are necessarily material production within which an apparently self-subsistent mode of production can alone be carried on' (Williams 1977: 93). Williams decisively opts for a theory of *hegemony* deriving from the Italian Marxist theoretician Antonio Gramsci. Indeed, Gramsci's notion of hegemony now seemed to Williams 'one of the major turning points in Marxist cultural theory' (p. 108).

Gramsci's central achievement consists in the articulation of a culturalist sense of the wholeness of culture with a more typically Marxist sense of the interestedness of ideology. Thus hegemony is 'in the strongest sense a "culture", but a culture which has also to be seen as the lived dominance and subordination of particular classes' (p. 110). For Williams, as for Gramsci, the counter-hegemonic moment is especially significant. Hence his attempt to expand upon Gramsci's initial distinction between traditional and organic intellectuals, so as to identify what he terms *dominant*, *residual* and *emergent* cultural elements (pp. 121–7). Williams is able to deploy this scheme with some panache in the analysis of particular cultural texts as, for example, in his essay on 'Forms of English Fiction in 1848' (Williams 1986). His reading of Gramsci almost certainly reconstructs the original authorial intention a great deal more successfully than did the Althusserian theory of ideology so influential on Australian sociology during the 1970s and early 1980s.

In the third and final phase of his work, that produced during the 1980s, the developing internationalisation of corporate capitalism, and the promise of a postmodern radicalism centred around the new social movements, each obliged Williams to think through the theoretical and practical implications of an apparent decentring of the British nation-state on the one hand, and class politics on the other. The key texts here are *Towards 2000* (1983) and the posthumously published and sadly unfinished *The Politics of Modernism* (1989a). Both books quite directly address the cultural politics of *postmodernity*. The more explicitly postmodern moments in *Towards 2000* are contained, firstly, in its sense of the contemporary world system as so radically internationalised, 'paranational' in Williams' phrase, as to undermine the cultural legitimacy of the 'official community' of nation-states such as 'the Yookay' (Williams 1983: 197–8); and, secondly, in its recognition of the peace movement, the ecology movement, the feminist movement and what Williams terms the movement of 'oppositional culture' as major 'resources of hope' for a journey beyond capitalism (p. 250). Williams is careful, however, to acknowledge the continuing importance both of localised communities (pp. 196–7) and of the labour movement, if not of the Labour party. For Williams it is a 'misinterpretation' to see the social movements as 'getting beyond class politics'. Rather, these 'new' issues, followed through, 'lead us into the central systems of the industrial–capitalist mode of production and . . . into its system of classes' (pp. 172–3).

In *The Long Revolution* and in *Culture and Society*, Williams had respectfully but determinedly aired his differences with the guardians of Leavis' minority culture. By *Towards 2000*, he had become much more dismissive: 'There are very few absolute contrasts left between a "minority culture" and "mass communications" ' (p. 134). Williams is insistent that the older modernisms, which once threatened to destabilise the certainties of bourgeois life, have become transformed into a new ' "post-modernist" establishment' which 'takes human inadequacy . . . as self-evident' (p. 141). He was thus already deeply sceptical of the 'pseudo-radicalism' of 'the negative structures of post-modernist art' (p. 145). In *The Politics of Modernism* he would state the case much more forcefully: 'If we are to break out of the non-historical fixity of *post-*modernism, then we must search out and counterpose an alternative tradition taken from the neglected works left in the wide margin of the century, a tradition which may address itself not to this by now exploitable because quite inhuman rewriting of the past but, for all our sakes, to a modern *future* in which community may be imagined again' (Williams 1989a: 35).

Much of the theoretical literature in cultural studies has revolved around a persistent contrast between 'culturalism' and 'structuralism' (R. Johnson 1979; Dermody et al. 1982), in which the former is typically represented by Williams, and perhaps by the historian, E.P. Thompson, the latter by an entire intellectual tradition reaching back from Althusser and Lévi-Strauss to Durkheim and Saussure. Poststructuralism has developed by way of a reaction against this structuralist intellectual tradition. But there is, in fact, a culturalist intellectual tradition behind Williams, the tradition reaching back from Eliot and Leavis to Arnold and beyond, the tradition which Williams himself had sought to map out in *Culture and Society*. Williams stands in relation to this tradition very much as a *post-culturalist*. This is so in more than the simply chronological sense. Where structuralism proper displayed a recurrent aspiration to scientificity, thereby attempting to discover the truth beneath the text, poststructuralisms have betrayed that aspiration by an equally recurrent insistence that there is no single truth in the text, that cultural meaning can never be pinned down, not even by structuralism itself. Practically, this had led to an emergent preoccupation with reader response, reception, the role of the reader, and similar, related concepts.

Before Williams, the culturalist tradition had typically subscribed, not to a scientism, but nonetheless to a kind of 'objective idealism' by which truth was seen to inhere in the cultural tradition itself. Williams' own deconstruction of this notion, through the idea of the selective tradition, effects a relativising turn similar to that of poststructuralism in relation to structuralism. It does so by virtue of an appeal to the role of the (collective) reader. It more than gestures in the direction of a recognition of the intrication of power within discourse as the later Foucault acknowledged; and a recognition of the materiality, historicity and arbitrary variability of the linguistic sign similar to that in both Derrida and Foucault. And all this remains coupled to a sense of genuinely free communicative action—a truly common culture—as normative, of which even Habermas might have approved. Little wonder, then, that Terry Eagleton would eventually conclude that 'Williams' work has prefigured and pre-empted the development of parallel left positions by, so to speak, apparently standing still' (Eagleton 1984: 109).

BIBLIOGRAPHY

Primary sources

Williams, R. (1952) *Drama from Ibsen to Eliot* London, Chatto and Windus
——(1954a) (with Michael Orrom) *Preface to Film* London, Film Drama
——(1954b) *Drama in Performance* London, Frederick Muller
——(1958) *Culture and Society, 1780–1950* Harmondsworth, Penguin, 1963
——(1960) *Border Country* London, Chatto and Windus
——(1961) *The Long Revolution* Harmondsworth, Penguin 1965
——(1962) *Communications* Harmondsworth, Penguin
——(1964) *Second Generation* London, Chatto and Windus
——(1966) *Modern Tragedy* London, Chatto and Windus
——(1968a) *Drama from Ibsen to Brecht* London, Chatto and Windus
——(1968b) (with S. Hall and E.P. Thompson) *Politics: The May Day Manifesto* Harmondsworth, Penguin
——(1971a) 'Literature and sociology: in memory of Lucien Goldmann' *New Left Review* 67
——(1971b) *Orwell* London, Fontana
——(1973) *The Country and the City* London, Chatto and Windus

——(1974a) *The English Novel: From Dickens to Lawrence* St Albans, Paladin
——(1974b) *Television: Technology and Cultural Form* London, Fontana
——(1976) *Keywords: A Vocabulary of Culture and Society* London, Fontana
——(1977) *Marxism and Literature* Oxford, Oxford University Press
——(1978) *The Volunteers* London, Eyre Methuen
——(1979a) *The Fight for Manod* London, Chatto and Windus
——(1979b) *Politics and Letters: Interviews with New Left Review* London, New Left Books
——(1980) *Problems in Materialism and Culture: Selected Essays* London, Verso
——(1981) *Culture* London, Fontana
——(1983) *Towards 2000* London, Chatto and Windus
——(1984) *Writing in Society* London, Verso
——(1985) *Loyalties* London, Chatto and Windus
——(1986) 'Forms of English fiction in 1848', in F. Barker et al. (eds) *Literature, Politics and Theory* London, Methuen
——(1989a) *The Politics of Modernism: Against the New Conformists* London, Verso
——(1989b) *Resources of Hope* London, Verso

Secondary sources

Barnett, A. (1976) 'Raymond Williams and Marxism: a rejoinder to Terry Eagleton' *New Left Review* 99
Dermody, S. et al. (1982) 'Introduction: Australian cultural studies—problems and dilemmas', in S. Dermody et al. (eds) *Nellie Melba, Ginger Meggs and Friends: Essays in Australian Cultural History* Malmsbury, Kibble Books
Eagleton, T. (1976) *Criticism and Ideology* London, New Left Books
——(1984) *The Function of Criticism* London, Verso
——(1988) 'Resources for a journey of hope: the significance of Raymond Williams' *New Left Review* 168
——(1989) (ed.) *Raymond Williams: Critical Perspectives* Cambridge, Polity
Garnham, N. (1988) 'Raymond Williams, 1921–1988: a cultural analyst, a distinctive tradition' *Journal of Communication* 38
Hunter, I. (1988) *Culture and Government: the Emergence of Literary Education* London, Macmillan
Johnson, L. (1979) *The Cultural Critics: From Matthew Arnold to Raymond Williams* London, Routledge & Kegan Paul
——(1987) 'Raymond Williams: a Marxist view of culture', in D. Austin-Broos (ed.) *Creating Culture: Profiles in the Study of Culture* Sydney, Allen & Unwin

Johnson, R. (1979) 'Histories of culture/theories of ideology: notes on an impasse', in M. Barrett et al. (eds) *Ideology and Cultural Production* London, Croom Helm

Jones, P. (1982) 'Organic intellectuals and the generation of English cultural studies' *Thesis Eleven* 5/6

Lawson, S. (1988) 'Raymond Williams' *Australian Society* April

Levy, B. and Otto, P. (1989) (eds) *Southern Review* 22 (2) Special issue on Raymond Williams

Milner, A. (1988) 'A young man's death: Raymond Williams, 1921–1988' *Thesis Eleven* 20

Neale, R.S. (1984) 'Cultural materialism: a critique' *Social History* 9 (2)

O'Connor, A. (1989) *Raymond Williams: Writing, Culture, Politics* Oxford, Blackwell

Sparks, C. 'Raymond Williams, culture and Marxism' *International Socialism* 2 (9)

Thompson, E.P. (1961) 'The long revolution' *New Left Review* 9, 10

Williams, P. (1978) 'Raymond Williams: the critic and society' *Arena* 51

Contributors

Malcolm Alexander researches and teaches in the areas of macrosociology, comparative studies and world system theory. He has made comparative studies of Australia, Argentina and Canada and is currently co-editor of *Australian–Canadian Studies*. He is a senior lecturer in the Division of Humanities of Griffith University.

Peter Beilharz teaches sociology at La Trobe University. He is the author of *Trotsky, Trotskyism and the Transition to Socialism* (1987) and *Labour's Utopias* (1991), and co-author of *Arguing About the Welfare State*. A regular reviewer and contributor to debates on socialism and the labour movement, he is an editor of *Thesis Eleven*.

Jan Branson teaches women's studies and the sociology of education at La Trobe University. She has conducted research in Australia and Indonesia and is currently engaged in research into the sociocultural construction of 'the disabled' in Australia with special focus on programs for the integration of the so-called 'disabled' into mainstream education and on the education of the deaf in Australia. She is the author of *Women's Studies and its Potential Role in the University*, co-author of *Class, Sex and Education: Culture, Ideology and the Reproduction of Inequality in Australia*, editor of *The Other Half: Women in Australian Society* and co-editor of *Development and Displacement: Women in Southeast Asia*.

Malcolm Crick, a senior lecturer in social anthropology at Deakin University, studied at the University of Sussex and then did research at Oxford University. His doctoral thesis was on the topic of social anthropology, language and meaning, work which was published as *Explorations in Language and Meaning. Towards a Semantic Anthropology*. Since the early 1980s his central field of research has been international tourism in the Third World. He is currently completing a monograph on international tourism in Sri Lanka.

Michael Crozier teaches political science at the University of

Melbourne. He has written major studies on Walter Benjamin and on 'The Architectonic Imagination: Aristotle, Aquinas, Alberti'. Presently he is engaged in an examination of the politico-philosophical dimensions of the eighteenth-century English landscape garden. He is also an editor of the journal *Thesis Eleven*.

H.A. Cubbon is a senior lecturer in the sociology department at La Trobe University. Formerly he was an industrial psychologist with the National Institute of Industrial Psychology, London; a research officer in the psychology department at the University of Melbourne; and a lecturer in the psychology department at Bedford College, London University.

David Ames Curtis, translator, editor, writer and activist, was born in Massachusetts in 1956. He studied philosophy at Harvard University. He was community organiser, Carolina Action/ACORN, Black Periodical Fiction Project Research Director and a union organiser at Yale University. The principal English-language translator of Cornelius Castoriadis, he has been published in American, European and Australian journals. He is the co-founder of Agora International, which examines Castoriadis' work.

Alastair Davidson is professor of political theory at the University of Sydney. He is the author of *Gramsci : The Man, His Ideas* (1968); *Antonio Gramsci : Towards an Intellectual Biography* (1977, 1987) and many articles on Gramsci and other related issues, e.g. *The Theory and Practice of Italian Communism* (1982).

Rita Felski teaches in the School of Humanities, Murdoch University, Western Australia. She is the author of *Beyond Feminist Aesthetics: Feminist Literature and Social Change* as well as articles on feminist literary and social theory.

John Gow pursued his undergraduate studies at Griffith University and the University of New South Wales. His major research interests encompass the historical development of the contemporary international economic and geopolitical orders and the economic and political dynamics of nation-states. He was awarded a doctorate by Griffith University for a world-historical study of Australian politics and external relations. He is presently employed as a lecturer in sociology at the University of Newcastle.

Russell Grigg is a lecturer in philosophical studies at Deakin University. A member of the Lacanian School, *École de la cause freudienne*, he is translator of *Seminar III. The Psychoses*.

Paul Raymond Harrison is a lecturer in sociology at La Trobe University. His main research interests are in the fields of social and cultural theory.

Kevin Hart is associate professor of critical theory at Monash University. He teaches in the English department and the Centre for General and Comparative Literature. His most recent publication is *The Trespass* *of the Sign: Deconstruction, Theology and Philosophy.*

Trevor Hogan is a tutor and postgraduate student in sociology at La Trobe University. He is currently engaged in a study of English traditions of ethical and Christian socialism.

Gisela Kaplan migrated to Australia in 1968, and gained her PhD at Monash University. Since 1983 she has lectured in Australia and been visiting professor in US universities. She is the co-editor of *Hannah Arendt. Thinking, Judging, Freedom* and the author of *Contemporary Western European Feminism, 1968–1988.* Her main research interests are in minority groups, political sociology, gender, and the sociology of welfare.

Douglas Kirsner is a senior lecturer in philosophy and history of ideas at Deakin University. In 1977 he founded the Deakin University Annual Freud Conference which he continues to direct. Douglas Kirsner has recently completed *American Psychoanalysis and its Discontents*, a book on the culture of American psychoanalysis to be published by the University of California Press in 1992. He is editor of *The Public Intellectual.*

Beryl Langer teaches sociology at La Trobe University. Her current research is on El Salvadoran refugee settlement in Melbourne, literary production in Canada and Australia, and the commodification of childhood. A former editor of *Australian–Canadian Studies*, she is not a Durkheimian.

Judy Lattas is a tutor in women's studies at Macquarie University. Areas of interest include anti-nuclear criticism and anarcha-feminist practices in Australia as well as contemporary French critical theory. She is currently writing a PhD on 'politics' and the writing of Jacques Derrida.

John Lechte, a former student of Julia Kristeva, is a tutor in sociology at Macquarie University in Sydney. He has published articles on Joyce, Rousseau and multiculturalism, as well as articles on art in light of Julia Kristeva's work. His book on Julia Kristeva was published by Routledge in 1990.

Kevin McDonald teaches sociology at Phillip Institute of Technology, Melbourne. He holds a DEA from the Ecole des Hautes Etudes en Sciences Sociales, where he is currently completing a doctorate on modernity, social movements and the 'information society'. He is an author of *Thesis Eleven.*

Stephen Mennell is professor of sociology at Monash University. He read economics at Cambridge University, was Frank Knox Fellow at Harvard University, and from 1967 to 1990 taught sociology at the University of Exeter. His books include *All Manners of Food* (1985), *Norbert Elias: Civilisation and the Human Self-Image* (1989) and *Human History and Social Process* (with Goudsblom and Jones, 1989).

SOCIAL THEORY

Don Miller teaches anthropology and sociology at Monash University. He has conducted research in India, Indonesia and Australia and is currently engaged in research into the sociocultural construction of 'the disabled' in Western societies and in Australia in particular. He is the author of *From Hierarchy to Stratification: Changing Patterns of Social Inequality in a North Indian Village*, co-author of *Class, Sex and Education in Capitalist Society: Culture, Ideology and the Reproduction of Inequality in Australia*, and editor of *Peasants and Politics: Grass Roots Reactions to Change in Asia*.

Andrew Milner has been director of the Centre for General and Comparative Literature at Monash University since 1985. He is the author of *John Milton and the English Revolution, The Road to St Kilda Pier* and *Contemporary Cultural Theory* and co-editor of *Postmodern Conditions* and *Discourse and Difference*.

Peter Murphy is a lecturer in politics at Ballarat University College. His work has appeared in *Thesis Eleven, Praxis International, Social Research*, and *Telos*. He has taught at La Trobe University, the University of Melbourne, and in the graduate faculty of the New School For Social Research, New York.

Daniel Ross has completed a BA (Hons) degree at La Trobe University and is currently working on a PhD degree at the same university. His main interests are the history and philosophy of social theory, the history of consciousness and ethical theory.

John Rundell is a lecturer in sociology in the department of anthropology and sociology, Monash University. He is an editor of *Thesis Eleven*, and author of *Origins of Modernity: The Origins of Modern Social Theory from Kant to Hegel to Marx*.

Michael Taveira is a postgraduate student in sociology at La Trobe University. He was educated at Loyola College (philosophy), the University of Melbourne (political science), the Ateneo de Manila University (theology) and La Trobe University (sociology).

Anna Yeatman is a social and political theorist who has been involved in contemporary issues of public policy and public management. She is the author of *Bureaucrats, Technocrats, Femocrats: Essays on the Contemporary Australian State* and is currently completing a book on *Feminism, Postmodernism and Social Science*. In 1991 she took up appointment as foundation professor of women's studies at University of Waikato, New Zealand.